Make Common Sense Common Again

Exploring Current Events in the Age of Mass Confusion

John Sheirer

ISBN: 978-0692693810

Published in the United States by Big Table Publishing.

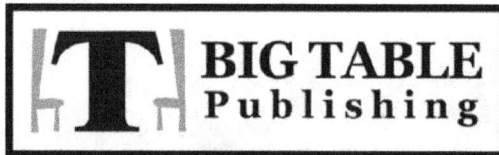

BIG TABLE
Publishing

Big Table Publishing
Boston, MA
www.bigtablepublishing.com

Dedication

For Matthew and Emily.
Let's leave them a better world.

Table of Contents

—
4

Make Common Sense Common Again

April 2016

As 2015 drew to a bumpy close, Republican presidential candidate Ben Carson tweeted his New Year's resolution: "Make common sense common again." Carson was, of course, making a clear reference to the ridiculousness of Donald Trump's "Make America Great Again" slogan. Just a few months later, after Carson's somnambulant campaign face-planted, he endorsed Trump for president. Since Carson clearly didn't take his own advice about common sense, I'm appropriating his tweet for the title of this book.

Many people in this country want basic common sense to guide our politics and government. We must speak up. That's what this book is all about. Injecting more common sense into our elections and policies would do far more to topple the dreaded "establishment" than any individual candidate ever could. We who embrace common sense have a few suggestions.

We want voting made easier, not harder. Voter fraud, as Republicans define it, doesn't really exist. Unfortunately, their voter suppression schemes are far too real. Common sense should spur people living in our representative system to involve more people in elections, not fewer.

We want the corporate media to stop treating elections like sporting events or celebrity gossip columns and start covering the issues in depth. Understanding the issues is the first step toward voting with common sense.

We want taxes made fairer for everyone, not used as giveaways for the wealthy and corporations. The Republican Party's obsession with redistributing wealth upward in the hope that it will eventually trickle down to the rest of us defies common sense, and it has been empirically disproven by economic reality for the last three decades.

We want the myth that so-called "lazy people" who only want "free stuff" from the government to end. That's a lie meant to distract Americans from unpleasant economic realities. Even after our economic recover from the financial crash at the end of the Bush administration, there are still more people looking for work than there are good jobs available. Common sense tells us that we need the private sector and government to work together in creating more good jobs and fully fixing the economy. We certainly don't need to blame the victims of tough economic times.

We want Wall Street and corporations to invest in the working class instead of padding their own fat wallets. Common sense tells us that a tiny ultra-wealthy class can't exist while everyone else struggles to get by.

We want Citizens United overturned to get secret money out of politics. The "corporations are people" view is the biggest violation of common sense in recent American history. Allowing such outsized corporate

PAC influence on elections has to end. All the conservatives ranting about imaginary "government tyranny" in this country really need to examine that way corporate power has developed an outsized boot heal in recent decades.

We want everyone to accept the scientific consensus that climate change is real and a potentially devastating problem that needs to be addressed now. The Republican Party is the only major political group on earth that still denies climate change—mostly thanks to the influence of billions of dollars in donations from the fossil fuel industry. Republican politicians are fond of saying, "I'm not a scientist" when questioned on the issue, but common sense tells us that we should at least listen to scientists when it comes to climate science.

We want war only as a last resort, not a permanent policy. Our Defense Department is funded ten times as well as our State Department. Where's the common sense in overfunding war and underfunding diplomacy?

We want veterans treated with respect, not used as props. When our citizens make the profound sacrifice to defend our nation, we need to take care of their needs after the battles. We don't need to wave the flag while obstructing every legislative effort to help veterans. Helping veterans is more than common sense. It's basic human decency.

We want women's choices not dictated by government or religious dogma. Common sense prevailed in the discussion of abortion and contraception decades ago. Let's not regress to the days of institutionalized misogyny.

We want guns regulated the same way other dangerous products are. Doing nothing to address gun violence while sending "hopes and prayers" after every tragic shooting is about as effective as a hair dryer in a sand storm. The only thing that can stop a bad elected official with a gun fetish is electing good officials with the common sense to work for stronger gun-safety laws.

We want marriage equality and LGBT civil rights to remain as the law of the land. No one with common sense uses the government to micromanage which bathroom people can use or who we can love.

We want everyone to continue working to recognize and overcome many decades of institutional racism and fear/hate-based politics. There's no common sense in the way Republicans blame the country's problems on immigrants, Muslims, or anyone who looks slightly darker than the average Norwegian skier.

We want the do-nothing Republican saboteurs kicked out of Congress and state governments. Democrats have been pushing common-sense policies while Republicans at every level have been obstructing anything that helps everyday Americans. Since the Republican Party shows no signs of fixing itself from within, the only way to get them to wake up is to send them home and let the grown-ups take charge.

We want the radical changes instituted years ago by Presidents

Reagan/Bush/Bush finally reversed. Common sense requires us to see where our problems originated and to clean up the messes rather than simply stepping around and over them as if they don't exist.

We want President Obama respected as the classy, effective president who brought our nation back from the brink of economic collapse and international embarrassment. Anyone looking at the past seven years with minimal common sense should realize that President Obama has been a strong voice for clarity in a very confused political system.

We want that huge liar Donald Trump to shut his dishonest mouth and the rest of Republican politicians to stop basing their policies on outright lies. Five minutes on legitimate fact-checking sites reveals what common sense has been telling us for many years: Republicans lie far more often than Democrats. America works best when both parties tell the truth.

We want Hillary Clinton and Bernie Sanders (and their stubborn supporters) to unite and keep us moving forward. Clearly, one party has plans that support opportunity for as many Americans as possible, while the other party drags us backward. The only way to defeat Republicans in November is for everyone in the American center-left majority to vote—not just for president, but for every office in Congress, statehouses, and local government. A real common-sense revolution can only happen in this country if we participate together at every level.

Common sense throughout American government isn't too much to ask in such a great nation. So let's ask for it with our votes.

I'm with Her

March 2016

The Massachusetts polls for our upcoming Massachusetts Democratic primary are a toss-up right now between Bernie Sanders and Hillary Clinton. The chatter I'm hearing around my home state is a pretty even split between Bernie and Hillary, with the general pattern being age (young for Bernie, middle and older for Hillary—with many exceptions, of course). Like a microcosm of my state, I was undecided between Bernie and Hillary for quite some time. I've loved them both for decades before this campaign began and will use their first names throughout this essay because I live in the fantasy that I'm close with them, as do millions of Americans. I doubt that either one of my buddies running for president is wondering about my endorsement, but I'll give it anyway.

First, though, I'm excited by all the young people who are energized for the 2016 election, in large part due to the excitement surrounding Bernie. But I'm also cautious. Any Bernie supporter over the age of 24 could have voted in the disastrous 2010 "Tea Party" election. And anyone over 20 could have voted in the equally terrible 2014 election. But young people are the least reliable voting block in the United States. A large percentage of young people didn't vote in 2010 and 2014. Where were they? Were they sitting at home playing X-Box while Republicans swept the midterm elections, giving us a horribly dysfunctional Congress? And for all the energy surrounding this election, turnout among Democrats in the early primaries is down compared with 2008. Where are the young people? Will they turn out for the general election in November? I certainly hope so. Huge crowds at Bernie rallies are great, but we need huge crowds at the polls far more. In this country, you can't have a revolution without people showing up to vote. Bernie and his supporters talk about a revolution, but in this country, revolutions don't happen when revolutionary voting bocks stay home. You can't even have a functional Congress or a reasonable president if people don't show up to vote.

Most Bernie and Hillary supporters have been civil to me as I made up my mind. Unfortunately, a fair number of Bernie supporters who I've talked with believe that Hillary is a crook and a liar, mostly thanks to decades of right-wing attacks. I'm constantly amazed when my liberal friends post links to anti-Hillary articles from right-wing websites known for mind-numbing dishonesty. One supposedly liberal Bernie supporter told me that all Hillary had going for her was an extra X chromosome, ignoring her long list of accomplishments. I hope his wife gave him a stern dose of reality in exchange for his sexist comment.

Some Bernie supporters also think Hillary is a conservative, thanks to direct comparisons with Bernie, but that's not even close to accurate. The nonpartisan "On the Issues" website rates both Hillary and Bernie as "hardcore liberal." Another nonpartisan analysis done by "Voteview" rated Hillary the eleventh most liberal member of the Senate during her time in office. Bernie supporters are often shocked when I point out that Hillary voted in line with Bernie 93% of the time when they occupied the Senate together. That's a solid A in any classroom. If there's a conservative out there who has voted with Bernie 93% of the time, then please show me that unicorn. I'm old enough to remember campaigning for Bill Clinton in 1992, waving signs on the Coolidge Bridge in Northampton, Massachusetts, and having a passing car stop so that the red-faced driver could tell me that Bill and Hillary were "pinko commie freaks." I just avoided his flying spittle and wished him a nice day. I doubt there's more than a dozen Republicans in the whole country who believe that Hillary plays for their team.

Just being undecided caused some Bernie supporters to call me a closet Republican sell-out for not being 100% in favor of Bernie and 100% in favor of sending Hillary to prison. Some said I was a fake liberal and called me a "Teabillery huckster" for even considering voting for "Shillary-Shrillary-Hellery" Clinton. One person called me a "neocon" and a "neoliberal" on the same day in the same Facebook comment twenty-seven words apart. Here's an online comment from someone has never met me and knows nothing about me, responding to my column endorsing Hillary as a good choice for president: "Those who support corporate capitalist candidates play the same role that apologists for segregation played in a generation past. I'm sure that John Sheirer is a decent, thoughtful person. But he stands on the wrong side of history." Wow. It seems that future historians will lump me right there with the racists of yesteryear. But at least I'm "a decent, thoughtful person"— like all those segregationists were, I guess.

The commenter is right that I'm a decent and thoughtful person. As a decent and thoughtful person, I object to being compared with segregationists because I endorse Hillary for president. That's an insult to her, to me, and, most importantly, to the millions of Americans who have been victimized by institutional racism over the years. I fully understand the suffering brought on by income inequality in this country. So does Hillary. She isn't a "corporate capitalist" in the sense the commenter implied. That would be the collection of Republican candidates running for president and leading the obstruction in Congress and many state governments. In contrast, Hillary is proposing strict, progressive financial reforms. We may not agree with all of her proposals, or we may think that her proposals don't go far enough, but we can't deny that they exist. Hillary has never burned a cross in anyone's yard or murdered human beings because of their race, as many segregationists did. I haven't either. The commenter may think that Hillary

———

10

and I are on the "wrong side of history," but that comparison is on the wrong side of reality, civility, and basic common sense.

The Bernie supporters who have an irrational hatred for Hillary and even for people who entertain the possibility of supporting Hillary need to learn that every time they use the term "Shillary," Donald Trump has a tiny organism in his micro-penis. Please stop doing the Republican hatchet-men's jobs for them. I haven't heard a similar level of vitriol from Hillary supporters, and Bernie himself doesn't indulge in such blatant attacks. Insulting both me and a candidate I was considering really wasn't a good way to campaign for Bernie. But I've put those attacks aside as best I could and focused on each candidate's positions on the issues and their overall experience in public service.

By the way, for any of my Republican friends who might have read this far by accident, if you object to Hillary because you think she stood by and let those brave men die in Benghazi (she didn't, according to nine investigations) or that she's about to be indicted because of her e-mail use when she was Secretary of State (she's been cleared of any wrongdoing) or that her work with the Clinton Foundation was all about corruptly enriching her own personal wealth (nope—it's a real charity that has helped millions of people) … umm, sorry. Those false claims are bird droppings on the windshield of reality. Please scrub away Fox, Rush, Drudge, and the other monosyllabic propagandists who are blocking your view of the real world.

It's easy for me to get behind both Bernie and Hillary because they both support positions on the issues that I agree with and care deeply about. Both support a minimum wage increase, voting rights, unions, campaign finance reform, Wall Street reform, LGBT rights, religious freedom, gun-safety regulation, equal pay, college affordability, education funding and reform, fair taxation, jobs programs, diplomacy over war, choice, criminal justice reform, universal health care, strengthening Social Security and Medicare, stem cell research, comprehensive immigration reform, veterans support, addressing climate change and protecting the environment, clean energy, and a host of other issues—many of which I detailed in a another chapter. The nonpartisan website "On the Issues" rates both Bernie and Hillary as "far-left liberals." They are happy siblings in the liberal/progressive family by any reasonable definition.

I voted absentee on the Friday before the Massachusetts primary because I work most of the Tuesday election day in Connecticut. Ultimately, I decided to vote for Hillary because I've admired her very progressive work for 25 years, her overall positions are a bit more practical than Bernie's, the depth and breadth of her public service experience is unmatched, her leadership style will be more effective in today's political climate, and she has a better chance in the general election than Bernie does.

Some Democrats are concerned about Hillary's electability, but those

---

concerns are overblown. Currently, Bernie is pumping iron in general election polls, besting most of the Republican candidates by several points. But Hillary is right there in those polls only slightly less muscular than Bernie's showing against the Republicans. And it's barely morning for general election sunset polls right now when the campaigns are just forming their strategies. Republicans themselves would much rather run against Bernie than Hillary. That's why Karl Rove's super PAC has been running anti-Hillary ads during the primaries. If Rove is against Hillary, then how can she be a terrible candidate?

For the most part, Republicans have barely tossed any pebbles at Bernie yet, but they'll catapult boulders on his head the second he approaches the nomination. Republicans are terrible at governing but fantastic at negative campaigning. Incorrect accusations that Obama was a socialist mobilized millions of right-wingers against the president. Does anyone believe that the Republican base will understand that Bernie's Democratic Socialism is different from Hitler's National Socialism? I don't have that much faith in the folks who waved posters of Obama with a photoshopped Hitler mustache.

Bernie could crater 20 points in a month without the time to counter Republican attacks and climb his way out of those lost points. Hillary has weathered such storms for decades and is still the perennial "most admired" woman in the world, according to polls. "Hillary hate" runs hot but not deep. Republicans have over flogged their wheezing attacks against Hillary. They'll certainly try to bring her down with new lies, but they'll just sound like the same stale lies. Fresh attacks against Bernie, by contrast, will be shiny objects flickering across the public mind and the lazy media from convention to election day.

Bernie hasn't always reacted very well to the relatively mild criticism he has gotten from Hillary during the primaries. That doesn't bode well for how he would handle the Republican crap storm headed his way. In debates, Bernie would certainly outpoint Donald Trump, the likely Republican nominee. But too many uninformed voters see Bernie and Trump filling the same populist role. With Hillary, the contrast is greater. And Hillary, with a tough streak developed from decades of having to deal with condescending men, is much better equipped to destroy Trump for both his issue ignorance and his obvious lack of presidential character. And she'll bring actual "class" to her Trump takedown, while Trump will only be able to display the last three letters of that word.

Yes, I know that Hillary gave speeches to Wall Street groups. So what? The First Amendment talks about freedom of assembly and freedom of speech. Is Hillary somehow not entitled to the same freedoms every other citizen is? Yes, she was paid for those speeches, and a significant portion of her earnings went to The Clinton Foundation, which is an actual charity that helps actual human beings and not the "slush fund" that her political opponents claim it is. In total, she donated slightly more than half of her speaking fees in 2014 and 2015 to various charities.

Is Hillary somehow not allowed to be paid for her work? How progressive is it for anyone to claim it's wrong for a woman to be paid to give a speech when a man would certainly be paid? If a Wall Street group called me and offered to pay me a large sum of money to speak, I would certainly do so. And that wouldn't make me less likely to work for strong regulations against corporate wrongdoing. Why do we expect that Hillary, a lifelong progressive, would change her views for a fee?

And why is Hillary the only candidate being subjected to demands that she release the transcripts of her paid speeches to Wall Street? Bernie was never asked to speak to Wall Street because they weren't interested in his opinion, which is Wall Street's loss because he has many good ideas that the folks on Wall Street should hear. So he has no transcripts to release. But is he being asked to release the transcripts of every speech he has ever given to every group? No. Why not? And what do people expect to find in Hillary's Wall Street speeches? Do they really think she would say something along the lines of, "So, when I run for president and say that I want to regulate Wall Street, remember that I'm just lying to get votes"? Do people think she's really that stupid or greedy or immoral? If so, then they've been bamboozled by Republican propaganda. By the way, in one Wall Street speech where video has been shown, Hillary spoke about the need to have women in positions of power and responsibility. What progressive would object to that?

Yes, Hillary's campaign received some donations from Wall Street employees. First, that's different getting money directly from Wall Street Banks or corporations, which she hasn't. The vast majority of those donations come from individuals who work in those industries, not the corporate entities. A small percentage comes form PACs aligned with the industries. The claim that "Wall Street banks" give money to Hillary is misleading. Second, Bernie has also received millions from employees of Wall Street and other industries—just not as much as Hillary. And third, Hillary's superior funding means she'll have the resources needed to run against the Republican nominee, who will certainly have untold billions in dark money PAC funding from Wall Street and far worse. Plus she'll have the funding to campaign for other Democrats in down-ballot races across the country. Many Democrats have taken money from Wall Street employees (including President Obama), and those same Democrats passed significant Wall Street reform. The worst elements of Wall Street that represent greed and corporate power will hate Hillary just as much as they hate Obama when she follows through with her proposed Wall Street reforms, which she will.

To hear Hillary's detractors, she must be almost totally dependent on Wall Street for her campaign and super PAC funding. But Open Secrets, the website that tracks campaign finance information, reported in December that only 7.2% of Hillary's overall funding (campaign and super PACs) comes from Wall Street sources. That's a pretty meager proportion considering how her detractors focus so much on Hillary's Wall Street funding. Just for comparison, the same Open Secrets analysis included the fact that Jeb Bush got a whopping 26% of his overall funding from Wall Street. Once again, the attempts to show that Hillary is "Republican lite" just don't bear fruit.

About her speaking fees and campaign donations, Hillary herself has said, "You will not find that I ever changed a view or a vote because of any donation I ever received, and there is no evidence to the contrary." Bernie's campaign circulated a 2004 video that they claimed showed Senator Elizabeth Warren condemning Hillary for changing a vote on a bankruptcy bill because of Wall Street influence. In fact, Hillary originally supported the bill in 2001 because she pushed for and got protections for women and children dealing with divorce added to the bill. When those protections were eliminated in 2005, she didn't support the bill. In short, she supported the bill when she was able to make it more progressive, and she withdrew her support when those progressive changes were withdrawn—not because she was bought off by campaign cash.

Kevin Drum recently published an examination of Hillary's supposed Wall Street connection in his *Mother Jones* article, "Just how Cozy is Hillary Clinton with Wall Street?" The answer he comes to is "if there's a strong case to be made for 'coziness,' I've failed to find it." He looked at the bankruptcy bill and many other legislative initiatives and didn't find any real evidence to show that Hillary is somehow a pawn of Wall Street. Hillary's contention that she hasn't favored Wall Street, despite her paid speeches or campaign contributions, is far closer to the truth than her detractors will ever admit.

Once the general election kicks in, Wall Street instantly will become a nonissue for Hillary's campaign. Republicans have been bending to the will of Wall Street for generations, so they won't be able to criticize Hillary on that subject. They've all voted for or cheered on lobbyists who wrote bills that favor big corporations. Ted Cruz's wife and John Kasich himself even worked directly for Wall Street companies. As for Trump—he actually *is* Wall Street in all its excesses. Hillary will look like Erin Brockovich by comparison.

The Wall Street issue also points to something important related to getting important things done for the American people. Bernie's leadership style is a bit too "all or nothing" for those of us with a practical-minded bent. Bernie's idea of Medicare-for-all, for example, is a great final outcome, but there is simply no way that it could happen right now or in the foreseeable future. Hillary, on the other hand, is proposing imperfect but desirable ways to improve the Affordable Care Act, and those proposals have a far better chance of actually happening. The old saying, "Don't let the perfect be the enemy of the good," has never been more applicable.

As a writer, I see how incremental improvements can be an effective process that leads to a strong result. The early drafts of my writing fall into the category that writer Anne Lamott describes as, "shitty first drafts." These drafts aren't close to a final product, but they can build to a much stronger final version through the process of revision. And even the "shitty first draft" is far better than nothing. By analogy, building legislation through incremental revision actually works. The Affordable Care Act isn't perfect, but it's a great first draft of long-term health care reform. It's helping millions of people now, and with some improvements, it can help even more people in the long run and eventually become something along the lines of Bernie's Medicare-for-all vision.

When I'm writing, I only have to deal with myself and few very helpful editors at a later stage in the process. Making legislation in the United States today involves dealing not only with friendly colleagues (other Democrats) who may have different ideas, but battling opponents with radically different views (so-called "mainstream" Republicans), and even worse, enemies who are fully investing in making government fail no matter what the issue (extremist Republicans who have taken over the actual "mainstream" of their party). As much as we wish it weren't true, those Republicans were elected by the American people (thanks in part to Gerrymandering, of course). But they were legally elected. We have to work with them, and they aren't going to support anything close to Bernie's all-or-nothing proposals.

Incremental reform is difficult but possible in this system. Revolution is impossible. Bernie wants a revolution against the 1%. Hillary wants substantial incremental reform for the 99%. I love the idea of revolution—who doesn't? But it's just not possible right now. Sustained reform over long periods is far better than failed revolution for a presidency benefitting the most Americans possible.

A friend of mine who supports Bernie keeps telling me that Hillary calls herself "a proud Goldwater Girl." He seems to think that this disqualifies Hillary from being a "true liberal." Yes, she said this once, twenty years ago, about her first political activity forty years ago when she was in high school. Her parents were Republicans, and that helped shape her early beliefs. I also campaigned for a Republican in high school, an obscure member of Congress named Bud Shuster. I did it to get a day off from school, a free meal, and the company of some of my cute female classmates. Hillary did it out of a budding sense of civic engagement that would soon become her life's work.

If Hillary's brief Republican youth keeps her from being a true liberal today, then does mine as well? How about Arianna Huffington, the liberal icon who runs *Huffington Post*? She was a Republican until she was in her 40s. That hardly means that *Huffington Post* is secretly conservative. Elizabeth Warren, perhaps the only politician who rivals Bernie's progressive credentials among those who administer ideological purity tests on the left, was a Republican until her 40s as well. Why do Huffington and Warren get a pass on being Republicans until well into their adulthood, but Hillary gets condemned for something she did in high school? The words "double standard" aren't strong enough for that level of hypocrisy.

We liberals scratch our collective heads when Republicans perform their right-wing purity tests. The idea that John McCain and Mitt Romney lost their presidential elections because they weren't "true conservatives" makes us double over with laughter. And when the dubiously named Congressional "Freedom Caucus" recently drummed John Boehner out of Washington for the sin of occasionally trying to do his job in concert with a Democratic president, we felt equal parts disgust at their extremism and hilarity at their circular firing squad. Yet here we are, liberals conducting liberal purity tests and claiming that Hillary fails. I wonder if the Republicans, all of whom view Hillary as an irredeemable far-far-far-far-left liberal, are laughing at us.

Hillary became a Democrat in college, just as I did. I've been a Democrat for decades because I believe in people coming together to support shared values, beliefs, and policies. I still believe in the two-party system—even if the Republican Party has lost its collective mind. Hillary has been solidly connected with progressive Democratic ideals through her entire adult life. I'm a Democrat for the same reason I'm a union member—because together, we are stronger. I've never worked around my union to negotiate my own contract. Hillary has worked within the Democratic Party to create sustainable progress in our nation, and she has tirelessly helped other Democrats raise money and become more skilled candidates for office. In 2015 alone, Hillary raised $18 million for other Democrats running for various offices. Bernie? Nothing. He hasn't even committed to raise money for other Democrats if he is the 2016 nominee, and that's one main role of a party's leader. Hillary has been strong and independent-minded while still supporting and connecting with other strong and independent-minded people in the Democratic Party.

Bernie, on the other hand, only became a Democrat for this election. It's stylish these days to be "anti-establishment" and to claim that party affiliation means nothing. Like many stylish viewpoints, this one lacks substance. Hillary has embraced her party because it reflects her values, and Bernie has avoided party affiliation for the same reason. And he has often criticized the Democratic Party, even equating it with the Republican Party on occasion—once calling the two major parties, "Tweedledum and Tweedledee" and another time saying both parties "are the party of the ruling class." He's even suing the Democratic National Committee over the data breech that his own campaign perpetrated. No one seems to understand what that's all about.

Bernie has caucused with Democrats while in Congress, of course, but he never embraced the party. He has admitted that he's running as a Democrat for the "media attention" that he couldn't get as an independent, and he has already filed to run for Senate reelection in 2018 as an independent. His current identification as a Democrat is temporary—perhaps even opportunistic. If independence from party is so important, then why didn't Bernie run as an independent from the start? Overall, creating positive change from within the system is less glamorous but can have a deeper effect than booing from the balcony.

On the issues, no candidate wears saint robes, of course, and Bernie (despite his monk-like appearance) is no exception. He voted to shield gun manufacturers from lawsuits and against the Brady Bill, actions he has yet to adequately explain. He voted for the 1994 Crime Bill that he criticizes as a regular part of his campaign. He helped block comprehensive immigration reform, and Republicans continue to use that issue to enflame our nation's worst ethnocentric impulses. He supports the F-35 bomber, a wasteful, trillion-dollar military/corporate pork project based in Vermont. He worked to locate a toxic waste dump for Vermont's nuclear plant in a poor Latino area of Texas. He has said that he will raise taxes on the middle-class, not just the wealthy and corporations. He said that President Obama should have had primary challenge in 2012. He claimed that Hillary only supports President Obama to court the African-American vote. In a recent debate, he seemed to equate poverty with being African-American. He reduces nearly every issue to "noun-verb-Wall Street," and his foreign policy recommendations lack specifics. His frequent "artful smears" of Hillary's integrity don't match his vow to run a positive campaign.

And, frankly, he can be a grump, which may work wonders at campaign rallies, but isn't the most practical or optimistic approach to governing. Just ask some people Bernie has worked with. Mickey Hirten, the former editor of the *Burlington Free Press* when Bernie served as Burlington, Vermont, mayor. Hirten recently wrote this about Bernie's less-than-cordial personality: "Bernie was always full of himself: pious, self-righteous and utterly humorless." Hirten said Bernie showed a "stick-it-to-them approach to politics," which doesn't bode well for the diplomacy required of a president. Chris Graf, another Vermont journalist who interacted with Bernie, said, "Bernie has no social skills, no sense of humor, and he's quick to boil over." As Hirten points out, such a rigid approach won't accomplish much in today's political environment. Liberal lion Barney Frank echoed that viewpoint when he said, "Bernie alienates his natural allies. He is completely ineffective as a lobbyist because he offends just about everyone." Bernie's grumpy complaints when Planned Parenthood and Human Rights Watch endorsed Hillary showed his tendency for alienation to a national audience.

Worst of all, after running a campaign based on not being an "establishment" candidate, Bernie started talking like what his supporters would call a "corrupt politician." A few days after he lost all five primaries on March 15, he and his campaign officials revealed their strategy of manipulating the superdelegates that his supporter had railed against for months. Bernie himself said that he would try to flip Hillary's superdelegates to his side even if he came to the convention behind in the popular vote. And Bernie's Senior Strategist, Tad Devine, even suggested that the Bernie campaign would try to get *pledged delegates* (the ones awarded based on votes in the primaries) to switch from Hillary to Bernie. In other words, Bernie and his campaign openly said that he would manipulate the political process in order to steal the nomination from Hillary even if she got more primary votes than he did. That was a shock.

Bernie also recently said that he would ask President Obama to withdraw his Supreme Court nominee if Bernie is elected president. Again, it's jarring when a "man of the people" behaves in a way that defies the will of the people. President Obama had nearly a year left in his term when the Supreme Court seat became open. The people elected President Obama to fill court vacancies during his term, among other Constitutional duties. Bernie isn't acting much differently from Republicans when he takes the position that President Obama doesn't have every right to nominate his candidate and have that person considered by the Senate. Hillary, on the other hand, said that she wouldn't ask President Obama to with draw his nominee. On this issue, Hillary is certainly showing more respect for the will of the people than Bernie is.

I still respect Bernie and will still support him if he wins the nomination. But we need to dispense with the myth that he has passed some kind of purity test while all other candidates are tainted. I won't belabor these points or flood Facebook with memes denouncing Bernie's entire campaign based on a few cherry-picked complaints as I've seen some Hillary-haters do to her. When we hold both candidates to the same standard of scrutiny, both come out very well overall. Hillary deserves that same level of respect as Bernie does.

In terms of respect, the vast majority of people who have worked with both Hillary and Bernie in the Senate have endorsed Hillary, which carries significant authority. In fact, just about everyone who has worked with Hillary praises her passion for serving the American people and making this country and the world a better place. She has been endorsed by hundreds of current and former elected and appointed Democrats, along with dozens of major labor unions and progressive organizations. These people and groups don't endorse "fake liberals" or "Republican lite" candidates.

On the other hand, the vast majority of the people who criticize Hillary as a liar, shill, criminal, opportunist, Wall Street toady, racist, fake anything—and whatever other random attack—are people who haven't actually worked with her. I'll take the word of the folks who have stood shoulder to shoulder with Hillary rather than the ones who just repeat right-wing propaganda, fourth-hand media attacks, and gossip.

Bernie has helped to push Hillary to the left, which is great, but she was at least 93% there already. Anyone who doesn't think Hillary is a progressive should watch her first major speech of the campaign again. That June 2015 speech is a blueprint for progressive American government. If Bernie gets the nomination, I'll support him with all my heart, but I support Hillary with my heart and my brain as well for her views, plans, connections, and experience. And, frankly, a fraction of my support comes from the fact that she's a woman. President Obama's election spurred a flare of racist attitudes and ugliness in some corners of our country, but, in the long run, his race will have a positive effect on American history. Just as African-American children can be inspired by an effective African-American president for generations to come, so too will young girls have an inspiring role model when they look to the White House.

Yes, a woman president will bring the undercurrent of sexism into the light, but that light will expose the ugliness of sexism. In the long run, a woman president will do far more to combat sexism than to foster it. Of course, I'm not saying that we should elect anyone just because of race or gender. Republican women and African-Americans are just as destructive as the rest of their party. But the election of a woman such as Hillary, who will be as excellent a president as Obama has been, is another step toward fulfilling the long-term equality promise of our nation.

When it comes to Bernie versus Hillary, there are no bad choices. Bernie is a strong left hand, and Hillary is an even stronger one. The only bad choice is not voting, be it the primary or, especially, the general election. And, as always, the worst choice of all is voting for a Republican come November.

Race, History, and Political Affiliation

February 2016

Last month, Martin Luther King quotes popped up on Facebook to celebrate the great civil rights leader's birthday. Now that we're in Black History Month, I'm pleased to see more of his words making the rounds in social media.

Unfortunately, along with King's inspiring quotes, I've read many comments claiming that King himself was a Republican who would oppose today's liberals. King generally kept his political affiliation neutral to appeal to the broadest range of people that he could, but calling him a Republican is simply ridiculous.

King voted for John Kennedy in 1960 and encouraged people to vote against Republican Barry Goldwater in 1964. He supported Planned Parenthood, unions, non-violence, and an increased minimum wage, among other liberal causes. How would those views play in today's Republican party? Not well.

If King were indeed a Republican, then we should expect that Republicans favored the holiday we celebrate in his honor, shouldn't we? Yet that was clearly not the case.

The law establishing Martin Luther King Day passed Congress in 1983 by a significant margin, primarily based on overwhelming support from Democrats. The president at the time, Republican Ronald Reagan, originally opposed the holiday, but he changed his mind and signed it when it passed with a veto-proof margin. A significant number of Congressional Republicans opposed the holiday, including six current Republicans still serving in Congress. Among them are such prominent figures as Steve Scalise, the third-ranking Republican in the House, and Orrin Hatch, the Republican chair of the powerful Senate Finance Committee.

The people who want us to believe the fiction that King was a Republican also like to claim that Democrats are the real bigots because they fought for slavery, founded the KKK, and opposed the Civil Rights Act.

These claims bear only a superficial resemblance to reality. Yes, Lincoln was a Republican, and some Democrats opposed civil rights half a century ago. But the geographical north/south and philosophical liberal/conservative distinctions are far more telling than party affiliation when looking at the complex history of racial issues.

Lincoln was a Northern liberal who liberated the slaves. (Yes, Republicans could be liberal back then, shocking though that may seem today.) Democrats of that era included many Southern conservatives who wanted to conserve slavery.

Democrats led the nation in addressing the issue of racism well before passage of the Civil Rights Act. In 1946, President Harry Truman, a Democrat, created the President's Committee on Civil Rights, to address the issue of racism in America. The commission condemned lynching and called for desegregation of bus, train, and air travel, along with protection of voting rights. Truman's support for, in his own words, "equal economic opportunities, equal rights of citizenship, and equal educational opportunities for all our people, whatever their race or religion or status of birth," is exactly where the Democratic Party still stands today.

Truman also fully desegregated the military for the first time in American history with his 1948 Executive Order 9981, which read, in part "It is hereby declared to be the policy of the President that there shall be equality of treatment and opportunity for all persons in the armed services without regard to race, color, religion or national origin." Truman had to use an executive order for the action because Congress, notably Republicans, had failed to act on the issue. I'm sure President Obama can relate to Truman's frustration with the "Do-Nothing Congress" of the day.

In the 1960s, the north/south, liberal/conservative divide was again a strong force. Northern liberals, both Democrats and Republicans, overwhelmingly supported civil rights, while Southern conservatives of both parties overwhelmingly voted against the Civil Rights Act. And a Democratic president, Lyndon Johnson, signed the Civil Rights Act into law. The Republican who lost to Johnson, Barry Goldwater, opposed the Civil Rights Act and voted against it in the Senate.

The racist Southern Democrats then became Republicans (Strom Thurmond, most famously) or joined third parties (George Wallace). Southern Democrats who renounced previous racist views (Robert Byrd) remained Democrats. Civil rights leaders from the 1960s who are still active in politics today (such as John Lewis) are all Democrats. Ask John Lewis if Martin Luther King would be a Republican today. Lewis has a great laugh and scathing glare for foolish questions.

Calling today's Democrats racist because of the party's past makes as much common sense as bragging that Bill Russell and Carl Yastrzemski will lead the Celtics and Red Sox to championships this year. That nonsense would get you laughed out of any tavern in Beantown. Teams change over time. Political parties do the same.

In recent years, the South has become reliably Republican. In fact, when you superimpose a U.S. map during the Civil War onto a map of the 2012 presidential election, the results are startling. Basically, President Obama dominated the Union, and Mitt Romney surged in the Confederacy.

That's not to say that today's Republicans are uniformly racist. The purpose of this article isn't to step in off the street and start shouting that all Republicans are racist. This article is in response to the false claim that

Democrats are racist. Obviously, not all Republicans are racist. But much of their rhetoric is racially charged, to say the least. Would the anti-Obama "birthers" have surfaced if his father had white skin and been born in, say, England? Not likely.

One current issue analogous to slavery and civil rights is immigration. Democrats have consistently advocated a path to citizenship for undocumented immigrants who follow the law and contribute to society. Republicans briefly flirted with that position a few years ago but now are overwhelmingly opposed to immigration reform. Their presidential frontrunner, Donald Trump, has based much of his campaign on deporting millions of brown-skinned immigrants and blocking Muslims from entering the country.

White supremacists recently sent out a wave of robocalls supporting Trump's candidacy, including the guy who inspired Dylann Roof, the racist shooter who murdered nine African-Americans in a South Carolina church in June 2015. Trump himself routinely retweets white supremacists without a second thought. One such tweet included a chart that blamed 81% of white murder victims on African-American killers, a stunningly racist lie considering the actual number is 15%. Hey, Trump was only off by a 540%. No one ever said his math skills were as "huge" as his ego.

What high-profile Democrats take such discriminatory positions, get that kind of racist support, or exaggerate racial crime statistics so ridiculously? None, obviously.

How many Republican civil rights leaders has our country seen in the past fifty years? How many Democrats have run a national campaign based on the "southern strategy" of appealing directly to racist white voters? How many KKK leaders have seriously endorsed Democrats for president in recent decades? None, none, and none.

What does it say about a party that has to go back to the 1960s or even the 1860s to find positive role models on civil rights issues? Nothing good.

How about the civil rights of LGBT people? The KKK has long hated gay people, and many conservatives love to rail against "the homosexual agenda" (an agenda that, in reality, actually recognizes gay people as fully human people). Democrats have consistently supported LGBT civil rights, while Republicans have opposed them, often with hell-fire rhetoric. Future generations will look back at today's anti-gay Republicans very much as we look back at the people who fought for slavery and segregation.

How do many Republicans respond to the "Black Lives Matter" movement? By ignoring the fact that African-Americans are far more likely to be victimized by bad apple law enforcement officers than white Americans are. Many Republicans are fond of retorting that "all lives matter!" as if an appropriate response to donating to the American Heart Association would be to object and claim that "all diseases matter!"

How do many Republicans respond to the shooting of Trayvon Martin, an unarmed African-American teenager walking in his own father's neighborhood? By calling him a "thug" and making a folk hero out of his killer, George Zimmerman, an obviously terrible person who has gone on to several subsequent arrests for violent acts.

How do many Republicans respond to the fact that African-Americans are statistically more prone to the economic inequalities of our corporate culture? By ignoring long-term institutional racism and claiming that there has been a "breakdown in the black family." Isn't that just a slightly more polite way of saying that African-Americans are somehow morally inferior? Yet Republicans toss around this "breakdown of the black family" claim as if it's a scholarly fact rather than a coded phrase to mask a racial insult.

Is voting a civil rights issue? If so, that's another area where Republicans have failed African-Americans. Since the 2008 election of President Obama, the Republican Party has been crying foul and making up charges of rampant voter fraud. The reality is that in-person voter fraud is extremely rare, almost to the point on nonexistence. That fact hasn't stopped Republicans from enacting voter suppression laws that, not coincidentally, disproportionately affect African-American voters. How many Democrats have pushed voter suppression laws? None. In fact, Democrats support laws that make voting easier for everyone.

How do many Republicans respond to the issue of the Confederate flag? By claiming that it's a symbol of cultural pride that has nothing to do with slavery or racism. Do they really expect us to believe that KKK members wave the Confederate flag to celebrate their culture rather than their hatred? Some Republican politicians have bowed to public pressure and changed their views on the Confederate flag, but the fact that the issue is still under debate among many Republicans is a clear sign of their confusion on the issue of race in American history.

Let's not forget that the KKK hates Catholic and Jewish people just about as much as they hate African-Americans. Catholics have long been supporters of the Democratic Party. That has changed in recent years as the Republican Party has fully embraced the Catholic Church's official position opposing birth control and abortion. Actual Catholic voters don't follow institutional dogma as closely, and Obama still won the Catholic vote over Romney in 2012 by a slight margin. Jewish voters have routinely favored Democratic Presidential candidates over Republicans by a three-to-one margin for more than a century. Are all those Catholic and Jewish voters secretly KKK members? Umm … no.

A white Republican friend of mine recently opined that African-Americans have been fooled into supporting Democrats by the lure of welfare and other giveaways supposedly promised by President Obama. Really? He was trying to make the case that he's not racist by claiming that nearly 95% of African-Americans voters supported Obama not because they gave his candidacy the same thoughtful consideration he assumes of every other voter, but because they wanted what Romney himself called, "free stuff." Does my Republican friend honestly believe it's not racist to imply that African-Americans are foolish, selfish, and lazy?

My Republican friend told me I was a typical closeted-racist Democrat for "playing the race card" by pointing out the racial implications of his claim. That's called "projection," a term that can be found in any dictionary of psychological terms. My Republican friend would rather no one questioned his views on race because those questions force him to face the fact that his political party has a very bad record on race. But silence on any issue is a form of consent. Should we give our consent to any form of racism, even when it's masked in obvious dog-whistle terminology? Of course not.

In the end, how can anyone possibly claim that the party that supports humane immigration and LGBT policies and that elected our first African-American president is bigoted while the party that demeans, marginalizes, and demonizes large groups of people is morally superior? How would Martin Luther King answer that question? I wish he were still here so that we could ask him.

The Sanders-Clinton Conundrum

January 2016

I'm a fan of Bernie Sanders. He brings an energy to the Democratic primary that we all would have missed if the only other contenders against frontrunner Hillary Clinton had been folks such as Martin O'Malley, Lincoln Chaffee, and Jim Webb. And Sanders has promoted several core liberal/progressive issues, especially income inequality, tax fairness, and college costs. I'll vote for Sanders in a heartbeat if he wins the Democratic nomination. I respect and share his supporters' passion. At this point, I'm honestly undecided for my vote in the upcoming Massachusetts Democratic primary.

But a disturbing trend has developed. Whenever I engage Sanders supporters in a discussion of the issues, they often voice distrust of Hillary Clinton with claims that she isn't honest, is too much like a Republican, and is too disliked to win the general election. None of these contentions are accurate. Clinton and Sanders are far closer on the issues than most people know, and both candidates fair extremely well in general election polls.

In fact, Clinton is a remarkably honest politician, especially for one with a trumped-up reputation for dishonesty. Just consult the leading political fact-checker in the country, PolitiFact.com. Clinton ranks slightly ahead of Sanders in PolitiFact's overall honesty ratings, and she has been evaluated on more than three times as many statements as Sanders. Both candidates are among the most honest major politicians rated by Politifact. Not surprisingly, all of the Republicans rank far lower than either Democrat. When Republicans claim that Clinton is dishonest, the irony flows like maple syrup at a New Hampshire campaign breakfast.

Many Sanders supporters call a potential presidential contest between Clinton and the Republican nominee, "the lesser of two evils." But lumping Clinton into the same category of "evil" with the truly horrible cadre of Republicans food-fighting for their party's nomination plays right into the Republican scheme. That's why the Republican candidates hardly mention Sanders but attack Clinton every chance they get.

Here's how it works: Republicans know that the vast majority of Clinton supporters, who tend to be practical by nature, will vote for Sanders if he is the nominee. Republicans also know that a significant number of Sanders supporters might not to vote for Clinton because she doesn't pass their candidate purity test. So Republicans constantly throw dirt at Clinton knowing that the mainstream corporate media will amplify the message to the airwaves, giving the impression that Clinton is roundly disliked while allowing Sanders to remain unscathed. CNN and the *New York Times*, for example, have flogged the twin fake scandals of Clinton's e-mail and her role in the Benghazi tragedy until even some Sanders supporters have used these attacks as evidence that Clinton can't be trusted. In reality, Clinton has been repeatedly exonerated on all counts. Republicans can't claim that Clinton has a fake birth certificate, but their attacks are no less absurd than the "birther" nonsense used against President Obama.

The contention that Clinton is "Republican lite" ignores the fact that Clinton and Sanders agree on about 90% of the issues, and both of them disagree with Republicans on about 90% of the issues. In fact, they actually voted together 93% of the time during the two years they served in the Senate at the same time from 2007 to 2009. The two candidates may differ on details, but on the broader issues, they are far more alike than different.

The details of their policy positions are available on each campaign's websites and through the excellent "On the Issues" website pages for Sanders and Clinton. Ten minutes of scanning those resources will show that Sanders and Clinton are both in stark contrast to any Republican candidate. Here are the major issues to confirm the fact that the two Democratic contenders are, in reality, very close.

Minimum Wage: Both Clinton and Sanders favor raising the minimum wage—Clinton to $12 per hour, Sanders to $15. All of the Republican candidates oppose raising the minimum wage, and some have floated the idea of eliminating it altogether. Trump even said, "wages are too high" during a nationally televised Republican debate.

Voting Rights: Both Clinton and Sanders favor restoring the Voting Rights Act, making registration easier, expanding early voting, and reducing wait times for voting. All of the Republican candidates have bought into the Republican Party's fake "voter fraud" scare tactics and favor legislation that makes both registration and voting more difficult in ways that disproportionately affect minorities, women, and young people.

Unions: Both Clinton and Sanders are long-time union supporters, and both have been endorsed by major national unions. The Republican candidates have all been active in efforts to weaken unions.

Campaign Financing: Both Clinton and Sanders want to repeal Citizens United and reform campaign finance laws. Most Republican candidates do not. (Trump is the exception because his own ridiculous wealth lessens his need for massive corporate contributions—although he will undoubtedly need corporate support for the general election if he is the Republican nominee.)

Gun Laws: Both Clinton and Sanders favor common-sense gun laws. Sanders, coming from the rural and somewhat libertarian state of Vermont, has actually opposed some gun regulations that Clinton supported. Sanders voted against the Brady Bill in 1993, and he voted for a bill protecting gun manufacturers from lawsuits as recently as 2005. But they are currently both very much on the liberal/progressive side of gun policy. Clinton's most recent rating from the National Rifle Association is an "F" while Sanders is close with a "D-." The Republican candidates all cling to the NRA and favor legislation that relaxes gun safety even more than the already loose laws that plague our country.

Wall Street and Banking Reform: Both Clinton and Sanders support Wall Street reform. Sanders focuses on the reinstating the Glass-Steagall law, breaking up the big banks, and reforming the Federal Reserve while Clinton has proposed a comprehensive reform approach that's stronger than the current Obama administration reforms. Yes, Sanders would be more hated by Wall Street, but the financial industry wouldn't be happy with most Clinton proposals either. Wall Street has donated to her campaign in the hope that she will be less reform-minded than Sanders, much as they supported Obama in 2008. But they pulled way back on their support for Obama in 2012 because he championed the Dodd-Frank reform bill, credit card reform, the Consumer Protection Bureau—and he won a $5.7 billion settlement for the financial crisis of 2008. Wall Street will similarly drop support for Clinton when she works for the reforms she has proposed. The Republican candidates, of course, want to deregulate their buddies on Wall Street as much as possible regardless of the consequences to everyday Americans.

LGBT Issues: Both Clinton and Sanders support LGBT equality in all aspects of life, from marriage to employment. Clinton may have come to her position on marriage equality later than Sanders, but she is there now. The same can be said of Obama, and he has become a champion for LGBT rights. Clinton has been endorsed by Human Rights Watch, the leading LGBT advocacy group. Republicans, of course, all seek to repeal the advances of recent LGBT rights victories and bring us back to the discrimination of darker times.

Religious Freedom: Both Clinton and Sanders support freedom of (and from) religion for all Americans as the U.S. Constitution outlines in the First Amendment. The Republican candidates have ignored the Constitution and behave as though Christianity deserves preferential rights regarding religious freedom.

Equal Pay: Both Clinton and Sanders support equal pay for equal work and have both supported legislation that supports gender equality. The Republican candidates pay lip-service to equality, but none of them has voted for any legislation that addresses the issue.

Deficit Reduction: Both Clinton and Sanders favor reducing the federal budget deficit through a combination of fair taxes and reductions to wasteful spending, particularly defense spending. Republicans have proposed cutting programs for the poor and middle-class, shifting tax burdens even more onto the poor and middle-class, and increasing defense spending. In short, their budget-reduction plans actually increase the budget deficit while comforting the comfortable and afflicting the afflicted.

Taxes: Both Clinton and Sanders have proposed tax increases for the wealthy and corporations to return us to the fair policies that helped to create the middle-class in the last century. Clinton, in fact, has promised not to raise taxes on people making less that $250,000 per year while Sanders proposals don't rule out increased middle-class tax rates to fund specific programs. The Republican candidates, of course, talk about lowering taxes on everyone, but the details of their plans reveal a far greater burden on the middle-class and the poor to fund giveaways to the wealthy and corporations.

College Affordability: Both Clinton and Sanders have proposed plans for no-debt college education. Sanders's plan calls for free tuition at public institutions while Clinton's plan calls for expanded work-study and grant opportunities for students to finance their education. Both plans would address the crippling student loan debt crisis. The Republican candidates view education as a commodity subject to the whims of the free market. Under their plans, student loan debt is just a profit source for the banking industry.

Marijuana and Drug Policy: Both Clinton and Sanders favor medical marijuana and reforming the criminal justice system with regard to drug laws and sentencing, although Sanders goes farther in the direction of legalizing recreational marijuana use than Clinton. The Republican candidates are split on medical marijuana, and all except Rand Paul support harsh penalties for recreational drug use.

Foreign Affairs: Both Clinton and Sanders emphasize that our nation's diplomatic role in the world is far more important than our military role. Clinton has a reputation as more of a hawk than Sanders, but her work as Secretary of State shows she understands the essential nature of American diplomacy as a way to encourage peace throughout the world. The Republican candidates (with the exception of Rand Paul) have all beaten war drums, particularly relating to conflicts in the Middle East. Most of them would have us escalate the conflicts in Iraq and Afghanistan while starting new wars in Iran and Syria.

Iran Nuclear Deal: Both Clinton and Sanders support the Obama administration's nuclear deal with Iran as the best chance for peace and nuclear de-escalation in the region. Clinton's work as Secretary of State during Obama's first term helped to lay the groundwork for the deal. All of the Republican candidates, of course, oppose the deal and would almost certainly kill it before even giving it a chance to work.

Terrorism: Both Clinton and Sanders support creating international coalitions that combine military action and diplomacy to fight terrorism. They both oppose torture and support programs aimed at reducing terrorist recruiting, cutting off funding sources for terrorists, and closing the offshore prison at Guantanamo Bay. The Republican candidates favor a return to the Bush administration's "us against them" mentality, they oppose closing

---

Guantanamo Bay, and they favor the use of torture.

Social Security and Medicare: Both Clinton and Sanders oppose privatizing Medicare or Social Security. Both support increasing benefits and coverage, especially through tax increases on the wealthy. Both oppose raising the retirement age (despite inaccurate reports that Clinton endorsed this idea). Most of the Republican candidates favor raising the retirement age, along with reductions and privatization of both Social Security and Medicare.

Abortion and Family Planning: Both Clinton and Sanders support comprehensive access to contraception, family planning, prenatal care, family leave, and continued federal funding for Planned Parenthood—which has endorsed Clinton. They both support a woman's right to choose what to do with her own pregnancy. All of the Republican candidates believe government should make reproductive choices for pregnant women and that insurance coverage for contraception access should be determined by an employer's religious beliefs. Republicans also oppose federal funding for Planned Parenthood, and most have told ridiculous lies as part of an organized right-wing smear campaign against the organization.

Stem Cell Research: Both Clinton and Sanders support funding for embryonic stem cell research because of the medical benefits in treating numerous diseases. Although Sanders joined Congressional Republicans in opposing therapeutic cloning in the early 2000s, he has come around to a more progressive and science-based view. All of the Republican candidates oppose embryonic stem cell research on confused anti-abortion grounds. Despite the hypocrisy of his stated opposition, Ben Carson has actually participated in medical research that used embryonic stem cells.

Universal Healthcare: Both Clinton and Sanders believe that healthcare is a human right. Both support Obamacare and have made proposals to improve the program. Sanders has long been a proponent of a single-payer system and would push for a Medicare-for-all system immediately. Clinton proposed a comprehensive program in her role as First Lady more than two decades ago. The Republican candidates universally oppose Obamacare and single-payer health insurance systems. They view medical insurance and healthcare as a product available to only those who can afford it.

Comprehensive Immigration Reform: Both Clinton and Sanders support comprehensive immigration reform, including a detailed path to citizenship for undocumented immigrants. One of the few times their votes in the Senate differed was when they disagreed on a the details of a proposed 2007 immigration bill, with Clinton voting in favor and Sanders against. Republicans in Congress ultimately blocked the bill. Some Republicans support minor, piecemeal immigration reform, but most of the Republican candidates are loudly anti-reform, especially Trump.

Refugees: Both Clinton and Sanders favor America's longstanding tradition of bringing refugees from troubled regions of the world into the

—
29

United States. Both candidates support the current rigorous system of screening refugees to ensure that people intent on committing terrorist acts do not gain entry into the country masquerading as refugees. The Republican candidates have been fear mongering about refugees coming to our country and don't seem to recognize that we even have a screening process. They've shown very little compassion for the plight of refugees fleeing terrorism. Trump's proposed ban on Muslim refugees is the most bigoted and xenophobic example of Republican views.

Trans-Pacific Partnership: Both Clinton and Sanders oppose the TPP. Sanders has consistently been against these types of major trade deals while Clinton, as a member of the Obama administration that was developing the deal, was an early supporter of the TPP process before she opposed the final form of the deal. Some Republicans have voiced support for the deal, but most oppose it, primarily out of automatic opposition to everything President Obama supports.

Keystone XL Pipeline: Both Clinton and Sanders oppose the pipeline because of its negative environmental impact. Clinton took longer to come to that position, but she is now in the same place as Sanders on the issue. All of the Republican candidates support the pipeline and downplay its environmental impact while wildly exaggerating the jobs and energy benefits.

Climate Change and the Environment: Both Clinton and Sanders recognize the scientific consensus that climate change is real and caused by human activity. They both support the Obama administration's recent international Paris agreement to reduce emissions. They both support efforts to promote renewable energy and reduce our dependence on fossil fuels. They both understand that climate change is an issue that affects the international security of the United States. The Republican Party is the only major political group on the planet that denies global climate change. Republican candidates downplay, dismiss, or ridicule climate science and promote fossil fuels over renewable energy. The Republican Party in general is against nearly all environmental regulations.

Veterans Programs: Both Clinton and Sanders have consistently championed programs that benefit American veterans and current military members. Both have spearheaded specific bills in the Senate to help veterans. The Republican candidates love to praise veterans, but they are far more likely to put more military personnel in harm's way for questionable goals, and they have consistently opposed programs that would help veterans after they come home from combat.

Despite all the areas where Clinton agrees with Sanders, she isn't perfect, of course. Sanders supporters raise legitimate questions about her corporate donors, her super PAC, her campaign tactics, and her connections with the party establishment. She is also against marijuana decriminalization and has been in favor of capital punishment in the past—although she hasn't said much on the issue in recent years. She favors extremely strict regulation of fracking while her favors an outright ban. But, after reviewing the list of views she shares with Sanders on so many crucial issues, it's just not credible for anyone to claim that Clinton has more in common with Republicans than with Sanders.

Here's another fact that Sanders "lesser-of-two-evils" supporters must understand if they are going to make a responsible choice in the event that Clinton secures the party nomination: Hillary Clinton is not evil, lesser or otherwise. Ample evidence exists from her long career in public service to support her candidacy from a liberal/progressive viewpoint. This evidence rarely sees the light in the scandal-obsessed corporate media, but Clinton's progressive record of accomplishments is clear for anyone who takes the time to look beyond the smear campaigns.

Clinton was an active and progressive First Lady during her husband's presidency. She chaired the task force that created the Health Security Act of 1993, dubbed "Hillarycare" two decades before "Obamacare." The proposal was eventually defeated by obstructionist Republicans and weak Democrats who didn't support the program. Those who today claim that Clinton is just a Republican in disguise would do well to remember the criticism of her health care plan all those years ago: "too liberal."

Clinton also went to China during her time as First Lady and spoke courageously about women's rights when China most certainly didn't want to hear about women's rights. Despite the defeat of "Hillarycare," Clinton fought while First Lady for the Children's Heath Insurance Program (CHIP), which continues to provide health care to millions of children. She helped pass the Adoption and Safe Families Act, improving the adoption system across the nation. She worked for veterans suffering from Gulf War Syndrome when they came back from the first Iraq war waged by the first Bush administration. In short, she was a progressive force as First Lady.

In less than two full terms as a Senator, she developed legislation to extend full military health benefits to National Guard members and reservists. Representing New York, she was instrumental in securing funding to address the medical needs of 9-11 first responders. And she strengthened the CHIP program that she helped found as First Lady. She also developed legislation that reformed immigration policies, improved flu vaccines, supported family caregivers, and expanded access to family planning services.

Coming on the heels of the Bush administrations disastrous foreign policy, Clinton joined President Obama to rebuild America's respect in the world community as Secretary of State. She renewed, improved, and established relationships with nearly every region of the world during her four years as our nation's leading diplomat. She negotiated a ceasefire between Israel and Hamas during an escalation in their conflict. She helped form the coalition that protected thousands of Libyans from genocide by Muammar

GADDAFI. She organized China, Russian, and the European Union to impose the sanctions against Iran that laid the groundwork for getting that nation to negotiate a nuclear deal.

In addition, her work with Bill Clinton through the Clinton Foundation helped improve the living conditions of millions of people in hundreds of countries. The foundation funds health care programs, disaster relief, education, women's rights, civil rights, and a host of other programs across the globe—earning praise (and donations) from even Donald Trump himself before his nasty run for the presidency. Republicans have alleged conflicts of interest between the Foundation and Clinton's role as Secretary of State, but they haven't provided a single reliable fact to back up their charges.

Overall, I have three requests for the Sanders supporters. First, please look at Clinton's positions on the issues objectively. Don't fall into the trap of right-wing rhetoric that began before some of today's voters were even born. Republicans have been attacking her since her husband ran for president in 1992, partly to damage him but also because they knew she would be a formidable candidate herself in the future. They were right. She was an active and passionate First Lady, an effective and progressive Senator, and a tireless and consequential Secretary of State. And she has been a career-long champion of progressive causes.

Second, please tone down the anti-Clinton rhetoric. In more than three decades of studying politics, I've never seen supporters of one candidate attack another so closely aligned to their own candidate the way a small but loud minority of Sanders supporters have attacked Clinton. I've personally been called as many foul names in recent months by Sanders supporters as I usually am by right-wingers—and I loudly proclaim my love for Sanders. My crime? I recognize that Clinton is better for the country than any Republican presidential candidate.

Please remember that people who are undecided between voting Democrat or Republican in November are listening to our discussions. When they hear nasty attacks, they assume Democrats are as bad as Republicans, get turned off, and don't vote. Don't let the normal squabbles of party politics (such as the nothingburger December data breech or the number of debates) take away from the fact that Clinton and Sanders have been refreshingly civil in their interactions with each other. Take your cue from Sanders himself and focus on Clinton's positions on the issues rather than personal attacks.

Third, and most important, if Sanders loses to Clinton in the primaries (which every poll shows will likely happen), then please do the right thing and vote for Clinton in the general election. She may not be perfect in everyone's view, but she's far, far better than any Republican candidate. Sanders himself has said so. So be like Sanders. In retrospect, one major reason we got two terrible George W. Bush terms is that people didn't think Al Gore and John Kerry were perfect enough. And a big reason we have a horrible Republican Congress and so many bad Republican governors and legislatures across the country is that people didn't think Obama was perfect enough in 2010 and 2014.

If Clinton gets the nomination, then we need all of the Sanders supporters voting for her and convincing their reluctant friends to do likewise. The "Sanders or Bust" movement is a sure way to lose the general election. Sanders himself will certainly endorse and vote for her if she's the nominee. He has vowed not to run as an independent, and he won't be writing in his own name or voting for third-party candidates with no chance to win. And he absolutely won't be staying home on election day. Some folks may still not completely trust Clinton, but she's on board with the vast majority of the Sanders policy positions.

Being an enthusiastic supporter of the candidate you lose to in the primaries takes class and dignity. And that's exactly what Clinton did for Obama in 2008. She didn't sulk or pout or mount a third-party challenge. She recognized reality and did what was best for the country. I have no doubt that she will do the same this time if Sanders is the nominee, and Sanders will do the same for Clinton if she wins. We should expect the same class and dignity from each candidate's supporters as well.

If Clinton is the nominee, then there's always the chance that she could ask Sanders to be her running mate. The conventional wisdom has Clinton selecting a young, dynamic candidate (Julian Castro, for example) to energize the youth vote. But Sanders has already energized the youth vote, so why not him? If Clinton becomes president and wins a second term, as most presidents in the past half century have, there would be plenty of time to groom younger Democratic candidates to hold onto the presidency in 2024. More likely, Clinton could immediately appoint Sanders to the cabinet as Secretary of Labor, where he could have an even bigger policy impact than he does in the Senate.

If people refuse to vote for her because she's not as good as Sanders, or if they write in Sanders rather than voting for Clinton, then we're much more likely to end up with a President Trumpcruzrubiobushpalinputin—along with more wars, more alienation of the world community, more tax cuts for the rich, more fights about marriage equality, no minimum wage increase, no reasonable improvements to gun laws, no improvements in health care reform, no sane immigration polices, lots of extremists in the cabinet and on the Supreme Court, and on and on. We thought George W. Bush was bad, but the people vying for the Republican nomination right now would be many times worse.

The core message here isn't that Sanders supporters should give up. By all means, please keep campaigning for him in the primaries. He's an outstanding candidate who would make a terrific president. The vast majority of Clinton voters will support him if he wins the nomination. The core message is that two very specific candidates, Sanders and Clinton, would be far better than any Republican in the race.

Listen to both candidates, compare and contrast, and vote in the primaries for the one you think should be the nominee. But the Democrats who don't vote in the general election if their favored candidate doesn't get the nomination could very well help Republicans win the White House and, even worse, win down-ballot Senate, House, Governor, and local elections as well. Republicans have proven that they get out and vote in Presidential elections even when their preferred candidate doesn't win the nomination. Democrats need to show the same commitment.

The bottom line is that Democrats must vote, whether we nominate Sanders or Clinton. If we don't, then Republicans will win. That's not fear mongering. That's basic electoral reality.

You Don't Build a Wall Around a
Shining City on a Hill

December 2015

Five minutes after the San Bernardino shooters were identified, a conservative friend of mine took to Facebook to say that all Muslims are killers. Funny, but he didn't say that all Christians are killers after a Colorado Planned Parenthood was attacked by a Christian a few days earlier. I come to Facebook for connection and community, not misinformed and nasty comments. Unfortunately, that kind of appalling ignorance is shockingly common these days.

Not surprisingly, my Facebook friend is a Donald Trump supporter. I asked him if his accusation that all Muslims are killers encompassed all three million Muslims in the United States, including the 5,000 Muslims serving in our armed forces. What about the Muslims I've known over the years—friends, neighbors, students, and colleagues? "Yes," he replied, "all of them." I asked if that included my dentist. He often puts dangerous instruments in my mouth, so if he's a terrorist, then he could inflict some serious dental terror on me. "Him too," I was informed. Who knew the battle against tooth decay was part of the global terrorist agenda!?

We all want to keep our country safe, but Trump and many Republicans these days have devolved into xenophobia and isolationism. They want to build a wall around our country, as well as reject Syrian refugees fleeing terrorism. When did Republicans go from seeing the United States as a shining city on a hill to a walled-off, three-little-pigs hut where we hide from the big bad wolf?

Guess who else wants us to build a wall and reject refugees? The terrorists who call themselves ISIS want us to isolate ourselves and turn our backs to the rest of the world. Daesh (a better name because the terrorists themselves hate it—and it sounds a little like "douche") is a tiny minority of extremists who want us to hide behind walls, real and imaginary. Daesh wants us to stop helping less fortunate people around the world so that they can have an easier fight against them.

I'm old enough to remember people talking about how Irish immigrants were all criminals who shouldn't have been let in the country. Some of my distant ancestors wouldn't have made it here if the people in charge took the view that Republicans are taking now.

Refusing refugees supports Daesh, pure and simple. The refugees we reject today could easily become the terrorists of tomorrow. The vast majority of these refugees are escaping from harm, not trying to do harm. If they're abandoned, they're far more likely to strike out.

Republican presidential candidates act like they're trying to recruit for Daesh. Jeb Bush wants refugees to prove that they're Christians. Seriously? I'm not sure Jeb Bush can prove that he's a Christian. Chris Christie says he wouldn't even accept a five-year-old orphan refugee. I thought guys from New Jersey were supposed to be tough, not quivering masses of jello that melt at the prospect of a toddler from another country.

No one wants to let any potential terrorists into the country. That's why we have a rigorous screening process that takes one to two years to consider each refugee—longer for Syrians. The process involves the United Nations, the Departments of Defense, State, and Homeland Security, and the FBI, among other agencies. Some Republicans seem to think that President Obama flies Air Force One into a refugee camp, plucks up a random few thousand people, and then drops them over the rainbow in Kansas. That's a fantasy world.

If any country can screen terrorists from refugees, we can—and we do. According to the Migration Policy Institute, the United States has cleared 784,000 refugees to enter the country since 9-11, and only three have since been arrested for terror-related charges, none of them Syrian. If only our weak gun laws were a fraction as effective, then we could surely reduce the shocking number of mass shootings.

Trump has said that President Obama is being too "politically correct" in fighting Daesh. "With the terrorists," he said, "you have to take out their families." Trump doesn't seem to understand that purposely killing civilians is an international war crime. Another word for killing family members of your enemy would be "terrorism."

It's not just Trump. Most Republicans say that President Obama is too soft on terrorism. Many claim he has done nothing to fight terrorism. Some even say that he sides with the terrorists. Those are lies. According to Defense Department sources, the Obama-led coalition has made more than 8,000 airstrikes and dropped 28,000 bombs on Daesh targets since Operation Inherent Resolve began in 2014.

We can debate the wisdom of this bombing campaign, but claiming it doesn't exist denies reality. Bombing terrorists is a strange way to be "soft" on terrorism. Bombs aren't soft. I'm just glad Obama doesn't like me so much that he sends a Tomahawk missile as a token of his affection. Thinking that Obama sides with terrorists while he's killing them to protect us is profoundly confused.

Many Republicans are confused enough think Obama created Daesh. They claim the group only came into existence because Obama "cut and ran" in Iraq. This theory ignores the fact that George W. Bush negotiated the timetable and conditions for the U.S. withdrawal from Iraq, and Obama followed through on that agreement. Republicans also ignore the fact that Daesh's leaders are members of Saddam's Bath Party and army that the Bush administration disbanded. Basically, when Daesh was born, Obama was a state senator in Illinois while George Bush and Dick Cheney were handing out cigars as the proud parents of baby Daesh.

The Republican word police also believe that if Obama just called these Daesh criminals "radical Islam," then that would somehow stop terrorism. Really? Do they think that calling the Ku Klux Klan or the Planned Parenthood murderer "radical Christian" would have stopped them? Of course not.

The terrorists who call themselves ISIS want us to label them "Islamic" for the same reason KKK meeting begins with a prayer and the Pledge of Allegiance. Klan members think they're Christian patriots rather than terrorists. Daesh members think they follow "true" Islam, but they don't. The vast majority of Muslims have been saying loudly and clearly that Daesh isn't true to Islam.

The rise of Donald Trump and his nastiness has intensified the backlash against Muslims, but it dates back nearly a decade, roughly to the emergence of Barack Obama as a national leader. A recent PPP poll showed that a majority of Republicans still believe the president is a Muslim, despite the fact that he is a lifelong Christian.

Republicans haven't always been this bad. President George W. Bush, to his credit, said many times that Muslims are peaceful and we are not at war with Islam. Today's Republican leaders seem to have lost that common-sense perspective in their quest to frighten people into voting for them. America deserves better.

Keep Guns Out of Our Schools

November 2015

After the mass shooting at Virginia Tech in 2007, my little community college in Connecticut had a training session about responding to a campus shooting. Before the session began, my colleagues and I chatted, shuffled papers, and made last-minute class plans as we always do before pre-semester meetings. I opened my laptop to multitask on some class plans.

Then the trainer began the session with these words: "When there's a shooting on campus, the teacher is always the first person murdered." The paper shuffling stopped. I closed my laptop. He had our full attention. This turned out to be one of the most useful (and most unsettling) training session any of us had ever attended.

School shootings have become all too common in recent years. Since Virginia Tech, there have been approximately 200 incidents of gunfire at schools, resulting in more than 100 deaths. Just last month, another major school shooting took place at Umpqua Community College in Oregon. As our trainer would have predicted, the teacher was the first person shot. In the face of all this violence, we have instituted many basic security upgrades at our small, one-building campus.

We started keeping most of our outside doors locked, instituted a key card system for employees, and tightened our guest check-in procedures. Our classroom doors now all lock from the inside. We reactivated our long-dormant public address system for both broadcasting and listening in the event of an emergency. We installed panic buttons inside and outside the building and added two dozen security cameras with live monitoring. We increased the number of security guards and improved our already strong relationship with the local police department.

One step we haven't taken is bringing guns to the college. Connecticut has no specific laws prohibiting guns on college campuses. That decision is left to the colleges themselves. In a nod to old-fashioned New England common sense, every public and private college in the state prohibits open or concealed carry of firearms. Even our security guards don't carry guns.

NRA leadership tells us that arming teachers would protect students. As a teacher for more than three decades, I can assure the NRA that teachers already have full-time jobs. We don't need to become armed guards as well. We belittle police officers when we say teachers can easily handle law enforcement duties, and we belittle teachers when we say that we should add complex security duties to their jobs. As an aside, I'm pleased to note that I don't see any NRA-style gunslingers who want to exploit our students as a way to live out unrealistic first-person shooter hero fantasies when I look around at our faculty meetings.

The NRA has fought every common-sense gun law proposed in recent years. There are many basic regulations that could help address school shootings, such as expanded and improved background checks, limits or bans on extended magazines and assault weapons, and more restrictive open- and concealed-carry laws. These laws could go a long way toward reducing the number of mass shootings and the death toll that results from these horrible crimes. Connecticut had the good sense to enact many of these laws after the Newtown shooting. But the NRA-controlled Republicans in charge of Congress and most state governments have made sure that reasonable gun-safety laws don't get the fair hearing they deserve.

Obviously, we all want to protect our students and everyone else on campus. But bringing guns to school isn't the answer. Do we really want our children and young adults educated in a militarized environment, growing up thinking that it's normal to have armed people patrolling civilian areas during peacetime? That sounds more like a third-world dictatorship than the greatest republic in world history.

The recent case of Ben Fields, the uniformed South Carolina school resource officer who slammed a disobedient young female student from her desk, isn't much better than a dictator's armed thugs terrorizing our schools. I recognize that such behavior shouldn't condemn the vast majority of police officers who view their careers as a public trust and perform their duties with honor and courage. But the Fields case illustrates the exact opposite of what we need in terms of law enforcement, authority, and security in our schools.

We need to take the concept of "resource officer" and amplify it by recruiting, training, and rewarding the best officers for this position. They should specialize in interacting with students and employees in positive and supportive ways. And these officers should be integrated into the school community enough to anticipate potential troubles and diffuse them before they can escalate to violence.

This should be a highly desirable job for only the best officers because they would be charged with protecting our young people and helping shape their lives, very much as teachers do. Only the best officers, those trained in working productively with young people, should be eligible to apply for these jobs. They should be evaluated closely, offered the support they need to perform their jobs at the highest level, and fired if they can't do the job. Officers with a history of disciplinary problems or excessive force shouldn't be allowed anywhere near our students.

These officers should be armed, of course, but with concealed, non-lethal (but still effective) weapons. The idea that safety is improved by introducing more guns to any situation is clearly disproven by basic criminal justice research. Far better that any collateral damage in the event of a

---

confrontation is from non-lethal weapons rather than guns. Our current technology for nonlethal weapons may be inadequate for this task, but that's no reason to reject the idea. If such weapons don't exist, let's make it a national priority to invent them.

Teachers may be the first victims of school shooters, but students are the most tragic victims. The presence of our best officers in the schools, far more than the presence of guns, would send the message that police are here to protect and support students, not enforce arbitrary authority over young people in inappropriate, stifling, or even violent ways.

Basically, that's the way the best local law enforcement works, with an emphasis on common-sense security measures, community engagement, respect, and collaboration. Our schools are our most important local communities. Why shouldn't they have our best officers?

Sending Good Vibes

October 2015

"Please pray for me." I see this request on Facebook more often than posts about food, puppies, grandchildren, politics, and the day's weather combined.

The reasons for these requests range from poignant to commonplace to outlandish. "Dad is going in for surgery today." "My little girl has her blood test this morning." "I see the doctor today at noon." My heart goes out to these friends without hesitation.

Then I read requests like these: "My class presentation is this afternoon—prayers please!" "Please send prayers for my job interview today!" "The plane is about to take off. Please pray for God to hold up the wings!" Okay. My heart flutters, but is it wrong that my empathy isn't as intense as it is for the folks with fathers in surgery or children who may face terrible diseases?"

Then there are the "vaguebookers," people who post cryptic requests. "I could really use some prayers right now!" I hope I'm not being cruel when I sometimes translate this request to, "I could really use some attention right now!"

My favorite prayer request arrived while I took a break from writing this column to scan social media. "Please send me some prayers. I'm going through a difficult time right now. I need to work but all of my Facebook friends are extra-interesting and amazing today, and I can't seem to get off the computer." Wow, she read my mind! Some good-hearted but irony-impaired folks said they would keep her in their prayers.

I've even read some recent requests to pray for Kim Davis, Mike Huckabee, Ben Carson, Ted Cruz, and His Excellency, Donald Trump. How do I pray for people who discriminate in the name of God or for disingenuous politicians who want to pull our country down a dangerous and regressive path? I was asked to pray for the sinners at Planned Parenthood who are killing babies and selling their body parts. How do I pray based on a vicious lie about people who have dedicated their lives to helping treat women's health needs?

I'm often unsure how to respond to any of these prayer requests. As a "nontraditional" Christian, I don't address God directly in my mind or aloud. I don't fold my hands or drop to my knees in the standard prayer position. Matthew 6:5 advises us not to pray in public like the show-off hypocrites. On the other hand, First Thessalonians 5:17 tells us to pray without ceasing. How do we manage to adhere to both Biblical messages?

My "prayers" may not be traditional, but I definitely keep "good thoughts" for friends and loved ones. I even think "good thoughts" for people I disagree with strongly—perhaps not "without ceasing" but often. Matthew 5:44 tells us to love our enemies. If love means wanting everyone to treat other human beings with more care and respect and believing that they can, then, yes, I love my enemies.

One Republican Facebook friend posted the message, "Pray for Obama" with a reference to Psalm 109. When I pointed out that praying for Obama's death wasn't very nice, he replied that he didn't know what I was talking about. So I quoted part of Psalm 109: "Let his children be fatherless and his wife a widow." To his credit, my friend had the common sense to apologize and delete his post once he knew the full context of his biblical reference. I sent him good thoughts.

Do my "good thoughts" count as "prayers"? Back in college, when I was active in Christian groups, I once told a friend that I was thinking "good thoughts" for him during a tough time. He was offended. "I'd rather you prayed for me, but if you don't care enough to pray, then I guess that shows me how you really feel." Ummm … I love you, too? I ended up on some prayer lists because my "good thoughts" weren't prayerful enough for some folks.

I'm still fond of the phrase "sending good thoughts" and use it frequently in social media and real life. Those three words are especially useful on Facebook because I follow them with a "lesser than" character and the numeral 3, which the Facebook angels convert to a heart so perfectly shaped and so deeply crimson that I can almost feel it bursting in my chest. Maybe it's the power of that bleeding heart, but I always get a "like" on my "good thoughts" comments, no matter the religious or political affiliation of the object of my good thoughts.

"Pray for me," Pope Francis said to adoring crowds during his recent visit to the United States. "And if some of you can't pray because you are not believers, send me good vibrations." There's a request I can support every time.

In fact, I recently put together my own "good vibrations" response for every Facebook prayer request. I assembled a couple dozen photos of 2004 Pontiac Vibes, the same car I've driven for a decade and will drive until it falls apart. Then I added the words, "Hey, you! I'm sending you a whole lot of good Vibes!"

And I mean it. Good Vibes for everyone! Hope it helps.

Who is the Democrats' Donald Trump?

September 2015

"Democrats and Republicans are all the same," is a fashionable lament, but it's one that doesn't stand up to basic scrutiny.

Recent years have brought us reality-challenged Republicans such as Sarah Palin, Michelle Bachmann, Allen West, Joe Walsh, Louie Gohmert, Steve King, and Paul LePage, to name only a few. I like to ask people who claim that both parties were equally bad, "Who's the Democrats' equivalent of these Republicans?" No one ever gives me an adequate answer. Obviously, no Democrat is even close to that level of absurdity.

The current Republican presidential front-runner destroys the false claim that both parties are the same. Every time someone sees an assessment of Donald Trump as a terrible candidate and then names Democrats who they think are somehow just as bad, it's hard not to laugh at the absurdity. It's like saying, "Sure, a tornado wiped out ten city blocks, but we had some drizzle in the next town down the road." Asking which Democrat running for president is the equivalent of Donald Trump is too easy. Clearly, no one is. The real question is this: Which elected Democrat at any level in the past decade is anywhere near as absurd as Trump? The only rational answer to that question is also, "no one."

Which Democrat made ridiculous "birther" accusations about President Obama and insisted that he would prove his claims—but never even tried? Which Democrat said that going to a rich-kid military school gave him as much training as members of our armed forces? Which Democrat held a fundraiser for a fake veterans' group? Which Democrat said he gets his foreign policy knowledge from TV shows? Which Democrat's approach to the Middle East can be summed up as, "bomb 'em and take their oil"? Which Democrat said he has a secret plan to destroy ISIS but will only reveal it if he gets elected?

Which Democrat is a reality TV celebrity? Which Democrat kicked off his campaign by calling millions of people "rapists"? Which Democrat's campaign slogan is as insulting to our nation as Trump's, "Make America Great Again"? If President Obama donned a baseball cap with Trump's slogan, Republicans would make "America's Already Great—Go Back to Kenya!" their convention theme.

Which Democrat defends decades of derogatory comments about women by claiming that it's okay because he was only talking about Rosie O'Donnell? Which Democrat feuded with a woman television personality by retweeting comments calling her a "bimbo"? Which Democrat makes comments about wanting to date his own daughter or insulted the appearance

---

of the only woman Republican running for president? Which Democrat has a long history of calling anyone he disagrees with "stupid" and "a loser"?

Which Democrat's speeches and debate performances have been analyzed by linguists and found to be at a fourth-grade level? Which Democrat is being sued over the unlicensed fake "university" that bears his name? Which Democrat brags about making money from his four bankruptcies and earned about the same from his multi-million-dollar inheritance as he would have if he had simply invested in the stock market and slept all day?

Which Democrat gives "policy" speeches with no actual policies? Which Democrat has never earned a "true" rating from PolitiFact, the leading nonpartisan fact-checker? Which Democrat shares Trump's PolitiFact rating of nearly 80% "mostly false," "false," and "pants on fire" statements? By contrast, less than a third of President Obama's, Hillary Clinton's, and Bernie Sanders's statements fall into those embarrassing categories.

Which Democrat has proposed a plan as cruel and impractical as deporting millions of people? Which Democrat ejected a respected Latino journalist from his press conference for questioning that plan? Which Democrat inspired two jerks in Boston to beat up a Latino homeless man and then claim, "Trump was right. All these illegals need to be deported."? Which Democrat running such an anti-immigrant campaign claimed, "I will win the Latino vote" while polling 14% approval among Latinos?

Despite the common-sense fact that Trump has no counterpart among Democrats, many ill-informed commentators still try to force the comparisons. For example, in his recent *Daily Hampshire Gazette* column, my columnist colleague, Jay Fleitman, compared Trump to Barack Obama and Hillary Clinton. Seriously? Fleitman couldn't defend his claim because even he must know it's as twisted as Trump's hair. Fleitman represents "establishment" Republicans who object to Trump's tone. In reality, however, most Republican presidential candidates are just as bad as Trump in their own ways.

Here are some examples: Carson and Bush have repeatedly lied about Planned Parenthood. Huckabee compared Obama to Nazis. Christie and Walker have been under investigation, and Perry is under indictment. Kasich proposed eliminating teacher's lounges as education reform. Paul (a doctor!) echoed Trump's false claim that vaccines can cause mental disorders. Fiorina fired 30,000 workers at HP before being fired herself. Cruz called Obama the world's biggest sponsor of terrorism. Rubio will keep denying climate change even after his Miami home is under water. And on and on. These folks aren't as loud as Trump, but they're equally terrible for the country.

Who is the Democrat's Trump? No one. Why? Because both parties aren't even close to being the same. Today's Republicans are far, far worse. Here's the real question: Which political party supports such unqualified, obnoxious, and dishonest candidates as Trump and the many Trumpettes in the Republican presidential field?

In one sense, I underestimated Trump. I thought he would poll poorly, drop out when things got tough, and then cravenly declare himself the winner because he made other candidates adopt his views. But that's what would have happened if he had run as a Democrat. In fact, I overestimated the Republican Party as a whole. I know many wonderful people who are lifelong Republicans, so I couldn't have guessed that a significant percentage of the party would be deluded, ignorant, and nasty enough to see Trump as their savior. The bottom line is that Trump and the rest of the Republican presidential candidates are the stinking head of a fish that's in danger of becoming rotten all the way to the tail.

Ben Carson is a Typical Republican Hypocrite

August 2015

Ben Carson was once a well-respected neurosurgeon. Then he started running for president and talking in public. I really don't care what Ben Carson thinks about the pyramids. He can hold whatever loony views he wants as a private citizen, no matter how wrong those views are. Ben Carson for president? Absolutely not, thank you very much.

Carson's ideas about the role of government are just as loony as his thoughts on the pyramids, and that's where he gets to be dangerous. He can't force Americans to believe that the pyramids were built by the Biblical Joseph to store grain. But, if he became president, Carson would try to force his views about government onto other Americans, and that's not acceptable.

For example, Carson believes that government assistance makes people too dependent to work for themselves. He's particularly focused on Obamacare, which he was confused enough to compare to slavery. Obviously, the Affordable Care Act, which is far from being the "welfare" program that Republicans have tried to make us believe, hasn't enslaved anyone. In fact, no welfare program enslaves people. Instead, welfare gives people the chance to make their lives better while they're in a difficult situation. Welfare gives people an opportunity. That's the opposite of slavery.

Carson's own life is a great example of the opportunity welfare can bring to people's lives. In his own books, Carson has written about how government assistance made a positive difference in his own life, rather than making him lazy. His mother held their family together in part because she received welfare and food stamps. Carson himself got free eyeglasses from a government program as a child, helping him to succeed in school and eventually become a doctor.

Carson wants us to believe that government assistance to people suffering from economic hardships is somehow ruining America—except the assistance he got, of course. That view makes him a typical Republican hypocrite. He's happy to take for granted what the government did for him, but he wants to deny similar help to everyone else. Democrats, on the other hand, believe that government should work for everyone, not just the chosen, entitled few.

Carson's views about government assistance are very common among Republicans. When I told a friend of mine (an ardent Carson supporter) that Carson himself benefitted from welfare, he replied, "Well, at least Carson did better and didn't become dependent on handouts like so many of his brothers and sisters. Welfare has become a generational curse for millions in this country."

"Brothers and sisters?" I assume my friend wasn't refereeing to Carson's biological siblings. It's amazing how some Republicans can so easily drop racial dog whistles and code words into any conversation.

Let's look at some facts to put Carson's claims and my friend's comments in perspective. The vast majority of welfare recipients get benefits for only a short time, on average only a few months. That's hardly the "generational curse" that Republicans like to call government assistance. Studies show that more than three-fourths of the households that get welfare include people who hold jobs. Unfortunately, those jobs don't pay enough to support a family. Fully half of fast-food workers get some form of government assistance. I worked in fast food as a graduate student. Anyone who wants to call fast food workers lazy is just ignorant.

Another Republican friend told me that almost every time she goes to Walmart, she sees someone with "a buggy full of food, like, a lot, usually as much as mine. And they always use their EBT card but I use my debit card. It's extremely frustrating when they dress nice and have their nails done. My husband and I work very hard to raise three daughters to always do the right thing but it seems like everyone else is doing the wrong thing and being rewarded."

Wow, that's a lot to unpack. First, our personal observations tell only a small part of what's actually happening in the world. When I go to the grocery store, for example, I see hard-working store employees and hard-working customers buying food for their families. My Republican friend sees welfare recipients with food, clothing, and nails that make her jealous. She sees "everyone else doing the wrong thing."

Whose observations are more accurate and more reflective of reality—hers or mine? It doesn't matter, because actual research on the subject shows that the vast majority of people on welfare are in need, not abusing the system. They're feeding their families, not getting special things that are somehow being denied to other, supposedly more deserving people.

Second, as I mentioned earlier, a majority of the households that get welfare include people who hold jobs that pay less than a living wage. The next time my friend goes to Walmart, she should take a look at the employees working hard there. A big percentage of them are getting government benefits, even when they work part-time or full-time, because their wages are so low that they can't even afford to shop at Walmart. Is that their fault?

I've worked hard all my life. Like Carson, I didn't grow up in a wealthy household. We received some government benefits while still working very hard on our little farm, and those benefits weren't even close to extravagant. I worked very hard in college and graduate school, getting by through jobs, academic scholarships, and student loans. I paid back every penny of the loans with interest. My wife and I taught our children to do the right thing as well. Now they're teaching their own kids to do the right thing.

But if my children or grandchildren ever needed government assistance for a short time to put food on their family's table, I wouldn't appreciate people who don't know anything about them judging them as somehow being less worthwhile human beings.

Of course, I don't approve of the small percentage of people who try to abuse the system. Those folks are criminals whose behavior should be stopped. But I don't peek over people's shoulders to see how they're paying at the grocery store. It's not my business to judge. An EBT card doesn't look much different from most debit cards, so someone has to look very closely and be very interested in judging others to tell the difference. I'd rather focus my energies on making the world a better place for everyone than on singling out people in tough circumstances and judging them based on preconceived notions that don't match reality.

And I certainly could never support a presidential candidate such as Ben Carson who lacks the common sense to understand that the same benefits that helped his family can also benefit other families. I'll support candidates who understand that the vast majority of people would rather work than get a handout. I'll support candidates who understand that anyone can fall on hard times and need help now and then. I'll support candidates who understand that one of the main reason we have government is so that it can be an instrument through which "we the people" can help each other through those hard times. And I'll support candidates who understand that the term "welfare" isn't some kind of dirty word. It's in our Constitution.

Misleading Reports About Planned Parenthood

August 2015

My conservative columnist colleague, Jay Fleitman, wrote a recent column in *The Daily Hampshire Gazette* about the infamous Planned Parenthood videos circling the internet and stirring passions on all sides of the issue. Fleitman's column echoes a wave of misleading media reports surrounding these videos. The worst coverage has been by Fox News and other right-wing media. These outlets dishonestly claim that the videos show Planned Parenthood profiting from the sale of abortion-related "baby parts." That's not remotely true.

In contrast, the most common-sense coverage comes from fact-checkers who show that the videos are deceptively edited and presented with obvious manipulations. Rather than "sale" and "profit," the videos actually show a discussion of reimbursement for storage, delivery, and other expenses associated with voluntary donation of fetal tissue by women having abortions, all completely voluntary and legal. Calling this the "sale" of fetal tissue is an outright lie.

Right-wing media claim that tone of the video discussions proves Planned Parenthood is an evil organization. That's a gross distortion. These people aren't talking with patients who are considering an abortion. They aren't even talking about the philosophical issue of abortion. They're medical professionals talking with people pretending to be other medical professionals about technical issues related to medical procedures.

I personally know several wonderful people who work at Planned Parenthood clinics. They're among the kindest and most caring people I know. They're nothing like the supposed "monsters" being turned into caricatures in these videos. In reality, Planned Parenthood employees deliver services to women with the compassion and dignity that all human beings deserve.

Fleitman raises several questions near the end of this column that are indicative of the right-wing distortions of the issue. He first asks if the women getting abortions at Planned Parenthood were "all informed that their pregnancy would be reprocessed for sale?" First, there is no "sale," just donations and legal reimbursements. More importantly, Fleitman ignores the basic fact that these donations of fetal tissue for medical research are voluntary and only happen because the women getting abortions request donation. The alternative is that the tissue would be disposed of as medical waste.

Fleitman then asks if the women getting abortions knew "that Planned Parenthood might be making a profit on the sale?" Again, there is no "sale" or "profit." He then asks if women getting an abortion were "offered a percentage of that sale?" Fleitman's multiple repetitions of his dishonest "sale" claim don't convert his lie into truth, and focusing on percentages and profits is particularly disrespectful of the women involved.

Fleitman then stoops to proposing the "unthinkable specter of poor women getting pregnant for profit." Republicans are fond of false claims that poor women have children to get increased welfare benefits. But I've never heard anyone denigrate women so harshly by saying that a woman would purposely get pregnant as a way to earn a few dollars by having an abortion. Such a prospect does seem "unthinkable," yet Fleitman himself raises it. Frankly, the idea is disgusting.

After demeaning women and repeating the lie that Planned Parenthood is selling fetal tissue, Fleitman's next questions make no sense coming from a medical doctor. He asks about the research being conducted with "formed fetal tissue" and how this research differs from supposedly "less gruesome" stem cell research.

Even a non-physician can find these answers through a basic online search on the subjects. Fetal tissue research has been conducted for decades and has helped advance the treatment of polio, Parkinson's, and muscular dystrophy, among other serious diseases. Fetal tissue is less prone to rejection than adult stem cells and also provides more information on how human organs develop and react to different diseases. Fleitman is a physician writing a column that directly relates to medical issues. Expecting him to understand pertinent medical information really shouldn't be too much to ask.

His next question returns yet again to the lie about sales and profits. "Is the apparent sale of fetal tissue for profit illegal?" Yes, selling fetal tissue would be illegal—but no such sale is in evidence.

Fleitman's final questions are, frankly, pointless. "How is Planned Parenthood funded?" Planned Parenthood's budget reports are public and easily accessible online. More specifically, he wonders if Planned Parenthood is funded through "bulk grants under which abortions are subsidized?"

Even Fleitman must know about the Hyde Amendment, which forbids federal funding for abortions and has been reauthorized multiple times since 1976. Some states legally allow Medicaid funds to cover abortions in cases of rape, incest, or life-threatening health risks to the pregnant woman, but that's a very small percentage of abortions.

The bottom line is that Fleitman and his right-wing media role models ignore how Planned Parenthood provides free and low-cost medical care to millions of women who wouldn't otherwise have access, services such as prenatal care, STD and cancer screenings, contraception, and health education. Planned Parenthood helps prevent unwanted pregnancies, which prevents thousands if not millions of potential abortions.

Abortion is actually a small percentage (3%) of Planned Parenthood's services—and it's performed as a legal, safe, well-regulated medical procedure. By contrast, thousands of American women died each year from unsafe abortions before Roe v. Wade, just as tens of thousands of women continue to die from illegal abortions around the world each year. Planned Parenthood and legal abortion saves women's lives.

We shouldn't accept deceptive and manipulative videos as evidence that Planned Parenthood is anything other than an organization that supports and protects women's health. But Republicans are already planning another disingenuous government shutdown attempt over Planned Parenthood funding. These videos are being used dishonestly to inflame maximum outrage with a minimum of facts while attacking an organization that does tremendous good for millions of women. That's a shameful way to approach important issues.

Touching the Past to Heal the Future

July 2015

My wife and I recently visited South Carolina and walked directly by Emanuel African Methodist Episcopal *CHURCH*. To be honest, I didn't notice this particular church. Charleston is rich in historic buildings and beautiful landmarks. Another nearby church made a bigger impression because dozens of children played in its courtyard—kids of all races, laughing together in the steeple's shadow.

Several weeks after that trip, when I woke to news of the stunning murders at Emanuel, one of my first thoughts was of a different landmark, Boone Hall, a slave plantation near Charleston that now serves as a tourist attraction. A row of slave cottages lines the long driveway leading to the main house. These small buildings made by the slaves themselves from bricks manufactured on the plantation were some of the South's best slave quarters. Yet they were cramped, uncomfortable places barely better than the wooden shanties where most of the plantation's slaves lived.

One of the builders had pressed three fingers into a brick on the outside of one building as a way of leaving a signature that survives to this day. I put my own fingers into the impression, reaching back more than a century to connect with the human being who had lived here, worked here, suffered here, and most likely died here as the property of other human beings who believed they were God's chosen masters while others had the divine fate to be slaves.

No one who hasn't lived in bondage could fully grasp how horrible a life of slavery must have been. But I felt far more empathy for the slave who had left that handprint than for the master who claimed ownership. I understand the argument that slave owners were a product of their time, but I still can't accept that excuse for their actions.

As news unfolded about the troubled, hate-filled white shooter who had murdered nine African-Americans during a prayer meeting at Emanuel, I wished he had been at the plantation with us that day. I wished he had seen the bare floors and brick walls where slaves lived out their days under the spirit-crushing boot heel of false ownership.

Had he seen these sights, how could the shooter possibly develop the racist views that led him the false belief that African-Americans are ruining our country? Slavery nearly brought our country to actual ruin. If the shooter had touched that handprint, surely he would have seen that our lives should be examples of why racism must not poison this nation.

When the shooter's website was discovered, I was shocked to see that he had posted a photo of himself at that same Boone Hall Plantation.

But while I had empathized with the slaves in their cabins, the shooter's picture showed him posing at the plantation's mansion. He identified with the slavers, not the slaves. He connected with the people who thought they were morally justified in owning other human beings. Instead of putting his fingers into that brick handprint, the shooter knelt before the "big house," probably imagining himself as the master.

The shooter allegedly purchased his murder weapon with birthday gift money when he turned 21. I wish his present had been a tour of Boone Hall's slave houses or a good history book instead. Perhaps someone could have enrolled him in a local GED program to earn the high school education he lacked. He might have developed the critical thinking skills needed to debunk the racist trash he devoured on right-wing websites.

Before the Civil War, many southern states banned educating slaves because slave owners thought learning would help slaves understand that slavery is morally wrong. While the Charleston shooter's morals were severely underdeveloped, the slaves, regardless of their education, knew well enough that their own captivity was unjust.

One of the slave cabins at Boone Hall doubled as a church. Many slaves found community and comfort in these early African-American churches, but slave owners often suspected church activities encouraged independence and rebellion against captivity. The shooter committed his horrible crime in an African-American church. Did he understand the symbolism of attacking people in a place that has inspired the culture and spirit of African-Americans since the time of slavery? Had he ever seen children playing at Emanuel?

The shooter certainly knew what his beloved Confederate flag symbolized. The flag that he waved in his online photos recalls a history of treason, racism, and slavery. What did he do with the American flag? He burned it. What did he think of equality, a founding principle that our nation hasn't yet fully realized? He hated it so much that he murdered nine good people to try to ignite another Civil War. He failed. Common sense and decency now prevail over false "heritage" narratives in the growing movement to remove the Confederate flag from public buildings.

We abolished slavery more than a century ago. Yet we still have racial problems in large part due to the institutional racism represented by the Confederate flag and mansions built on the labor of people held in immoral captivity. Our nation is not yet perfect, and we can't forget the worst aspects of our history. But we should all touch that handprint as we strive for what our Constitution tell us is the founding purpose of the United States: to form "a more perfect union."

Youth Isn't Wasted on the Young

June 2015

Commencement ceremonies are a way of life here in education-rich Western Massachusetts this time of year, with our excellent colleges, universities, and many fine high schools. Those ubiquitous ceremonies raise an inevitable question about our youth: How will these capped-and-gowned youngsters carry our world into the future as we older generations settle into our real and metaphorical rocking chairs on the back porch?

Throughout history, oldsters have fretted that youngsters may not be up to the task. I remember long ago being struck by a quote attributed to Plato: "The young people of today think of nothing but themselves. They have no reverence for parents or old age. They are impatient of all restraint. They talk as if they alone know everything." Of course, my teenaged self considered Plato just a pompous old jerk. Apparently, irony was a concept I hadn't encountered back in those days.

The quote's exact origin has since been called into question, and most historians now believe Plato isn't the true source. But if those were his words, then the young punks who worried the great philosopher would now be approaching 2,500 years of age. Those whippersnappers have long ago ceased snapping their whips.

Early in my teaching career, I attended my first academic conference. I wasn't much older than a college student myself, but my prematurely gray temples led everyone to assume that I was a veteran of the teaching trenches. One tweedy professor took me for a peer and asked me over lunch, "Do this year's student seem worse than ever to you?"

I had very little data to compare at the time, but I've heard the same question repeatedly during my more than three-decade career since then. My whole head is gray now, so no one could ever mistake me for a student or wide-eyed rookie. I've been at the same happy little community college for nearly a quarter century, longer than 95% of my colleagues and about half the plumbing. My students don't know who's older, Plato or me.

It's always fashionable to claim that this year's students are worse than ever, but I don't see a big difference between now and thirty years ago. The emphasis on standardized testing has had a numbing effect on learners, but those contemptible tests have been with us for decades. They're just more official now with more consequences. That's a shame, of course, and the worst aspect of education today—but that's certainly no fault of the students.

As my writing students did thirty years ago, today's young folks still have the same problems with basic skills (punctuation, grammar, etc.) and with much more important concerns, such as organization, specificity, critical thinking, and creativity. But they end up grasping these ideas big and small at about the same pace they did many years ago.

Of course, students throughout history share the same issues of maturity, which is the main reason that some of them do poorly while some do well. Such was probably true of Plato's young students. They'd all just rather be anywhere other than the confines of school most days. Who can blame them? They live in an exciting world.

Thirty years ago, they longed to hang with friends, play sports or video games, experiment with saying "yes" to everything they had been told to "just say no" to, and, of course, explore their budding sexuality. Now they do the exact same things—except the ever-present smart phone facilitates whatever less-than-smart distraction they choose.

Sure, young people text and tweet too much for my taste. Evolution may lead to human beings developing huge thumbs and rear ends if that trend continues. And I certainly wish they read more books and voted in higher percentages, but those same problems have existed for decades.

Here's what seems more important to me: Young people generally disapprove of war, particularly with the tragedies of our recent conflicts so fresh in their hearts. The young today don't prejudge other people by their race or ethnicity nearly as much as previous generations did. They favor civil rights and marriage equality. They see religion as personal spirituality rather than dogma to impose on others. They care about gas mileage and carbon footprints. They recycle. They believe in science, evolution, and global climate change—and worry for the sanity of people who doubt such basic realities.

They know that comedians such as Jon Stewart and John Oliver provide far more accurate information about current events than Fox News does. They distrust most "establishment" politicians and know that the Republican Party is just a tool of the wealthy. They grasp with clarity the common-sense truth that corporations are not people. They want to do well financially but not at the expense of other people, other nations, or the planet as a whole. For all their individualism, they understand that we are all in this life together, family, community, society, nation, and world.

When I find myself stuck in traffic with multiple out-of-state license plates on those big college graduation dates, and I ponder the state of today's youth, I'm not overly worried about the future. I refuse to become the old dude who laments the shortcomings of the young. Instead, I'll celebrate their potential and try my best to offer the guidance I wish I had gotten at their age. Of course, I don't really expect them to listen. I'm no Plato, after all.

Burying the Lede About Hillary Clinton's Lead

May 2015

"Burying the lede" (or "lead" as it is sometimes called) is a concept in journalism that involves not focusing on the most important aspect of a story at the beginning of a report. It's a mistake most often made by inexperienced journalists.

Sometimes a writer might purposely bury the lede to push readers one way and then dramatically pull them back to the main point later in the article. That's what I'm doing here, giving the impression that this column is about a basic journalistic mistake. In reality, this column is about purposely bad journalism at the highest levels of the American media.

Such a failure took place at CNN.com recently in an article headlined: "As Campaigns Launch, CNN/ORC Poll Finds GOP Field Stays Tight." Most of the article focused on Republican candidates, few of whom even reached double-digits in the crowded field. If readers happened to zone out halfway through the article or clicked on another link, they would miss some truly newsworthy facts. CNN's own polls showed that Hillary Clinton destroys potential Democratic candidates by 58-68%, and she dominates Republican candidates by 14-24%. A sensible headline would be, "Clinton Crushes All Other Candidates in Latest Poll."

After dropping Clinton's name in the opening paragraph, the article doesn't even mention her again until the twelfth out of sixteen paragraphs. Any high school journalism student could identify this textbook example of burying the lede. But CNN writers are accomplished, professional journalists. Why would they make such a basic mistake?

The real problem is that this wasn't a "mistake." CNN buried lede because political journalism has become a ratings-focused pursuit that has more in common with sports journalism than it does with actual news reporting. CNN and the rest of the corporate media are invested in keeping the public focused on the politics as if it's a push toward the World Series instead of an examination of important issues facing the nation.

We New England fans might enjoy the headline, "Red Sox Overwhelming Favorites to Win World Series," but that wouldn't boost nationwide interest, improve ratings, sell advertizing, or, in the words of the great writer Charlie Pierce, "move units." Sports journalists love to focus on the underdog, partly because everyone loves the underdog, but mostly to increase interest. The idea that a scrappy bunch might slay a heavily favored giant is irresistible.

The current rag-tag Republican presidential hopefuls are the most under-the-dog underdogs imaginable. Rand Paul is a serial plagiarist and

---

conspiracy monger. Ted Cruz is hated by Republicans almost as much as by Democrats. Marco Rubio opposed his own immigration bill. Scott Walker compared union members to terrorists. Ben Carson compared Obamacare to slavery and America to Nazi Germany. Mike Huckabee promised to call down "fire from heaven" for some vague reason. Carly Fiorina laid off thirty thousand workers at HP. Rick Perry is under indictment. Chris Christie is a bully. Jeb Bush is a Bush. All of them get tripped up by a question as simple as, "Would you attend a gay wedding?" Yet CNN loves to promote them as viable candidates.

Oddly enough, conservatives often label "mainstream" corporate media outlets such as CNN as "liberal." One of my Republican friends calls CNN the "Communist News Network," and another calls it the "Clinton News Network." That might come as a surprise to Clinton herself as CNN buries her huge polling lead deep within its article. But CNN is simply a corporation that focuses on ratings and sales.

For the same reasons, the corporate media seems intent on pushing whatever Clinton "scandals" they can drum up, just as they have done for years with President Obama. Real issues such as affordable health insurance, ending wars, and peace negotiations don't boost ratings, so the media focuses on fake scandals instead. Nonsense about birth certificates and death panels grabs the casual viewer and generates far more interest with far fewer facts or consequences.

CNN knows that scandals, whether fake or real, bring ratings. They're happy to engage in the lazy dishonesty of fake scandals, which leads to trickle-down lazy dishonesty. For example, my conservative *Daily Hampshire Gazette* columnist colleague Jay Fleitman's recent column was another nutrition-free serving of fake Clinton scandals sprinkled with fake Obama scandals, providing more media failure empty calories.

We recently saw national headlines such as, "Will Clinton Foundation Sink Hillary's Campaign?" The common sense answer is an emphatic "no"— just as it has been for the non-scandals involving e-mail and Benghazi. The corporate media will undoubtedly keep flogging these non-issues because they attract viewers. It doesn't matter that none of these fake scandals actually rise to the level of the real scandals associated with Republican presidential candidates. The underdogs get a pass while the favorite is scrutinized and important issues ignored. Lazy journalism has become so much the norm that consumers don't even expect more from the profession so essential to Democracy that the First Amendment to our Constitution protects freedom of the press.

Will Hillary Clinton be our next president? Any honest headline would note that she's currently well ahead. Can you imagine any candidate actually winning by 14-24%? That's not likely. Polls more than a year ahead of the election haven't always been predictive in the past, so the presidential

---

polls will certainly narrow in the many upcoming months leading up to the election. But CNN and the rest of the corporate media are taking no chances. Misleading headlines about a supposedly tight presidential race serve to pump those ratings, sell those products, move those units. When burying the lede helps, the corporate media is happy to break out the shovels.

When Religion is Manipulated

April 2015

To commemorate Easter in the context of current politics, a progressive Christian friend of mine recently posted a picture on Facebook that depicts Christ's crucifixion with the fake Fox News headline: "Socialist Hippie Executed."

My friend noted that she thought long and hard about whether or not to post the picture and, if she did, what to say about it. In the end, she simply said that she wanted to post it because she thought it was valuable to her understanding of Easter and the overall Christian message.

I understood her trepidation. I've been derided and unfriended by people on Facebook for posting far less controversial political or religious material. Common sense tells us that my friend's satirical post about the way Fox News manipulates the issues is very telling—but it's also very easy to misunderstand, especially for people who still believe the obvious falsehood that Fox News is "fair and balanced."

A mutual friend who is a conservative Christian made the first comment after only a few minutes: "I wish you had thought about this more before posting something so tasteless." But isn't that the true "thoughtless" view? He quickly condemned the picture without refection because he completely missed the point that much of religious belief is being manipulated these days for political purposes that are actually the opposite of the Christian message.

The picture originated in a Facebook community called "If Fox News was Around." The group creates satirical pictures showing moments in history as Fox News and conservative media might have been misconstrued them.

I certainly don't find this particular picture very tasteful. And I imagine anyone who actually thinks that the right-wing propaganda outfit known as Fox News accurately reports on current events would find this picture quite objectionable. But satire is, by its nature, often not very tasteful. Jonathan Swift's "Modest Proposal" is far from tasteful, but it's a classic.

Tastefulness aside, this picture definitely raises some insightful points. For example, the life and teachings of Jesus are not compatible with the not-very-Christian extreme right-wing views that are now very popular among Fox News viewers and the Republican Party. Christ didn't praise unregulated corporate capitalism or call poor people lazy or advocate war over diplomacy or condemn gay people or support the death penalty (which was imposed on Jesus himself after all). These anti-Christian views are common among the American right and heavily promoted on Fox News.

And Fox News is very fond of falsely portraying Democrats as socialists for caring about how our government treats the poor and the oppressed, despite the fact that caring for the poor and oppressed was a central component of Christ's teachings. Overall, Fox News also doesn't seem to have much respect for the Ninth Commandment as the network bears false witness against its political opponents and falsifies Christian beliefs at an alarming rate.

Of course, Fox News weighed in frequently on the recent controversy about the "religious freedom" laws in Indiana and other states, laws that are obviously meant to discriminate against gay people. Fox News portrays Christians as the real victims of discrimination, as if their right to discriminate somehow deserves protection. The reality is that the anti-gay fever sweeping the religious right is based entirely on a few lines cherry-picked from the Old Testament, not on anything Jesus ever said. Fox News is once again manipulating so-called "religious" beliefs to promote a political agenda that has nothing to do with actual Christianity.

So, while I did find the satirical interpretation of Christ's crucifixion distasteful, I can see beyond my distaste and recognize that it makes a very good point. My progressive Christian friend was far from "thoughtless." She clearly put a great deal of consideration into what to make of this picture before posting it, and I support her right to free speech in posting it for us to consider and form our own opinions. I also respect my conservative Christian friend's right to free speech, but I soundly disagree with his views and wish he had put more thought into his thoughtless accusation of thoughtlessness.

Moreover, I wish the people on Fox News, most of whom make claims to being champions of Christian values, would put some real thought into what they say with the dishonest pretense of presenting "news." I watch Fox News regularly (distressing and mind-numbing though it can be) and closely follow the websites that fact-check Fox News's rampant dishonesty. The bottom line is that Fox News itself is far more tasteless and a far worse affront to Christianity than the satirical picture in question.

In the end, I thanked my progressive Christian friend for posting the picture. I still find it distasteful, of course, but personal taste isn't the point. I appreciate the deeper meaning behind the satire—and I certainly appreciate that my friend gave us the opportunity to think about these important issues. When we stop thinking and simply accept the kind of propaganda that Fox News and the conservative media distribute, we lose the reality-based critical thinking and common sense that defines America at its best.

A Message to Obamacare Opponents

March 2015

Last month, I wrote about a Facebook discussion in which I was called a baby-killer for being pro-choice. Ever the glutton for punishment, I recently engaged in a discussion of Obamacare on Facebook. Guess what? I was called a baby-killer for being pro-Obamacare. A guy just can't win sometimes.

The biggest eye-opener in this discussion was the fact that the vast majority of people who ranted against the Affordable Care Act had no idea what it actually does. The law's conservative opponents spent the entire discussion snowplowing enough false claims to bury poor Jay Fleitman's driveway: Obamacare mandates abortions, exempts the president and members of Congress, eliminates private insurance, has led to more people being uninsured, is the first step toward dictatorship, is unconstitutional, only benefits illegal immigrants, and was created by some evil supervillain named Gruber.

My head is still spinning.

I made one simple request that ground the discussion to a halt. I asked the opponents of Obamacare to summarize the law. A few people regurgitated more right-wing talking points from Fox News, but no one was even close to a factual summary of the law.

So I pointed out the six major aspects of the ACA:

1. Consumer protections that help all of us who have health insurance, whether it's through the ACA or not.

2. Private health insurance through the exchanges with subsidies for middle-income individuals and families to help make coverage affordable.

3. Expansion of Medicaid and CHIP to help provide very low-cost health insurance to low-income individuals and families.

4. Funding mechanisms to pay for the law's benefits, such as savings from Medicare over-reimbursement and taxes on very high incomes and highly profitable medical, pharmaceutical, and insurance companies. (Long term, ACA funding actually reduces the federal budget deficit by hundreds of billions of dollars.)

5. A business mandate that requires large companies to provide employees with access to health insurance rather than treating them and non-benefitted temps.

6. A personal-responsibility mandate to assure that everyone has health insurance and doesn't try to freeload off of the system

I referenced ObamacareFacts.com, a great source that explains this complicated law in clear detail.

Criticizing the law is fine, but not knowing the basics makes people sound confused at best, ludicrous at worst. We all need to educate ourselves about the law to have an informed discussion instead of sounding like children who cry about hating lima beans without ever actually tasting lima beans.

The ACA is far from perfect. (Single-payer would be considerably better, but that's still a few decades off.) Plenty of aspects of Obamacare should be improved, of course. But arguing from knowledge instead of ignorance is simply basic common sense. Nothing will get fixed by ranting about non-issues and false claims. Gruber is a jerk but irrelevant. Congress and the president aren't exempt. No one shoved the law down anyone's throat. Legislators actually read the bill. It's not Socialism, Communism, Fascism, or Rubberchickenism. It's not a government takeover or an attack on freedom. It's not a giveaway to lazy people. Republicans aren't going to get it repealed, and they don't have a workable replacement plan. The legal challenges won't win.

People who really want to improve health care access for all Americans need to stop repeating misinformed distractions and focus on facts.

I urged everyone to please stop relying on agenda-driven, right-wing sources for information about important issues such as the ACA. Does anyone really think a source that calls itself "Pissed Off Right Wingers," for example, is going to be unbiased? Being educated about how the media works means getting information from a variety of reliable sources, especially those that have a history of being accurate over the long term.

I shared four nonpartisan sources that use facts to debunk the biggest myths about the ACA: The Kaiser Family Foundation (Not affiliated with Kaiser Health Insurance), DailyFinance.com, PolitiFact.com, and the Lawyers.com blog. I even referenced ThinkProgress.org, a liberal site that takes on the myths as well. If people want to call liberals "libtards" and claim that we're evil people who hate America, at least be brave enough to read something written by actual liberals and not by right-wingers dishonestly putting words in our mouths. A simple Google search of these sites and the words "Obamacare myths" can provide more facts in five minutes than Fox News has provided in five years.

I also asked people to please discuss the ACA like adults. All of the insults and name-calling in the discussion made people look like immature jerks who were more interested in being on the *Jerry Springer Show* than in trying to make the world a better place. That's terrible citizenship and just creepy behavior in general. Don't try to show how terrible other people are by acting like a terrible person yourself.

Calling me a baby-killer because I support a law that actually reduces abortions and increases health care coverage for contraception, pregnancy, and childbirth is about as wrong as people can be. If people are angry, then they should use that anger as motivation to learn about the issues and make positive changes to the law—not to show how great they are at insulting people who disagree with them. None of us learn anything from each other's insults.

I finished the discussion by telling everyone to enjoy the latest snowstorm, stay safe, and have a great day. Maybe that message got through, at least.

Diving into the Abortion Debate

February 2015

I recently immersed myself in a week-long discussion of abortion while visiting the comment section of a conservative Facebook page. I was nearly the only pro-choice voice to stay in the discussion while surrounded by a dozen or so anti-choice people, which is fine because we can always grow by engaging with other views on any issue. I'm sure that the folks in this discussion don't encompass every aspect of the anti-choice view, but they seemed to represent the main anti-choice tenants. I learned a great deal during the discussion. Unfortunately, much of what I learned was unsettling for anyone who values civil discussion and public policy based on common sense and reality.

For many on the anti-choice side, the debate boiled down to one word: "life." They claimed that a fetus is alive; therefore, it must not be tampered with in any way. They also stated that pro-choice people don't think that a fetus is alive. When I pointed out that I did, of course, believe that a fetus was alive, they were shocked that I could kill anything living. When I pointed out that the food they ate for dinner was once alive, as were the skin cells they lost when they showered, they accused me of changing the subject. "Life is life," one person claimed. "Ending life is murder." I guess he must have eaten rocks for dinner to avoid becoming murderers.

The subject these folks wanted to discuss most often was what they saw as my obvious approval of murder—not just approval, but actual participation in murder. Anti-choice people view pro-choice people as murderers, and they're not bashful about calling us murderers. I was called a "baby killer" dozens of times during the debate, often with added insults about every aspect of my character. When I brought up the essential question of when a fetus becomes a fully realized human life, they always defaulted to conception and could entertain no other viewpoint. No one seemed willing to accept the idea that I might be a moral person who could see other sides of this complex and personal issue. Nope—just a murderer.

One person insisted that every physician he had ever asked told him that abortion is murder. When I pointed out that the American Medical Association officially considered abortion an acceptable medical procedure, he called me a murderer. Another person said we need a federal law prohibiting all abortions because anyone in favor of abortion is a murderer. When I pointed out that the Supreme Court ruled in 1974 that abortion is constitutional, he called me a murderer. Can you see the pattern? Is it really too much to ask to have a civil discussion without being repeatedly called a murderer?

64

I recently had the beautiful experience of holding my newborn granddaughter in my arms. This might surprise the anti-choice people attacking me, but I didn't once look into her beautiful blue eyes and consider killing her. Instead, I felt the joy of knowing that she is wanted and will be cared for by her parents who love her and chose to exercise the reproductive freedom to plan their family. That's what "pro-choice" means: choosing when to have a family. That's called freedom. The United States was founded on that concept.

Is it hard to understand that screeching "murderer!" at me isn't going to make me change a position that I've invested with serious thought? This issue should be treated with a better quality of discourse than the typical Jerry Springer episode. If I screeched back, "You just want to force women to be your barefoot, pregnant, sex slaves and baby factories!" then would they be likely to change their opinion? If I called them "baby starvers" for wanting to cut food stamps, would they suddenly say, "Oh, gosh, I guess you're right"? Of course not. Screeching and name-calling never solves anything.

Despite their view that abortion is murder, these anti-choice people don't want to talk about the penalties if abortion were to actually be outlawed. No one in the discussion would equate the penalties for abortion with their chosen penalty for the murder of a person who has already been born (the death penalty, of course). That's been the case with every abortion discussion I've ever had. They like to call abortion clinics "murder factories," but the don't like to talk about the punishments for these supposed murders. One man said, "Let's let God sort it out." No, sorry, but this is a nation of laws. We can't expect God to do our job of making laws.

If people believe that abortion really is murder, and they believe that murderers should always face the harshest penalties possible, then why do they hesitate about assigning those harsh penalties to women who have abortions, the doctors who perform them, the nurses who assist, the receptionists who book the appointment, the janitor who cleans the building, and the parent/friend/husband/boyfriend who brings the woman to the procedure? Even pressing the issue, I couldn't get anyone to see the contradiction in different penalties for two crimes they equated as murder. Perhaps at a deep level, they actually understand that killing an actual person and ending a pregnancy really aren't the same—even if they can't admit it.

They also insisted on calling me "pro-abortion," despite my view that I hope no one ever has to get an abortion. They didn't want to accept the idea that being "pro-choice" isn't the same as cheerleading for abortion. Being pro-choice means that I want pregnant women to have the right to make up their own mind about what to do. As Bill and Hilary Clinton have said for years, I think abortion should be "safe, legal, and rare." I certainly don't want to force women to have an abortion any more than I want to force women into an unwanted, full-term pregnancy. The "pro-life" view takes away this choice from all women. They should be called "anti-choice" because that's far more accurate than "pro-life."

When I pointed out that their anti-choice view called for government legislation that forced pregnant women to give birth without a choice in the matter, no one saw that kind of government control as a problem. Of course, they thought having the government require insurance companies to cover pregnancy and birth was an attack on their freedom. Nothing says "pro-life" like making sure medical care for pregnancy and birth is harder to get.

The term "pro-life" became even more muddled when I asked about government programs that supported parents and children. These "pro-life" folks were steadfastly against welfare in any form. They offered two reasons: fraud and dependency. They believed that for every truly needy person "deserving" of government assistance, another hundred were defrauding the system. I pointed out that studies show a very low fraud rate for these programs, but this fact didn't get in the way of their certainty that they were somehow being swindled. The also claimed that recipients of support programs became dependent on those programs and lost the will to take care of themselves. Again, the fact that most people are on welfare for only a short time didn't faze them. They simply decried programs that helped parents and children after they were born as the big government "nanny state," blissfully unaware that they were employing a parenting-related metaphor to trash government programs that actually benefit actual parents and children.

On the issue of government, many anti-choice people were outraged that their tax money might be going toward abortion. They didn't seem to care that I didn't like my tax money going toward war or corporate welfare. When I also noted that it had been illegal for federal funds to go toward abortion since the "Hyde Amendment" of 1976, they told me that they knew Obama (the "baby-killer in-chief" according to one person) had forced through Obamacare, which they viewed as an oppressive government attack on their freedom because it required doctors to perform abortions (it doesn't) and it mandated employers to pay for abortions (doesn't do that either). These false attacks on Obamacare are common on right-wing websites that put agenda over reality. In fact, Obamacare helps to lower the abortion rate by increasing access to contraception. As expected, these anti-choice folks were also against increased access to contraception.

Another logical inconsistency of the folks in the discussion was their view that we must make abortion illegal to reduce the number of abortions. Curiously, I'd been in previous discussions with many of these same people on the issue of gun-safety legislation. On that subject, they were quick to point out that laws wouldn't stop anyone from getting a gun, so we shouldn't even have such laws. They didn't see the obvious fact that this line of thinking is the exact opposite to their views on making abortion illegal. I jokingly mimicked a line from gun-rights advocates: "If abortion is outlawed, only outlaws will have abortions." They didn't get the joke or the basic logic behind it. In their minds, somehow abortions laws will stop abortions while gun laws won't stop guns.

Our discussion turned personal on several occasions—you know, in addition to their accusations that I was a baby killer. One man went on at length about how wonderful his wife was and how happy he was that his wife hadn't been aborted. This view has obvious emotional appeal because no one wants someone's beloved spouse to have never existed. The flaw in this emotional argument, of course, is that it must also apply to people who are not our beloved spouses. So I asked him if he was equally happy that Adolf Hitler had not been aborted. Usually, I avoid bringing Hitler into a discussion, but it was apt here. I explained that I wasn't equating his wife with Hitler, but he still informed me that I was a scumbag for my comment. In fact, his point about full-grown adults who were not aborted as fetuses opened the line of reasoning that led to Hitler popping up in the discussion. I didn't stoop to calling him a scumbag for subjecting his wife to the comparison, but he refused to even consider my point anyway.

The anti-choice people who came to the discussion with a religious viewpoint insisted that abortion is a central issue in Christianity. But when I asked them to tell me where in the Bible Jesus spoke out about abortion, they were at a loss and reverted to their focus on murder by quoting the Old Testament commandment, "Thou shalt not kill." In fact, the New Testament doesn't show Jesus ever mentioning abortion. When I referred people to some very informative websites that explored a Biblical justification for abortion rights, they accused me of perverting the Bible and hating God. When I referenced how the political right adopted a fervent anti-abortion crusade for political reasons less than fifty years ago, they accused me of being a brainwashed liberal.

While religion is often a major influence, some anti-choice people believe that science is also on their side. The same folks who routinely reject climate science, evolution, and vaccination have formed what they see as a scientific argument against abortion. They say that because an embryo has DNA distinct from the pregnant woman carrying that embryo, that embryo is a distinct and separate individual. Therefore, the woman has no right to decide what to do about the pregnancy. This argument breaks down for at least three reasons: Cancer cells inside the host's body have distinct DNA but aren't considered separate individuals. And identical twins, who start with the same DNA in the womb, aren't considered to be one individual. Also, a rare genetic condition called Chimerism endows a single human with two distinct DNA sequences. No one would consider someone with this condition to be two distinct individuals with two souls. On the subject of abortion, as in every other subject, science is clearly not on the side of anti-science reactionaries.

Anti-choice people have the incorrect impression that most

Americans share their views, and only liberal extremists think abortion is ever acceptable. Several people even sent me to Gallup polls that they said proved this point. In reality, the polls showed just the opposite. The most recent Gallup polls show that the nation is more-or-less even split between self-identified "pro-life" and "pro-choice" people, but more than three-fourths of Americans believe that abortion should be legal in some or all circumstances. That means three-fourths of Americans are, essentially, pro-choice. These folks believed so firmly in their position that they even misread straightforward polling data.

One of the most disturbing aspects of the discussion was that anti-choice people believe women have abortions casually, without much or any personal struggle. They seem to think that women (and the male partners or family members who support them) simply jot an abortion into their appointment calendar as they would a trip to the shopping mall or beauty parlor. (Yes, one person really used the term "beauty parlor"—no surprise that he was male.) That's absolutely not the case for any woman I've ever known who has chosen to have an abortion. This inability to acknowledge the deep thoughts and emotions experienced by these women—who are, by the way, fellow human beings—seems to be a gross failure of empathy at best and cruel psychopathology at worst.

While I respect the passion and conviction of anti-choice people, I deplore their nasty accusations that I kill babies, their mischaracterization of the pro-choice view as pro-abortion, their insistence that government force their will onto people who disagree with them, their over-reliance on very flimsy connections to religious doctrine, their shallow interpretation of science, their dismissal of the deeply personal and private nature of abortion, their myopic refusal to see any other sides of the issue, and their poorly constructed overall arguments for their views. This is a serious moral issue that requires a depth of thought, not rigid, reactionary condemnation.

My biggest takeaway from this abortion discussion is that anti-choice people are generally not open to persuasion. In fact, they're downright rigid and insular. When I pointed out that Ohio Congressional Representative Tim Ryan had recently switched from an anti-choice to a pro-choice position, they claimed that he was just a lying politician trying to keep his job. Ryan actually invested a great deal of moral reflection on his decision, writing in an op-ed about his change of view, "I am not afraid to say that my position has evolved as my experiences have broadened, deepened, and become more personal … I have come to believe that we must trust women and families—not politicians—to make the best decision for their lives."

Representative Ryan's change of heart gives me hope after a mostly depressing week of diving into the abortion debate. I only wish that the folks I encountered in that discussion had put Ryan's depth of thought into their own views on the issue.

Not-So-Shocking Predictions for 2015

As the new year begins, let's look into our fake crystal ball and predict some of the biggest news stories of 2015.

President Obama will take executive action to help the American people, and most Republicans will pretend that no president in history ever took any similar actions, and they'll shout that Obama is an evil dictatorial mastermind who somehow also simultaneously happens to be a clueless pawn manipulated by special interests.

Critics of the president will claim he should be both nicer and tougher on Republicans. They will not see the slightest contradiction in their views.

Clear evidence will show that Obamacare continues to help Americans get high-quality, affordable health insurance, saving millions of dollars and thousands of lives. Republicans will continue to claim that the law is a Socialist train wreck meant to destroy American and kill Grandma.

A plane will crash somewhere the Eastern Hemisphere under mysterious circumstances. Within hours of the first reports, someone will claim that President Obama is happy that a plane crashed so the media will be too distracted to ask questions about Benghazi.

Despite multiple investigations that have shown no wrongdoing by the presidential administration, Republicans in Congress will spend millions of taxpayers' dollars to convene more Benghazi hearings, asking questions that have been repeatedly answered while casting blame where none exists and trying to score cheap political points from a tragedy. Coincidentally, their blame-game will shift from Obama (who isn't running for reelection) to Hillary Clinton, the leading Democratic candidate.

The evidence that global climate change is already affecting us will be overwhelming, but people addicted to the conservative agenda and fossil fuels will rant that common-sense climate reality is a liberal hoax.

An exotic disease that causes untold suffering in other parts of the world will make a brief appearance in the United States. Our public health system will prevent the disease from spreading, but elected Republicans and conservative media pundits will fearmonger and blame President Obama for an outbreak that doesn't happen.

Marriage equality will bring an improved level of civilization to many states and simultaneously bring cries of the end of civilization from many conservatives.

Several truly terrible former, current, and prospective politicians will be the focus of speculation about a run for the Republican Presidential

---

nomination. None of these people will ever be president, thank God.

Some conservative pundits and Republican presidential candidates will make offhand remarks implying that Hillary Clinton is too old to run for president. Most of the people making these comments will actually be older than Hillary Clinton.

Some reality-impaired commentators will go on obscure right-wing talk shows to warn everyone that President Obama plans to cancel the 2016 elections and stay in the presidency. Thousands if not millions of gullible people will nod their heads in agreement. At least one Republican member of Congress will repeat this laughable claim as if it deserves serious consideration.

Vladimir Putin will continue to defy international common sense and run the Russian economy into the ground while many fake-patriot Republicans will praise Putin as somehow superior to our own president.

Extremist Muslims will kill innocent people, and many conservative pundits will blame an entire religion. Extremist Christians will kill innocent people, and many conservative pundits will call them "lone wolves."

After a shooting, Republicans will tell everyone that mental health, not guns, is the real issue. Then these same Republicans will try to destroy Obamacare, the largest expansion of mental health treatment access in American history.

Several rouge police officers will kill or injure unarmed civilians, and anyone who demands that these bad apples be held accountable will be accused of hating all police officers.

Some Democratic candidates for office will pretend that they don't support many of President Obama's positions. They will lose. Some Republican candidates will pretend that they support many of Obama's positions, being careful not to name the president. They will win.

A dwindling but loud contingent of insecure conservatives will claim that the phrase "Happy Holidays" is oppressive to the hundreds of millions of Americans who freely celebrate Christmas with no hint of actual oppression.

Some elected Democrats and liberal commentators will make occasional remarks that are not completely accurate. Hundreds of elected Republicans and conservative pundits will frequently make blatantly false statements. Instead of researching the issues and pointing out falsehoods, the mainstream corporate media will coddle both sides equally as if equating truth and lies makes their reporting unbiased.

Fox News will make many ridiculous claims about President Obama—that he's trying to ban cupcake sprinkles, for example. Yet Fox will still be the highest-rated "news" network in the world because dishonesty and fake outrage have always been components of Fox's successful business model.

Obviously, we really don't need a crystal ball to predict what will happen in 2015. The best predictor of the near future has always been the recent past. All of the predictions listed here are actually events that happened in 2014. Many also popped up in 2013. And 2012, 2011, 2010, 2009, etc. You get the idea.

A good New Year's resolution might be to recognize the pattern. Let's stop being surprised and call out these events in the coming year, holding the misinformers accountable. Better yet, let's work to prevent as much of this insanity in 2015 as we can.

Amnesty, Shamnesty

December 2014

Since President Obama announced his executive actions on immigration, the word "amnesty" has been flying around more frequently than flakes in a New England snowstorm. Social media and the news are full of rants about "Obama's amnesty." All of this attention ignores a basic fact: The president's executive actions don't come close to actual "amnesty." I'm reminded of the great scene in the movie *The Princess Bride* when Inigo Montoya says to Vizzini, "You keep using that word. I do not think it means what you think it means."

"Amnesty" is a pardon. In 1977, President Jimmy Carter granted actual amnesty in the form of an unconditional pardon to people who fled the Viet Nam draft. President Obama's immigration plan is far different.

The president's actions do not make undocumented immigrants into citizens or even absolve them from addressing their legal status. His actions simply provide the opportunity for some undocumented immigrants who have been in the country for more than five years to apply for temporary relief from deportation—but only if they have documented children and pass a background check. This will keep those families together and bring them into the mainstream of society where they can fully pay taxes and contribute positively to American culture. That's not amnesty.

"Amnesty" (like "Socialism" and "death panel") is another inflammatory term used by Republicans to agitate their base. Republicans want people to say, "Hey, I don't get amnesty, so why should illegal aliens?" Republicans know that people who actually understand the issue won't say, "Hey, I don't have to go through a complicated enforcement and application process to stay in the country, so why do some illegal aliens?" The boring facts don't stir enough anger, so Republicans prefer a rabble-rousing fiction to pit "us" against "them."

In addition to misusing the term "amnesty," opponents of the president are wrong about the policy itself. Republicans have falsely claimed that the president's actions are unprecedented. In reality, *every* president (Republican and Democrat) since Eisenhower has taken executive action on immigration.

Republicans claim that Obama's actions are unconstitutional, but the courts have affirmed that all presidents have wide-ranging legal authority to prioritize law enforcement. Recently, more than one hundred legal scholars and immigration experts signed a letter stating that the president's actions are entirely legal, despite the outcry from Republicans that the president is acting like a king who rules by decree. In fact, President Obama is on pace to issue the fewest executive orders per year of any president in more than a century.

Senator Ted Cruz (R-TX) claimed that Obama's actions reject the will of the people, especially considering the 2014 election. The fact-checker PolitiFact gave Cruz a "false" rating, noting that 2014 voters actually support the policies enacted by the president. Only extreme partisans such as Cruz are claiming that an apathetic midterm election with 37% voter turnout represents the will of the people.

Republicans also claim that Obama's action will hurt the economy, but actual economists say immigration reform boosts economic growth. Republicans have cited a widely discredited report from the conservative Heritage Foundation that claims immigration reform will cost trillions of taxpayer dollars in government benefits doled out to undocumented immigrants. In fact, that's completely untrue because the people covered by Obama's plan will not be eligible for the vast majority of government benefits, and they'll sow more in their own tax payments than they reap in very limited benefits. Obama's actions won't even add a penny to the deficit because the Citizenship and Immigration Service, which carries out the actions, is self-funded though application fees.

Reform opponents also claim that Obama should "secure the borders" before anything else. This view ignores the fact that the president's executive actions include increased border security provisions. The Obama administration has actually been strict about border security. Approximately two million people have been officially deported under Obama's watch, more than under President Bush. We can debate whether or not these deportations are a good idea, but we can't pretend they don't exist. And fewer people have entered the country illegally in recent years than during the administration of Republican hero Ronald Reagan.

Speaker of the House John Boehner claimed that Obama's actions would "poison the well" for immigration reform in Congress. In truth, Republicans themselves have been pouring the poison for years. Boehner won't bring bipartisan immigration reform that passed the Senate to a vote in the House—even though the bill would certainly pass. If Republicans hadn't also blocked immigration reform under President Bush back in 2007, then we would now have better laws that actually addressed the problems associated with illegal immigration, rather than the current inadequate laws.

Republicans rail that Obama himself has said for years that he can't unilaterally change immigration law. Of course, changing the law is Congress's job—a job Republicans have blocked. The president's executive actions don't change the law—they focus on common sense enforcement of existing laws. That's a big difference Republicans hope their followers are too angry and confused to notice. In their most desperate criticism, Obama-bashers cynically claim that his immigration actions are meant to create more Democratic voters. That's absurd considering the people affected can't even vote until completing a years-long process of gaining citizenship.

When I share these facts with my Republican friends, they cling to their cries of "amnesty" and rants about a dictatorial president. They call me an "Obamabot" with blind loyalty to the president. But I'll remain loyal to the verifiable facts about the president's actions, not Republican misinformation. And I'll be loyal to the basic definition of the word "amnesty," knowing that the false resentment it engenders, like so much Republican outrage these days, simply doesn't reflect reality.

Political Incivility and Intolerance

November 2014

A recent Pew Research Center study showed that 44% of liberals have blocked or unfriended someone on social media for political reasons, compared to 31% of conservatives. Some folks heralded the study as proof that liberals are intolerant. But that interpretation misses the obvious, common-sense interpretation: Conservatives deserve to be unfriended far more often than liberals do.

I'm very active in social media, particularly Facebook, where I've seen plenty of rudeness and incivility from both conservatives and liberals. Online discussions too often resemble the basement of an outhouse. But I've noticed a distinct difference between conservative and liberal incivility. When conservatives are intolerant, they're also usually wrong on the facts. When liberals get rude, it's usually in reaction to conservative ignorance and incivility.

I administer a Facebook page named for one of my books, *Tales of a Real American Liberal*, a collection of personal essays on political and social topics. You could call it a prequel to this book. Like both that book and this one, the Facebook page connects my personal experiences with politics and current events, always supported by facts rather than unfounded speculation. Naturally, the page attracts a fair number of contrarian conservative comments.

Occasionally, these conservative visitors are polite and open to civil discussion. Far more often, unfortunately, the conservative side of the conversation is represented by rude jerks who drop in with hit-and-run insults, profanity, copy-and-paste misinformation from right-wing websites, and accusations that I'm a baby killer who hates God and America, blah, blah, blah. I have zero tolerance for this kind of behavior, so I begin every discussion with this disclaimer:

"Comment guidelines: Please keep the comments civil and on topic. Honest disagreement is fine, but anyone who just wants to hijack the discussion with ignorance, insults, or debunked misinformation will be deleted and banned. This isn't censorship or denial of free speech. It's promoting a productive discussion. So please don't waste everybody's time. Thanks."

I can't really use such a disclaimer on my personal Facebook account where I've sometimes unfriended and been unfriended—almost always for political reasons. A few examples from my own personal social media experience can be illuminating on the subject of political incivility and intolerance.

I unfriended one guy I know from the gym after he claimed that the Sandy Hook mass shooting was a "false flag" staged by "Odumbo" to stir anti-gun feelings. Before unfriending him, I replied firmly but politely with references to several online debunkings of his theory. His ranting, paranoid reply ended by calling me another one of "Obalmer's sheeple." Was I intolerant for unfriending someone who insists that the mass-murder of children was faked?

Another unfriending occurred when a former coworker posted a link to a Fox News article with the headline "Obamacare Price Hikes Hit Red States Hardest." Here's her comment about the article, verbatim: "Obummers death panels are just for real americans in red states. Lets impeach this kenyen basterd before he kills us all!!!" When I pointed out the obvious fact that Republican elected officials in those red states had sabotaged the law's benefits, she immediately called me a "libtard." It's a shame that's not a real word because it's one of the few she spelled correctly. Was I intolerant for unfriending someone so rude?

A third unfriending happened when a high school classmate posted a completely false claim that President Obama's first-term stimulus program had created more jobs in China than in the United States. I sent him several sources showing that economists said the stimulus created or saved millions of American jobs and saved us from another Great Depression. He replied that he always knew I was a "commie homo" and insulting my wife and family. Was I intolerant for unfriending someone who told me I should move to China where I belonged?

A typical case where I was unfriended happened when an acquaintance posted an unflattering photo of Michelle Obama with claims that the First Lady was born a man. I immediately commented that this claim was misogynist, immature, and intolerant. Strong words, yes, but was I being intolerant for pointing out his gross intolerance?

One college classmate objected to my posts praising Connecticut's recently expanded gun-safety laws. He sent this message before unfriending me: "Maybe you shouldn't flaunt your gun-grabbing BS to someone who owns as many guns as I do and can find out where you live." Was I intolerant for not wanting to be the target of his implied threats of violence?

I was once even unfriended over the course of a full year. A college classmate posted misinformation several times each day, flooding his Facebook page with obviously false claims from right-wing websites. I painstakingly and politely explained the countervailing facts and provided nonpartisan references as often as I could. He rarely responded to my comments, and when he did, he usually threatened to block me. One day, out of the blue, he sent me a message that he was unfriending me for harassing him and being "a closed-minded liberal."

Ironically, "open-minded" is one of the primary definitions of the word "liberal." I've actually studied conservative claims and policies with a fully open mind. That's how I've discovered that they're often fact-free, ineffective, beneficial mainly to the wealthy and powerful, and counter to the best of American values, traditions, and history. If I had studied conservative claims and policies with a closed, intolerant mind, I probably would have liked them more.

If anyone wants to unfriend me for writing this book, please proceed.

Liberals Brought us the Best of America

October 2014

One of the strangest aspects of political discussions these days is that the word "liberal" gets tossed around as an insult. Some people even believe that calling someone a liberal automatically wins an argument. They don't bother with facts, reason, common sense, or compassion when a mindless insult is all they have.

As one famous liberal, Martin Luther King, once said, "The arc of the moral universe is long, but it bends toward justice." The folks who use "liberal" as an insult would do well to learn an important fact: At every significant moment in American history, the liberal view has propelled our nation along that arc toward justice.

Liberals brought us the American Revolution while conservatives believed that we should remain subjects of the British Empire instead of becoming an independent nation.

Liberals brought us a unified American nation while conservatives believed that we should be a grouping of separate, loosely connected states.

Liberals brought us the Bill of Rights while conservatives believed that defining our rights as Americans was redundant and unnecessary.

Liberals brought us an end to slavery while conservatives believed that some people have the right to own other human beings.

Liberals brought the right to vote to working-class whites, women, and African-Americans while conservatives believed that only property-owning white males should choose our representatives.

Liberals brought us public education for the betterment of our whole nation while conservatives believed that education should be a product bought and sold like a commodity and reserved for only a wealthy elite who could afford to be educated.

Liberals brought us the National Park system while conservatives believed that the most beautiful American lands should be sold to the highest bidder and enjoyed only by those who could pay for admission.

Liberals brought us the job programs that kept millions of Americans afloat during the Great Depression while conservatives tried to repeal those programs and called them socialism.

Liberals brought us food, workplace, and product safety while conservatives believed that there is an acceptable level of preventable illness, accidents, and death to ensure maximum corporate profit.

Liberals broke up monopolies to protect small businesses while conservatives have always supported large corporations that drive out mom-and-pop entrepreneurs.

Liberals brought us rural electrification while conservatives believed that there wasn't enough profit in bringing modern advances to parts of the nation that couldn't afford to purchase them.

Liberals brought us freedom from child labor while conservatives believed that there was nothing wrong with corporations exploiting children at farms, factories, and other dangerous jobs.

Liberals brought us an eight-hour workday, forty-hour workweek, and weekends while conservatives believed that American workers should serve the unrelenting demands of their corporate employers.

Liberals brought us the minimum wage while conservatives believed that corporations should be able to pay workers as little as they could possibly get away with.

Liberals brought us Social Security to lift millions of aging Americans out of poverty while conservatives didn't think it was the government's business to care whether or not people could survive once they were too old for the work force.

Liberals brought us basic civil, legal, and human rights for African-Americans, women, and gay people while conservatives considered these basic rights to be special gifts that no one deserved but white males.

Liberals brought us Medicare and Medicaid to guarantee basic health care to senior citizens and the poor while conservatives believed that health care should be a product that only those wealthy enough to afford should be able to access.

Liberals brought us an overall social safety net to protect our most unfortunate citizens while conservatives dismissed anyone who wasn't financially successful as lazy or irresponsible.

Liberals brought us the opportunity for all Americans, including women, African-Americans, and gay people, to serve their nation in the military while conservatives fought for the discriminatory idea that serving our country should be a special privilege reserved exclusively for white, male, heterosexuals.

When confronted with the fact that liberals have always represented core American values, people sometimes tell me that liberals might have been okay at some fuzzy point in the distant past, but today's liberals hate American and are trying to destroy our nation. Nothing could be further from the truth.

Today's liberals have brought us affordable health insurance, programs that staved off another Great Depression after the crash of 2008, Wall Street reform, and marriage equality. We also keep fighting for immigration reform, campaign finance reform, expanded educational opportunities, minimum wage increases, pay equity, Internet accessibility, common-sense gun safety regulation, tax fairness, and smarter military interventions.

Meanwhile, today's conservatives continue to fight against those advances while promoting regressive policies such as suppressing voters, creating the fiction of corporate personhood, restricting reproductive choices, cutting education, shredding the social safety net, shifting the tax burden even more to the working class, keeping big-money corruption in politics, and waging unwarranted full-scale wars that squander our blood and treasure.

Basically, liberals want to keep us arcing toward justice with optimism, equal opportunity, and facts while conservatives campaign on scapegoatting, fear, and misinformation.

So, please, go ahead and call me a liberal. I'm thankful for the compliment.

Stop this Liberal President!

September 2014

My friends, like so many of you, I was appalled when our nation elected a liberal legislator from Illinois to the highest office in our land. I joined you in our chorus of protest because we knew that this usurper would never cease his efforts to tear our country apart from within. Now we all know that his reign of terror has, indeed, come to smite all of us who truly love the very bosom of our homeland and who wish to conserve all that is good and decent in our great nation. How he bewitched and hypnotized the voters to reelect this liberal president during these days of national strife is one of the great mysteries of our time.

This liberal president attacks our divinely inspired founding document, the Constitution, with his boot heel twisting to trample its most fundamental precepts into the dust.

This liberal president uses dictatorial executive powers to grant amnesty to dark-skinned hoards of foreigners and set them loose to terrorize our native citizenry.

This liberal president takes up the weapons of war against the most patriotic of our own citizens simply because he cannot abide our economic traditions and religious liberty.

This liberal president haunts us with the nightmare of a federal income tax that chips away the very bedrock of our entrepreneurial freedoms.

This liberal president pours our nation's wealth into the vessel of an educational system that he will use to indoctrinate our apple-cheeked youth into his leftist agenda.

This liberal president steals the rightful role of private industry and grants government unprecedented power to control our lives by building controversial mass transportation systems. What are we, Europe?

This liberal president gives extraordinary free gifts to the least deserving occupants of our nation, letting them clutch the great properties of our land in their dirty fingers without paying for them—as God intended when He blessed the wealthy among us with material treasures to match our eventual treasures in heaven.

This liberal president pays but lip service to our Christian heritage, while his true religious beliefs, if indeed he actually has any, are as ambiguous as they are cloaked beneath the shroud of his private life rather than unfurled for all to see.

Yes, my patriotic friends, we must labor like noble *SISYPHUS* to stop this liberal president from violating the most sacred Article 1, Section 2, Paragraph 3 of our Constitution that values the soul of a Black person as three-fifths of a White person.

We must stop this liberal president from emancipating the slaves out of their rightful place as the property of our plantation owners.

We must stop this liberal president from waging his War of Northern Aggression (which some dare to call a "Civil War") upon our proud southern states.

We must stop this liberal president from funding his lawless war by confiscating the sweat of our brow through the taxation of his demonic Revenue Act.

We must stop this liberal president from erecting a system of Land Grant Universities to perpetuate his liberal ideology through inexpensive access to the blessings of higher education.

We must stop this liberal president from dragging us down the slippery slope toward a Socialist infrastructure by using the government to build a transcontinental railroad.

We must stop this liberal president from enacting his heinous Homestead Act, an obvious welfare giveaway of forty acres and a mule to his lazy political cronies.

We must stop this liberal president from making a mockery of Christianity by saying such demeaning statements as this recent utterance: "When I do good, I feel good. When I do bad, I feel bad. That is my religion." How sacrilegious. Any Muslim, Jew, Buddhist, Hindu, Sikh—or even atheist—could say as much.

Imagine, my friends, the light of our once great nation's future extinguished if we allow this liberal president to continue the darkness of his attack on our founding traditions. Those who do not share our views could one day in the not-so-far-off future be insane enough to carve this liberal president's face into the side of a mountain, as outlandish as that may seem to right-minded individuals like us.

Worse yet, in a century and a half, we might even see the cataclysmic day when a mixed-race commoner, perhaps even another legislator from Illinois, a man with a foreign-sounding name and exotic birthplace, might be elected president as a slightly left-of-center moderate with common-sense plans to bring our nation to its knees by pursuing such apocalyptic policies as immigration reform, a slight tax increase on the super rich, education funding, infrastructure improvements, a social safety net for the most vulnerable among us, and—oh, worst of all—respect for the separation of Church and State. Horrible! The very bile of my innards rises to fill my throat at the thought and threatens to expel itself upon the world.

The stench of that sickening vision, my dear friends, should make all good citizens tremble in our beds each night and hold tight to our stockpile of weapons each day. We can only hope that true patriots like ourselves will fight that future president tooth-and-nail, just as we now wage our own holy war at this tipping point in our great nation's history, in this the Year of our Lord, One Thousand Eight Hundred Sixty Four, our holy war against this current liberal president, the scoundrel Abraham Lincoln.

Thank you, my friends. Thank you. And may God bless the Confederate States of America.

Update: In April 2015, I performed this little piece of satire as a dramatic monologue at the Easthampton Massachusetts Book Festival. I originally recruited an amateur actor to do the job, but he had to pull out a few days before the event because his massage therapy licensing exam was rescheduled for the same night. So I got to be an actor for the first time since high school. It was an exhilarating, fun, and enlightening experience—and I'll probably never do it again. Oh, yes, and I know a guy who owes me a massage.

House Approves Absurd Lawsuit

August 2014

When I first heard that Congressional Republicans were planning to sue President Obama, I immediately checked to see if the information came from a satire outlet. The current crop of reality-impaired Republicans has given *The Onion* plenty of material since President Obama's election. Suing the president would be as mind numbing as claiming Obama inherited a successful Iraq War from President Bush. (Oh, wait … I know a conservative columnist who actually made that claim.)

The proposed Republican lawsuit, unfortunately, is not satire. In an all-too-real July 7 editorial on the CNN website, Speaker of the House John Boehner rambled about how President Obama has "consistently overstepped his authority under the Constitution." A reasonable person might expect examples of presidential overreach, but Boehner's editorial was about as specific as a toddler's explanation of where babies come from.

Carl Sagan of *Cosmos* fame was fond of saying, "extraordinary claims require extraordinary evidence." Speaker Boehner clearly does not subscribe to Sagan's theory. Of the 553 words in his editorial, not a single syllable indicated a specific case of the President exceeding his authority.

Republicans have been trying to label President Obama a dictator for years. The usual right-wing fringers on talk radio, the fever swamps of the Internet, and Fox News have ranted about how the president is a ruthless tyrant for the grave sins of trying to help people get health insurance or protect children from gun violence. But Republican luminaries such as Paul Ryan and John McCain repeated these accusations, bringing the fringe to the mainstream.

The weeks following Boehner's CNN editorial saw the proposed Republican lawsuit praised by conservative media outlets that promoted the Obama-as-tyrant narrative. Right-wingers connected any news event with Obama's fictionalized dictatorial tendencies. That passenger jet shot down over Ukraine? Obama did that to distract from the investigations of his many unconstitutional abuses—obviously.

Responsible members of the media, on the other hand, rightly pointed out Boehner's vagueries. So in a July 27 editorial in *USA Today*, Boehner finally revealed the specifics of President Obama's alleged crimes against the nation. After telling three outright lies about the president's actions relating to the environment, POW Bowe Bergdahl, and welfare, Boehner claimed that he must sue the president because he had delayed one provision of Obamacare, the mandate that requires companies with more than fifty employees to provide health insurance for their full-time workers.

Here's a fun fact: Republicans in the House had voted just last year that the president should delay that same employer mandate. Wait … what?

Let's be clear: Republicans planned to sue the president for doing what they wanted him to do—which is awfully nice for a dictator. House Republicans then passed a resolution for their lawsuit on July 30, interrupting their plans to jet off on yet another of their vacations away from the burdensome task of ignoring the nation's real problems. Almost immediately afterward, Republicans shredded the fabric of reality by criticizing the president for not taking executive action to address the border crisis that they have failed to address with legislation for comprehensive immigration reform.

I'm not an attorney, but I can read. The legal analysis I've read shows that the Republican lawsuit is completely without merit for at least two basic reasons. First, the courts have given presidents plenty of latitude to enforce laws as they see fit. Obama's delay of the employer mandate falls comfortably within that standard. Second, House Republicans must prove the president's actions have caused them damage. The president has lately been pointing out Republican incompetence, but Republicans' own actions and inactions have far more frequently brought that condemnation upon themselves.

Is this silly lawsuit a prelude to or substitute for the lunacy of impeachment? Despite their recent denials, many Republicans have brought up impeachment practically since Obama's first election. Now that Democrats have been calling them out on their impeachment rants, Republicans have taken offense and tried to deny their previous statements. Fortunately, inventions such as sound and video recording technology have captured their impeachment fantasies for rebroadcast on magical television and computer devices. Perhaps Republicans will also sue the inventors of these technologies that highlight their dishonesty.

Will the absurd Republican lawsuit even be filed? Probably. Republicans are fond of carrying on narratives that have long since been disproven. They keep trying to repeal Obamacare even though it has helped insure millions of Americans. And after every investigation has shown no wrongdoing in the Benghazi tragedy, the GOP is gearing up for yet another set of hearings to rehash their baseless attacks.

As my friend Naomi Minogue of Liberal Fix Radio says, Republicans keep throwing spaghetti at the walls. None of it ever sticks, but that never stops them from throwing more spaghetti. Naomi's analogy for today's Republican Party is fitting: tantrum-throwing children flinging half-baked pasta around the Capitol Building.

The Republican lawsuit against the president raises more questions that the obvious, "WTF?" Here are a few: Aren't Republicans supposed to be against frivolous lawsuits? Didn't they trumpet tort reform as a cure-all during the health care debates? How much will this lawsuit cost American taxpayers? What actual issues will Republicans continue to ignore as they pursue their witch-hunts? Will the lawsuit further damage Congress's single-digit approval rating? Is it mathematically possible for approval ratings to dip into negative numbers? What should we call this Congress when it has done far less that the historically inept Republicans that President Truman dubbed the "Do-Nothing Congress"?

Most important, will Americans reward Republicans for their insulting and embarrassing lawsuit at the voting booth in November? If so, maybe it's time to sue Republican voters for civic negligence.

We the Neighborhood

July 2014

On the Fourth of July, my wife Betsy and I walked the hilly driveway to our neighbors' house. Using the key that they had left for us, we let ourselves in so that we could water their plants and feed their cat while they were away for the holiday.

When we're away for a day next weekend to go to our granddaughter's baptism, those same wonderful neighbors will walk our dog for us. We look out for each other. That's what neighbors do.

For a small but vocal minority in America, unfortunately, the concept of being a good neighbor seems to have gotten lost. They've abandoned the civic ideal that our government is, like our neighborhood, "we the people."

When Betsy and I returned home from our neighborly errand, I signed onto Facebook and was promptly informed that I was a crazy liberal who would turn over control of everybody's lives to an all-powerful federal authority. What prompted such an accusation? I had posted to Facebook an Independence Day message that I believe our government is "we the people" and can have a positive role in the lives of American citizens.

I had been involved in an extended Facebook debate about the Hobby Lobby Supreme Court decision. I said it was a loss for actual human beings and a victory for corporate power. I said that our government, "we the people," should protect the rights of individuals, not treat inanimate corporations as if they could hold religious beliefs. That's when someone chimed in with an assessment of my obvious liberal insanity.

This gentleman ranted that all liberals were "sheeple" who wanted a tyrannical government to control everyone. He went on to say that "we the people" should refer to "God and the free market" as our nation's source of freedom. I was dumbfounded that anyone could so badly misinterpret the first three words of the United States Constitution. "We the people" references the formation of our government, not religion or economics. That's not liberal propaganda. That's just a basic fact that we should have learned in our neighborhood middle school social studies class.

How has our country gotten to the point where corporations can be considered "people" who have religious views about women's health? And how have Christian "religious" views been so corrupted, considering Jesus said nothing about contraception or abortion? Why are some people so offended by the thought that our government is "we the people"? Why are they so worried that a federal law requiring health insurance to cover contraception is somehow a terrible assault on religion or a sign of dictatorship?

Have the people who worry about tyranny looked at corporations lately? Corporate taxes are the lowest they've been in decades while corporate profits have exceeded their pre-crash levels. Have corporations expanded American freedoms by creating good-paying jobs to foster a robust American middle-class? Of course not. They've outsourced our neighbors' jobs, cut wages and benefits, and fought common-sense healthcare regulations while parking their profits in offshore accounts.

By comparison, liberal government "tyranny" sounds far better than corporate tyranny. Liberal government fosters job creation, decent wages, a safety net in hard times, and doesn't let your boss impose religious beliefs onto you. As tyranny goes, that's downright neighborly—"we the neighborhood."

On July fifth, Betsy and I climbed another hill, this one at one of the many wonderful state parks nearby. The trails are maintained by government employees who work very hard to keep the parks beautiful and safe. In fact, these government workers had recently installed a set of rough wooden stairs at a particularly steep portion of the trail. My aching knees appreciated the new stairs, and my sense of "we the people" did as well.

Can you imagine what our neighborhood parks and trails would be like if corporations owned and operated them? We would certainly have to pay a hefty admission fee, not to mention have our view blocked by giant billboards attached to every other tree. We'd exit through a combo gift shop and fast-food chain. For anyone who thinks that's an exaggeration, please do some research about how America's natural wonders were exploited for profit before the government established our national and state park system.

The folks who rant about government tyranny confuse me. Would they call my neighbors "freeloaders" and tell them to hire someone from the free market to water their plants? That seems absurd, but if the concept of "we the people" is actually free-market capitalism, that's what our neighborhood would be like. Good luck getting invited to the next backyard cookout. Maybe their favorite corporation could sell them some new friends—at a tidy profit, of course.

Don't they know that government actually exerted far more control in the past? They've forgotten the days when our federal government broke up monopolies in favor of neighborhood small businesses and set the top income tax bracket at three times what it is today. Will they continue screaming about the horrors of government tyranny as corporations cut their jobs? How about when five free-market conservatives on the Supreme Court rule that their employer's views trump their own convictions?

Betsy and I got a wonderful thank-you note from our neighbors for watering their plants and feeding their cat. I'm sure the corporate CEOs will be sending thank-you notes to the folks blaming the government any day now.

Republicans are Leaving American Values Behind on the Battlefield

June 2014

As I was finishing my monthly newspaper column about the Republican politicization of the Veterans Administration problems, America was hit with another astonishing reminder of how hypocritical Republicans can be about our military. This one was so horrendous that I didn't even see it coming.

In early June, President Obama announced the release of the last POW from our war in Afghanistan. Sergeant Bowe Bergdahl would be coming home after five years in captivity. I had heard his name in the news now and then, usually when a Republican was falsely claiming that President Obama had forgotten about him—yet another part of their vicious "Obama-hates-the-troops" propaganda.

My first thought was that I didn't think there was any way Republicans could turn the POW release into an attack on the president. I certainly didn't expect Republicans to thank the president for his efforts to bring Bergdahl home. That's well beyond their capacity. Instead, I assumed they would treat the issue in roughly the same way they did when President Obama oversaw the killing of Osama bin Laden. I thought they would say that the result was good, but that it was a victory for all Americans, doing whatever they could to make it look like any president would have done the same thing, and Obama just happened to be lucky enough to be in office and get the credit.

At worst, I figured they might concoct a story about how President Bush had somehow actually secured Bergdahl's release, or perhaps Dick Cheney had waterboarded the right brown person a decade ago to make the release possible. Republicans can be excellent fiction writers.

Oh, how wrong I was.

Almost within minutes, Republicans were criticizing everything relating to the release. Obama had given up too much. Obama had broken the law. Obama was the first president in history to negotiate with terrorists. Obama was trying to deflect attention away from problems with the Veterans Administration problems or Benghazi. Bergdahl's father looked like a Muslim. Bergdahl himself was a deserter and possibly a collaborator with the enemy. The attacks were swift, vicious, and fact-free—pretty much standard fare from the extremists who have taken over the Republican Party.

Many Republicans actually scrubbed their previous support for Bergdahl from their websites and social media. George Orwell would recognize their *1984*-like double-speak. Republicans before Obama rescued POW Bowe Bergdahl were saying, "Bowe Bergdahl is a hero who must be freed from Eastasia." Republicans after Obama rescued POW Bowe Bergdahl changed their tune to, "Bowe Bergdahl is a deserter who should have been left in Eurasia." They might as well be repeating the novel's catchphrases: "War is peace. Freedom is slavery. Ignorance is strength."

Looking back, I now confess that I'm embarrassed by my naiveté. What could I have been thinking to assume that Republicans would act with basic common sense and just be glad that an American soldier was home from captivity? I study politics closely, but I was still shocked by the craven behavior I saw. The exact same Republicans who had criticized Obama for not rescuing Bergdahl were now criticizing him for … guess what? … doing exactly what they wanted him to do.

High-profile conservatives in elected office and the media are now on record criticizing Obama for not bringing Bergdahl home and then later criticizing Obama for bringing Bergdahl home. Daily Banter writer Bob Cesca chronicled the flip-flops of Sarah Palin, Allen West, Kelly Ayotte, James Inhoff, Michelle Malkin, Jim Hoft, Oliver North, and Rich Nugent, to name just a few. It's as if these people don't understand that their previous words have been recorded and can be compared with their current words. Someone needs to teach Republicans that words are tangible things that don't just disappear like ghosts into the mist.

Senator John McCain (famously once a POW himself) was one of the worst but certainly not the only one. He ranted about how terrible the deal was, releasing such dangerous prisoners in exchange for Bergdahl. He even falsely claimed that these prisoners had masterminded the 9-11 attacks. In an uncharacteristic show of journalistic competence, the media immediately found video of McCain saying he would be in favor of just such a prisoner exchange only a few months before. Fact-checkers actually called out Republican dishonesty for a change.

Some basic research also indicated that the five released prisoners—while not model citizens—were far from the dangers that McCain claimed. These are middle-aged guys who had been out of the action for years. Their positions have long ago been taken over by younger cogs in the Taliban machine. While their release might be a terrorist morale booster at best, their strategic value is very low.

Also, they weren't going directly back to their homeland to immediately begin killing Americans. Instead, they were going to Qatar, the U.S. ally that had been the intermediary in the negotiations that ultimately freed Bergdahl. The five would be monitored closely by Qatari officials and, presumably, by United States intelligence. If ever there was a purpose for drones, it would be keeping track of these guys and taking them out if they warranted it. No one can say that the U.S. is not willing and able to use drones to kill known terrorists.

There are even calls for impeachment against Obama from some

Republicans who say that he broke the law by not giving thirty days notice to Congress. That claim is superficially true, but the Obama administration had been negotiating for Bergdahl's release for two years and had kept Congress informed. Video evidence suggested that Bergdahl's health was deteriorating, so the administration acted quickly on the last stages of the negotiations. And our current Congress, dominated in one branch by Teapublican lunatics and in the other branch by filibuster-happy obstructionists, simply can't be trusted to do what's right in a timely manner, especially with an American POW's life at stake.

Some critics of the president have said that he changed America's basic position of not negotiating with terrorists. Senator Ted Cruz, for example, made that claim and was quickly rebuffed by fact-checkers in another unexpected outbreak of responsible journalism. The United States has negotiated with criminals, terrorists, and rogue nations in order to secure the release of Americans throughout our history. Presidents Washington, Adams, and Jefferson did so at our nation's founding, and Johnson, Nixon, Carter, Reagan, Clinton, and G.W. Bush have done so recently. Some Republicans even claimed that terrorists were now more likely to capture Americans, as if the idea had just now occurred to the terrorists thanks to Obama's deal for Bergdahl's release.

Republicans immediately began criticizing the deal based on the obvious uneven numbers. Yes, five-for-one seems like a bad deal. But keep in mind that the United States has long had a solemn commitment to bringing back our prisoners. One American is worth five enemy prisoners if it means meeting our solemn commitment. The Taliban has no such commitment. Their POWs are considered more like pawns in a greater game. And we have, to put it bluntly, more bargaining chips than the Taliban does. We have more of their prisoners, and we only had to give up five to get 100% of the American POWs back. To make a chess analogy, we sacrificed five pawns to checkmate the opponent.

Republicans frequently trumpet their admiration for Israel's military stance. Here's a fact that might blow their minds: In 2011, Israel traded 1,027 Palestinian prisoners (including many convicted terrorists and murderers responsible for the deaths of 569 Israelis) to Hamas for Gilad Shalit, a former member of the Israeli military. Think about that ratio for a moment 1,027:1. Imagine the Republican freak out if President Obama had done what right-wing hero Benjamin Netanyahu did in the Bergdahl case.

The right-wing media jointed forces with the likes of Cruz and McCain to do what they do best: smear. Within days, a former Bush administration official had rounded up some of Bergdahl's fellow soldiers to criticize him on Fox News. They claimed he was a deserter who had cost the lives of several soldiers who were killed while searching for him. They had absolutely no evidence for that claim, but Fox News ate it like sugar pudding.

Some even implied that Bergdahl must have collaborated with the enemy, even though no evidence points in that direction. In fact, Bergdahl was tortured and had tried to escape his captors on more than one occasion.

Fox News didn't reveal what had already been detailed in 2012 by the late *Rolling Stone* journalist Michael Hastings. Bergdahl's unit suffered from notoriously bad leadership, and many of his fellow soldiers were far from ideal. Bergdahl was, by most accounts, at first a motivated soldier, but he grew dissatisfied with the weakness of his unit and eventually questioned the purpose of the war and his role in it. That same pattern—from supporting the war to questioning it—is very similar to American public opinion. Are millions of Americans somehow unpatriotic because we've also soured on the unnecessary, misguided, and mismanaged war?

Bergdahl himself hasn't been able to give his own story because he has been in captivity for five years. Fox has chosen to defame him rather than wait for his account. Fox also hasn't reported on a *New York Times* investigation that called into serious question the claims that soldiers had been killed while searching for him. Why would Fox let facts stand in the way of a good false narrative while smearing an American POW and the president who helped free him?

Fox even attacked Bergdahl's father, Bob Bergdahl, who had grown a beard and learned to speak basic Pashto in hopes of communicating with his son's captors. Republicans were outraged. Bill O'Reilly even said that the senior Bergdahl "looks like a Muslim," as if looking like a Muslim is some sort of crime. John Stewart pointed out the obvious, that Bergdahl would look right at home with Republican heroes, the cast of *Duck Dynasty*. His primary sin seems to be appearing with President Obama when Bergdahl's release was announced, making him guilty by association in the feverish Republican mind. The Bergdahl family has even gotten death threats thanks to the Republican smear campaign. By the way, the man being smeared for collaborating with President Obama, Bob Bergdahl is a registered Republican. After his treatment by Republican attack dogs, that may change.

Ultimately, none of the accusations against Bergdahl or his father are relevant to whether or not he should have been rescued. As President Obama has repeated, we don't leave our men and women in uniform behind. Why have Republicans abandoned this commitment simply because President Obama is taking it seriously? We don't apply arbitrary tests to see if we should rescue American soldiers. We don't say to our soldiers that we're committed to rescuing them only if they of their family members meet the Fox News criteria of being worthy of rescue. That's just crap.

A friend of mine posted his astonishment at Republican behavior on his Facebook page. "I'm wondering where all this outrage was when President Bush released 532 Gitmo prisoners." According to a report by the Director of National Intelligence, Bush's released Guantanamo prisoners reverted to terrorism at a rate of about 32%. Of the 82 released by Obama, the recidivism rate is less than an 8%. On top of that, no one seems to be talking about the intelligence value Bergdahl might be able to provide to the U.S. after seeing the Taliban close up for five years.

"To be totally honest," my friend continued, "if it were my son being held for five years, I wouldn't really give a damn what had to be done to get him home." He makes an excellent point. Bowe Bergdahl, like the veterans waiting for care at the VA, isn't some abstract political concept. He's a human being, the son of two human beings, who has been tortured in captivity for five years. "If it were my son" is a very empathetic statement—one Republicans seem incapable of making.

Imagine your own son or daughter being held captive by the Taliban. When Fox News attacks his or her actions and then suggests that there should be no rescue because of your hair or the words you've said, how would you feel? If my son or daughter were a POW, would Fox News attack them because I've written extensively in support of President Obama's policies and against the Republican Party and its propaganda wing, Fox News? You bet they would. And if you think you've got nothing that Fox News would criticize for political gain, then you haven't been paying attention to the Fox News business model: propaganda for profit.

My Facebook friend went on to comment, "I'm not a liberal bleeding heart. If he walked away from his post or is found to be a deserter (by a military court), then I definitely think he should be prosecuted and sentenced." Well, I am a liberal bleeding heart, and that's exactly my position as well, and the position of every liberal I know. There should be an investigation—a real one, not the one going on in the agenda-driven right-wing media right now. If he deserted or put his unit in danger, he should be punished accordingly. But he definitely should be back in the U.S. to face the consequences of his actions, not rotting away as a POW or being attacked in Fox News kangaroo court.

No one in an American uniform should be left behind. No one. Republicans believed in that promise at one time—until President Obama actually fulfilled it. Republicans should be ashamed of how quickly they turned against an American soldier and left American values behind.

Veterans Deserve Support, Not Petty Politics

June 2014

During his Memorial Day trip to visit troops in Afghanistan, President Obama said, "When it comes to supporting you and your families, the American people stand united. We support you. We are proud of you. We stand in awe of your service."

The president has strong personal credibility when he praises our veterans. He personally made significant donations to Fisher House Foundation, a program that provides support to wounded soldiers and their families. And his administration has improved veteran services in a number of ways, especially in the areas of veterans' employment and medical care.

But some won't accept that the president joins all Americans in supporting our veterans. Since President Obama first came to office, viral right-wing messages during the president's first term claimed that he was trying to cut military salaries, had threatened to withhold military pay, and refused to honor veterans on Memorial Day. These claims are completely false, as five minutes of using that liberal tool called "research." will reveal.

Another part of the Republican efforts to paint the president as anti-military is their obsession with recasting the Benghazi attacks as a scandal. Rather than honestly investigating the attacks to find ways to prevent future attacks, Republicans have made dozens of false accusations against the president, none of which have proven accurate.

As their latest attempt to make Benghazi into a fake scandal once again falters, Republicans have turned to problems in the Veterans Administration for their next attack on the president. Their scapegoatting conveniently ignores the fact that the VA problems date back to well before Obama took office and are rooted in the two wars that were launched and mismanaged by the previous administration.

Both Democrats and Republicans need to work together to address the VA problems. Democrats and the president need to make this issue a higher priority, not for political reasons but because it's the right thing to do for the men and women who put their lives on the line for our nation.

Republicans have a much harder task that mostly involves abandoning their usual petty political games. I doubt they'll welcome advice for a liberal like me, but Republicans need to make several difficult changes if they hope to lend a hand in addressing this issue.

First, Republicans need to stop using the military and veterans as pawns in their attacks on President Obama. They need to accept the fact that he isn't running for a third term and pivot from their worn-out strategy of claiming that every issue is somehow the president's fault. They need to stop trying to say that President Obama and Democrats do not support the American military. That's a battle that they've lost with all but a confused minority of hard-right ideologues.

Second, Republicans need to cooperate with Democrats in taking action to support America's veterans. Republicans have blocked several bills for veterans, including a veterans' jobs bill and an expansion of VA medical centers. These weren't blocked for policy reasons. The current Republican agenda simply cannot allow cooperation with the president and Democrats for fear that successful policies might be viewed as a political victory for the left. Republicans must accept the fact that good policy is a victory for all Americans.

Third, Republicans need to stop using the VA problems as a knee-jerk excuse to claim that government never does anything right. The tired conservative philosophy that government is the enemy can't guide the Republican Party's efforts to serve veterans. Like it or not, Republicans must understand that the military is part of the government. Republicans need to stop making the false and absurd claim that the VA problems are proof that Obamacare can't work either. No government program can be fully effective when it's being sabotaged, and Republicans have gleefully become the saboteurs of American government.

Fourth, Republicans need to remember that wars and their consequences aren't free. Lincoln paid for the Civil War with tax increases, and taxes paid for subsequent wars. But the Bush administration pushed through the first wartime tax cut in American history. Those who got the bulk of that tax cut, the wealthy and corporations, also benefit the most from America's military protection. The direct consequences of tax cuts are reductions in services, and the VA has been hit especially hard by that basic reality.

Finally, Republicans need to alter their war impulses. Many high-profile Republicans have criticized the common-sense foreign policy that President Obama recently outlined in a speech at West Point as "weak" or "appeasing." Some have even condemned the president for his lack of military actions in Syria, Iran, Russia, and elsewhere. Is the Republican memory so poor that they have forgotten the lessons of recent wars? Those lessons include the fact that war is very costly, certainly in terms of dollars, national image, and, most important, human lives. Most Republicans seem to have forgotten that the long lines of veterans who now need the services of an underfunded VA are the direct consequence of wars they helped start in Iraq and Afghanistan.

Despite the complexity of the VA issue, the bottom line is simple: Those who wish to honor and support veterans must understand the consequences of war, work for peace, and forget petty political games. The president and Democrats are on that path. Can Republicans follow?

An Affirmative Action Reaction

May 2014

"I'm sorry," said the voice. "We hired someone else."

The call came more than twenty years ago on an ordinary morning several weeks after the interview for a teaching job. This was far from my first rejection and certainly not my last. I rebounded from the initial blow quickly, but the inevitable awkward pause led to equally awkward words to fill the silence.

"We had to give the job to a minority," the conspiratorial voice whispered, as if to assure me that they were on my side, the defenseless, put-upon white man. I hung up, stunned and angered, not by some imagined unfairness against me, but by the ignorant assumption behind the comment. How could someone in a position of authority at an educational institution be so confused about hiring practices?

Like many people, I was appalled by the recent Supreme Court decision regarding affirmative action. Though the decision focused on college admission, some are hailing it as a death blow to affirmative action in general. Still others have even said that the decision is a rebuke to "whiny" minorities who simply want special rights that they don't deserve.

That view is even worse than the whispering telephone voice.

Not long after that rejection call, I received a much happier call for my current teaching job. I eventually met an administrator just months from retirement who told me in confidence that affirmative action policies forced him to hire "dozens of unqualified minorities." He had coordinated many hiring committees before I arrived. I looked around at my wonderful new colleagues and had no idea what he was talking about.

He called affirmative action "discriminatory social engineering," forgetting about the decades of actual systematic discriminatory social engineering that led to minorities and women being denied educational and career opportunities.

His rant struck me as absurd because noting about affirmative action leads to bad hiring decisions. If followed correctly, the basic tenets of affirmative action involve recruiting and considering a diversity of applicants who would otherwise have been shut out of the process.

When I became a Department Chair, I served on dozens of hiring committees and took affirmative action efforts seriously. We've never hired anyone unqualified, minority or not. Many qualified people have been turned down, as I was when I received that rejection call. That's unavoidable with so many talented applicants for every job.

Sometimes bad hires happen for many reasons, none of which are the fault of affirmative action. At any place of employment, a variety of people aren't good at their jobs. All of these folks made it through a hiring process of some kind or another. Blaming affirmative action for bad hiring decisions shows about as much common sense as blaming sour milk on UFOs.

The recent Supreme Court decision seems to be based on the conservative claim that racism no longer exists. If true, that would be wonderful, but the evidence against that claim is abundant. For example, how many witch doctor photos of the president or shots of watermelons growing on the White House lawn have been circulated since 2008? Enough to be shocking.

Recently, a freeloading rancher elevated to hero status by conservative media blurted out his views on "the Negro" perhaps being better off under slavery when they were taught to pick cotton so they didn't have to loaf the days away on concrete porches. Everyone acted stunned, but those comments aren't much different in content from Paul Ryan's absurd claim that "urban culture" has no work ethic or Mitt Romney's divisive "47%" condemnations.

The main difference is that politicians usually appeal to racist attitudes through the use of "dog whistle" code words to send their message, as Romney and Ryan did. Most prejudice is subtle. A young white student recently came to me to question his instructor's qualifications. He actually asked me if she was "an affirmative action hire." What had this young man been learning in his home to make him believe that a fully qualified teacher with strong work experience and excellent educational background was somehow only chosen to teach his class because of the color of her skin?

I'm fortunate that I've never had to live with that kind of prejudice. My worst worry as a white male instructor came when I first entered the profession. Only a few years older than the students, I fretted that they would misjudge me for my youth. Now I have the opposite worry as they see my gray head enter the classroom on the first day of the semester. But these concerns are inconsequential compared to racial biases.

Author and basketball legend Kareem Abdul Jabbar recently responded to a team owner's racist comments by saying that white people are more likely to believe in ghosts than in racism. That's a sight exaggeration, but he has a point. Some people's racial attitudes haven't changed much since I heard, "we had to give the job to a minority" more than two decades ago. Five conservative, white, male Supreme Court justices may believe racism is less tangible than ghosts, but that doesn't make it true.

We've made progress on racial issues in this nation, no doubt, but there's still much work to be done. Because I've never had to face racial prejudice doesn't give me any excuse to assume that racism no longer exists. I'll keep fighting for equal opportunity every chance I get.

The Myth of Lazy People

April 2014

Government benefits have long been stigmatized. When I was young, one particular family was teased because they were "on welfare." I remember hearing a chorus of "Farewell, welfare!" when these kids trooped, heads down, off the school bus.

I asked an older kid what "welfare" was. He said it was free government money for lazy people. The family in question, he informed me, spent their welfare on an expensive sailboat that they displayed outside their house for everyone to see.

That didn't make sense to me, so I visited the family's neighborhood after school. A ratty rowboat with duct-taped, hubcap-size holes leaned against the tiny house where two parents and five kids lived. I found better boats discarded along the banks when I explored the local streams.

Years later, I learned that the family father had lost his factory job for health reasons, so he did odd jobs for cash around town when he could. The mother labored raising five kids in cramped conditions with limited means. If ever people needed help, here they were. The kid who called them "lazy" and described their "expensive sailboat" was full of crap.

Many prominent conservatives today seem as reality-challenged as the bullies on the school bus. Republican Representative Paul Ryan claims that people are abusing our social safety net as a "hammock." Ryan himself went to college partly with government benefits after his father died, but he enjoys accusing others of taking advantage of the system.

Republicans praised Former House Speaker Newt Gingrich for telling people protesting economic conditions to "*GET* a job after you *TAKE A BATH*" and for calling Barack Obama the "Food Stamp President," referencing the increase in SNAP beneficiaries. Gingrich conveniently ignored the SNAP rate increase under President Bush, and that the economic downturn that made increased government assistance necessary predated the Obama administration.

The idea that people receiving SNAP benefits are lazy holds about as much water as that rotting rowboat. In fact, 75% of SNAP benefits go to households with veterans, children, senior citizens, or disabled people. Many SNAP recipients actually have jobs, but their wages are so low that they still need government assistance. The vast majority of able-bodied people getting benefits would rather work, but America still has three applicants for every job opening. Meanwhile, corporations that bankroll people like Ryan and Gingrich have fully recovered from the recession and are hoarding huge profits but not hiring.

In short, there is no hoard of unwashed lazy people. That fantasy exists only in the fact-free minds of Republicans who oppose not just our nation's safety net, but every job-creation and job-training bill that Democrats and the president propose.

Some loud voices want us believe that welfare fraud is rampant and bankrupting America. They rant that their cousin's neighbor's sister's boss's little league coach's hairdresser knows someone who heard about a "welfare queen" trading food stamps for candy bars, cocaine, and an iPhone—and, therefore, America is broke.

How can people believe such nasty bunk? Unfortunately, people believed the fake sailboat story of my youth and Ronald Regan's original "welfare queen" story, which was debunked long ago. No one ever offers proof but still demands that these ridiculous claims be honored as obvious truth. We shouldn't base public policy on eighth-hand anecdotes, especially when hungry children are involved. And the millions of needy families helped by the social safety net never make the gossip grapevine or the local news.

Actual research estimates social service fraud around 1-5%—similar to fraud-rate estimates for private businesses. And administrators more often perpetrate welfare fraud than recipients, so the omnipresent welfare cheat is a baseless myth.

Most important, the federal government spends about twice as much on corporate tax breaks, grants, and subsidies as on social service programs. And hungry children don't dump coal ash into our rivers as a corporation in North Carolina recently did.

Some people take advantage of the social safety net, of course. Let's find and punish these fraudsters. But a small percentage of fraud doesn't justify severe cuts. We don't dismantle the entire energy industry because some terrible companies pollute rivers. When Republicans use their "hammock" analogy to justify budgets that damage the safety net, I question their motives and their common sense.

Let's end on a positive note. I work at Asnuntuck Community College in Enfield, Connecticut, where we are partnering with the Connecticut Department of Social Services to offer a terrific program. SNAP recipients are eligible for scholarships to enroll in our career programs as a way to help them secure better job qualifications. They can study hard and earn an advantage in applying for competitive jobs where they can work hard and overcome the need for government assistance.

Too many Republicans repeat Reagan's fantasy mantra: "Government is the problem." They fail to grasp that one central role of government is to look out for our least fortunate citizens during tough times. I'm proud to work at a government-funded college connected with a government agency that offers government benefits to help people secure jobs.

Believing that SNAP benefits enable lazy people to lead an extravagant life is wrong. SNAP feeds hungry people and, through our scholarship program, helps people get jobs. The program doesn't reward lazy people with fictional hammocks or sailboats. Gingrich can call us the "Food Stamp College" if he likes. We'll wear his ignorant insult as a badge of honor.

Obamacare Works

March 2014

A Republican friend recently showed me his new bumper sticker: "Obamacare only works for people who don't." He beamed. I gave him a questioning look.

"Obamacare is just another giveaway to lazy people," he explained.

"You paid money for that?" I asked.

"No," he gushed. "I got it for free!" Unfortunately, Obamacare doesn't cover treatment for people who are "irony deficient."

Obamacare (the Affordable Care Act) isn't perfect, but it's now the law of the land that already works for Americas, despite the bumper-sticker mentality of those who attack it and the confused corporate media pundits who bungle reporting on its success. The vast majority of Americans who benefit from Obamacare actually do work, despite my Republican friend's absurd claim that only lazy people who forego getting jobs benefit from the law.

Misinformation and misunderstandings about Obamacare are still rampant four years after the law was passed, so we need an accounting that addresses the multitudes of ways that the law helps working Americans.

What about all the working Americans with pre-existing conditions who now can't be denied coverage? That's thanks to Obamacare. Does my Republican friend think these Americans are lazy?

What about all the working Americans who can now have their kids on their insurance to the age of 26 thanks to Obamacare? Are these Americans lazy? I don't think so.

Are all the working Americans whose insurance providers must now spend at least 80% of income from premiums on actual health care coverage lazy?

What about all the working Americans who will now have no yearly or lifetime limits on what their insurance will cover?

Are all the working Americans who now can't have their insurance coverage cancelled on a made-up technicality when they get sick lazy?

What about all the working Americans who will now not have to face extra costs and limited coverage just because they're women? My Republican friend can call those women lazy if he wants, but I certainly wouldn't. If he does think women are lazy, he should seek counseling because Obamacare is the largest expansion of mental health coverage in American history.

What about all the working Americans who now have no copayments for preventative care?

Are all the working Americans who now won't get scammed by

insurance companies selling junk policies with high prices that don't provide adequate coverage lazy?

What about all the working Americans who are now guaranteed the right to appeal if their claims are denied?

Are all the working Americans who will now not be subjected to arbitrary health insurance rate increases lazy?

What about all the working Americans who have already saved more than $2 billion in health insurance premiums thanks to Obamacare's premium-controls?

Are all the working Americans who run small businesses who will now have better, more affordable options for covering their employees lazy?

What about all the working Americans whose employers don't provide insurance coverage who can now get affordable plans on the healthcare exchanges?

Are all the low-income working Americans who are now eligible for insurance due to the Medicaid expansion lazy?

What about the half a million working Americans who the Congressional Budget Office says can now get affordable health insurance through the exchanges rather than holding onto jobs they don't want just to stay covered?

What about the half million unemployed Americans who will be happy to work at those half million jobs that people will leave because they can now get non-employer health insurance?

What about the vast majority of unemployed Americans who desperately want to work but can't get a job in bad economic times? They can now get affordable coverage for themselves and their families thanks to Obamacare.

Are all the working American taxpayers who benefit from the fact that Obamacare cuts the federal budget deficit by billions of dollars over the next decade lazy?

What about all the working Americans who labored for decades and can now have more secure Medicare thanks to Obamacare's cost-saving measures and closing of the Part D "donut hole"?

My intellectually lazy Republican friend thinks that there's an overall laziness epidemic in America, but he's absolutely wrong. The vast majority of Americans are not lazy. Anyone who thinks they are has blinders that block the view of 150 million Americans marching to work each day. The tiny percentage of people who might try to abuse the system does not trump the rest of our hard-working multitudes.

I enjoy a good bumper sticker as much as my Republican friend does, but my favorites are the ones that are based in facts, not ideological fantasy. Here's a good one: "Obamacare: Signed, Sealed, Delivering." The law has been passed, upheld, and is now working for America. Fact, fact, and fact.

The people who object to Obamacare the most seem to be the ones who know the least about the law—and the ones with the least common sense. It's time for Obamacare haters to put away their bumper stickers, stop calling our fellow Americans lazy, and join the rest of us in the real world.

Obama's State of the Union Address was More than a Model Speech

February 2014

The new semester began recently at my community college, and I happily met my new classes, including several sections of Public Speaking. The students range from age 18 to 50, with a wide array of interests and experiences, but they share a common anxiety about presenting speeches.

These students arrived bundled against the frigid January winter, but their shivering might have had more to do with their fear of public speaking than with the cold. By the time they finish the course in mid-May, I hope they leave in t-shirts and shorts with a newfound confidence that they can face public speaking situations with productive strategies for success to combat the inevitable shaking knees and voices.

The first week of classes coincided with the annual State of the Union Address by President Obama. This is perhaps the highest-profile speech in the nation each year, so we discussed it in class.

Some people who don't know much about me like to accuse me of using my position as a teacher to indoctrinate my students into believing liberal views. Needless to say, those people have never set foot in my classroom. The only "liberal" view I stress in class is that students should learn to think effectively for themselves. I want them to be able to see through the filters of media, propaganda, agenda, and bias to find common-sense reality.

I asked my students to put aside their own political views and simply watch as students of public speaking, looking for both an example of strong speaking skills and for how public speaking can be so much more than just a school assignment. Sometimes students believe that public speaking has nothing to do with life beyond the classroom, that it's just another box they have to check off on a list of graduation requirements, a painful band-aid that they have to pull slowly from a healing scab.

But President Obama's speech proved that public speaking can be a powerful way to engage in good citizenship by advocating for policies that move our nation forward and improve the lives of everyone around us. Members of my classes were impressed.

We discussed the president's technical strengths as a speaker: eye-contact with his audience, a clear and steady voice, gestures to emphasize important ideas, a strong sense of authority to go with a ready smile and good humor, organized and logical ideas, common sense and clear thinking, smooth transitions, specifics to develop the big ideas, respectful treatment of those who disagree. All in all, this year's speech was a clinic in how to be an excellent public speaker.

Then some students brought up the media reactions. "Why are they so mean?" one student asked. "Did they actually watch the speech?" another wondered.

Most of the students are busy adults, and, by their own admission, they don't follow politics as closely as they should. After returning home from classes and a job to do homework at the kitchen table while breastfeeding one child and helping two others with their own homework, and then rising before dawn to shovel snow from the driveway and drive off to work again—let's just say that watching C-SPAN isn't always atop their to-do list.

Another reason they often don't bother with politics is the relentlessly negative media. Reporting on scandals (or, in the case of right-wing media, fabricated scandals about the president) draws more ratings than coverage of government programs that actually help people or elected officials who follow their conscience and make difficult decisions.

Reporting on the State of the Union Address followed the usual negative pattern. The media loves to repeat the theme that Americans hate politicians, including President Obama. So they buried the news that people watching President Obama's State of the Union Address shared my students' positive reaction.

A CNN poll showed that 76% of viewers liked the speech. Unfortunately, CNN's own online and on-air analysis was mostly negative. And that's CNN, the supposedly "mainstream" media, not the ridiculous Obama-hate-aholics on Fox News and talk radio. Brit Hume of Fox News called the speech the "State of Confusion." Should badly rhymed superficial negativity pass as actual journalism these days? Unfortunately, Fox News seems to think so. Bill O'Reilly's disrespectful and interruption-filled Super Bowl Sunday interview of the president continued the network's pursuit of media-invented controversies at the expense of actually discussing the issues facing our nation.

Even if my students didn't have such busy lives, it's no wonder they tune out politics. As President Obama himself wrote about the negative media coverage of politics in one of his books, "I wonder who would spend their precious evenings with such sourpusses?" I advise my students to avoid the sourpusses and go straight to the public servants themselves. People have a great ability to judge which politicians are dedicated to helping the American people and which are simply interested in pushing their own ideology. It's too bad the media doesn't help enhance rather than obstruct citizenship.

When media pundits talk doom and gloom about the president's poll numbers, we need to keep in mind that those same polls show that President Obama is by far the most popular and respected major figure in American government today, especially compared with Republicans in Congress.

Americans support the same policies the president supports, and the nation generally likes him as a person—despite the relentless negative media narrative.

When my students watched President Obama's speech, they saw more than just a role model for their own public speaking efforts. They saw a role model for what participation in the American experience can be.

Putting My Values Where My Roof Is

January 2014

While sifting through tattered old boxes recently, I came across my own seventeen-year-old face beaming from a yellowed newspaper clipping. As a high school junior in 1978, I was named a top science student and invited to an energy conference at Penn State University. This was the first time that my picture appeared in the paper, the first time I spent a night away from our little farm without my family, and the first time I heard about the infant field of solar power.

An area coal company sponsored the conference, so solar was presented as a strange, possibly dangerous, far-too-expensive alternative to fossil fuels. But I was intrigued.

When I went to college, I learned that President Jimmy Carter (a trained engineer who understood the need for energy conservation) had mounted solar panels on the White House roof. In those formative years, I imagined my future in a forest cabin powered by solar panels like Carter's. I pictured driving my truck along rutted mountain roads to teach science at the local high school.

As many youthful dreams do, mine followed tangents both predictable and surprising. Middle age now finds me teaching, yes, but teaching writing and communication rather than science. My venue is a community college, not a high school. My truck is a four-wheel-drive hatchback, my mountain road the interstate. My forest is a wooded development not far from town, and my cabin is a pleasant contemporary farmhouse. All in all, a good result.

And I've finally come to realize one specific aspect of my vision: solar power.

My wife Betsy and I heard about the Solarize Northampton initiative last summer, so we made an appointment. We planned to listen politely, and then find a reason to decline the expense and trouble. We're frugal people who weren't interested in making a major investment at the time.

A nice young man from Real Goods Solar visited us in August, enjoyed the attentions of Libby, our overly affectionate dog, and pitched his product. We kept asking questions and getting good answers. To our surprise, we couldn't find a reason to decline. Our house was at an ideal angle for the sun. The roof would accommodate twenty-seven panels in three rows of nine, a perfectly pitched rectangle to greet us as we drove up our street. We could easily generate enough energy to cover our full bill and sell electricity back to the grid.

Another nice young man came, scratched Libby behind the ears, and laid out the finances. The project would be expensive, yes, but no more than a modest new car. With low-interest loans, state and federal tax rebates, increased home value, and, of course, no electric bill, the cost was manageable. With no reason to say no, we found ourselves saying yes.

With solar projects in high demand, our installation couldn't be scheduled until just after Christmas. Several more nice men showed up to brave snow, cold, and wind atop our roof. A few days later, the installation was complete, just in time for our tax rebates to be credited for 2013.

When Betsy and I drive around the area, we keep an eye out for solar projects. We've seen dozens of houses and even a few fields lined with panels, some blending with the architecture, some jutting like ragged rock formations. Of course, we think ours is the prettiest.

When I think back to my younger days, I remember the disappointment of Ronald Reagan removing Jimmy Carter's solar panels. But last year, common sense returned as Barack Obama commissioned a new solar installation on the White House, a project that must please Carter as much as it annoys Reagan's acolytes.

Betsy and I try to live our values by keeping our footprint small. We turn off lights, keep our heat low, recycle, reuse, and compost. And now we've gone solar, a smart and ethical choice.

That teenager in the old newspaper photo will never inhabit a forest cabin—and that's okay. In our pleasant farmhouse, beneath those solar panels, we have a small, widow-lined sunroom that houses my writing desk, Betsy's reading chair, and a pet bed where Libby watches for squirrels, the occasional family of deer, and even a few bears on rare occasions. I'd call that the grown-up fulfillment of my youthful dream.

PolitiFact's 2013 "Lie of the Year" is Actually "Half True"

December 2013

The fact-checking service PolitiFact.com just lost a major chunk of its credibility when they named President Obama's "If you like your health care plan, you can keep it" as their "lie of the year."

First, PolitiFact actually rated Obama's statement "half true" when they did their initial analysis. They name their "lie of the year" based only on an online poll, not on the actual analysis of the statement. Common sense tells us that something rated "half true" shouldn't even be in contention for lie of the year.

All of the other choices in the poll, mostly outright lies by Republicans, were rated "false" or "pants on Fire." How does a reputable fact-checking organization let an online poll determine its lie of the year instead of actual analysis of the statement? Anti-Obama forces marshaled their troops to vote in the PolitiFact poll, making sure that Republicans were able to crow about their shallow victory.

Second, less than 2% of insured people had their policies cancelled by their insurance company. How can predicting a 98% success rate at keeping policies be rated as the lie of the year?

Third, if people already had purchased those junk policies before the Affordable Care Act was passed, they could keep them—just as the president said.

Fourth, most of the cancelled policies were junk policies with little coverage and high costs that were sold after the Affordable Care Act was passed. The insurance companies knew they wouldn't meet the legal minimum requirements for acceptable policies that kicked in this year.

Fifth, most of the reports of people angry about their policies being cancelled were lies from the right or sloppy journalism. The people whose policies were cancelled could usually get better policies at less cost under the Affordable Care Act.

Here are just a few of the much bigger right-wing lies about health-care reform that PolitiFact had to choose from:

- Obamacare exempts Muslims. (pants on fire)
- Obamacare exempts members of Congress. (false)
- Obamacare will question your sex life. (pants on fire)
- The IRS will administer Obamacare, know all your personal information, and deny health care to conservatives. (pants on fire)

- Obamacare means forced home inspections by government agents. (pants on fire)
- Doctors who went to American medical schools won't accept Obamacare. (pants on fire)

Earlier this year, a study of PolitiFact's findings by the Center for Media and Public Affairs (CMPA) at George Mason University showed that Republicans lie far more often than Democrats. Yet PolitiFact let an online poll choose Obama's statement, which was an exaggeration at worst, as the lie of the year. PolitiFact's ridiculous selection of the president's statement as "lie of the year" simply gives credibility to a Republican Party that bases much of its politics and policies on dishonesty.

Adding further embarrassment to PolitiFact's lie of the year for 2013 is the fact that PolitiFact could have checked its own rulings to see President Obama's overall honesty. All politicians, pundits, and activists stretch the truth to some extent. But President Obama has been remarkably honest, according to PolitiFact itself.

PoltiFact has checked the president approximately 500 times over his career, more than twice as often as any other politician, and he has been rated "half true," "mostly true" or "true" 73% of the time, a far higher percentage than most other politicians or media figures.

Anyone who thinks the president is some kind of pathological liar is misinformed. We desperately need fact-checkers in our world of dishonest public figures and sloppy journalists, so when a big-name fact-checker such as PolitiFact gets its "lie of the year" so wrong, it damages public discourse in countless ways. In this particular case, in the words of Rachel Maddow, "PolitiFact, you're fired."

An Optimistic Look at 2013

December 2013

I recently told a friend that I planned to write about the good news of 2013, and he asked, "Was there any?" Actually ... yes.

Anyone who knows me knows that I'm a liberal. But sometimes I have to help define "liberal" in the wake of decades-long right-wing attacks on the term. Liberalism is optimistic at its core, which is at odds with current political pessimism. But liberals see the good in people and the potential for good government as "we the people." Yes, we see the reality that not everything in the world is wonderful, but we don't ignore the positive.

And 2013 saw far more positives than the typical news reports would lead us to believe.

Topping the year's list of good news is Obamacare. Yes, that's correct. Obamacare is good news! The over-criticized HealthCare.gov website is vastly improved after only two months. Consumer Reports calls it "terrific." The Congressional Budget Office recently reported that the law has already saved hundreds of billions of dollars more than originally predicted. And, best of all, the insurance exchanges are helping Americans all over the nation get affordable coverage.

In the blue states that cooperated with the new law by setting up state exchanges and accepting the federally funded Medicaid expansion, Obamacare has thrived. Even in red state Kentucky, where the governor is a Democrat, the law is a big success. Hundreds of thousands of uninsured people nationwide have already signed up for insurance, and millions more will follow.

Now that people are actually getting insurance through Obamacare, Republicans in Congress might finally abandon their nonsensical fake-repeal efforts. It's one thing to vote dozens of times for symbolic repeal, but it's completely different to try to take actual health insurance away from people who vote.

Can you imagine the positive impact if Republicans had helped instead of obstructed, and if the media had done its job? Initial reports about the people being hurt by Obamacare were a combination of sloppy journalism and right-wing propaganda. The thousands of Obamacare "good news" stories hardly get covered because they don't fit the narrative that "If it bleeds, it leads." Attacks generate ratings far better than reporting that a government program is actually helping people.

The good news is that the attacks were debunked within days. The vast majority of people wailing about losing their coverage got better policies for less money through Obamacare. In the reality where human beings actually live outside the 24-hour news cycle, the vast majority of Americans will pay less or be unaffected under Obamacare. Only 1-3% of Americans might have to pay more—while getting far better coverage than the junk policies they had before. Unfortunately, the media counts on people remembering the attacks and ignoring the corrections.

The law has actually been providing good news for several years now, curbing insurance company abuses with common-sense regulations, such as 80% of premiums going toward actual heath care, not being denied coverage because of pre-existing conditions, and women not being discriminated against or forced to pay more for insurance. Basic regulations might not be as gripping a headline as made-up death panels, but they're fantastic victories for everyday citizens trying to navigate the David and Goliath world of health care.

Despite the negative media narrative, the public is actually optimistic about Obamacare. A recent CNN/ORC poll showed that 54% of Americans favored the law or wanted it to do more, while only 40% opposed it. More good news about the start-up of Obamacare is that people are again discussing single-payer reform, something that has a far better chance to become a reality in the foreseeable future because of Obamacare's 2013 advances.

There's other good news on the foreign policy front, as the nation overcame extremely difficult circumstances in Syria and Iran. The media would have us believe that President Obama lucked into the Syria deal or that the Iran deal was merely an attempt to distract from initial problems with Obamacare. That's just unrealistic pessimism.

In reality, both the Syria and Iran deals resulted from long-term diplomatic efforts conducted outside media scrutiny. The president, Secretary of State John Kerry, and countless diplomats worked against deep resistance to broker groundbreaking deals and avoid the military actions that so many right-wing voices have cheered.

The early benefits are heartening: Syria's chemical weapons facilities have already been destroyed, and Iran recently invited independent nuclear inspectors into their nation, outcomes even the most optimistic observers wouldn't have predicted. These are victories far more meaningful than a million bombs dropped on foreign soil.

In judicial matters, the Supreme Court made a landmark marriage-equality ruling, taking some of the sting out of the terrible Voting Rights Act decision. Several new states have followed our New England lead by legalizing same-sex marriage. The court's ruling was especially important because it should pave the way for legalization in more states and perhaps even more far-reaching Supreme Court verdicts in the future. Also, federal benefits are now legally guaranteed to same-sex couples no matter where they live. Even Texas now recognizes same-sex couple military benefits, something that would have seemed impossible just a year ago.

At the voting booth, the 2013 off-off-year elections saw much good news at the state and local levels. Democrats swept statewide elections in the swing state of Virginia, defeating a slate of far-right candidates. New York elected a liberal mayor, as did Charlotte, Dayton, and Houston. New Jersey residents were confused enough to reelect Republican Chris Christie, but they resoundingly overturned Christie's earlier veto of a minimum wage increase.

In economic news, the unemployment rate just dropped to 7%, the lowest since the economic crash five years ago. The nation has had 45 straight months of private sector job growth, a stark contrast to the millions of jobs lost as the economy fell like lead through pudding at the end of the Bush presidency. And the stock market seems to hit a new record high every other day.

The economy should and could have been far better this year, as it should have been in previous years. The 2013 improvements would have been far greater—especially for the middle class—if Republicans had not obstructed every job-creating measure simply because they view economic improvements as a political victory for the president instead of something everyone wants and needs.

The year 2013 has been a bit like the classic question of whether the glass is half full or half empty. Republicans believe the glass once contained shining water on a hill but is now contaminated by socialist fluoridation. The tea party variety of Republican believes lazy poor people, aided by their Kenyan president, are drinking all their hard-earned water. Liberals see 2013 as a glass half full. Yes, we see a layer of scum on top of the water, but that's what the 2014 elections should be all about: skimming the scum.

One aspect of being an optimist is that you must be a realist first. Yes, the reality of 2013 had many shortcomings. I won't name them here because they dominated the media's fascination with negativity. When optimists see the reality of 2013's problems, we acknowledge that bad things happened, but we go a step further and ask how we can solve those problems. Being a liberal optimist isn't about making up good things—it's about accomplishing good things.

Nelson Mandela once said, "I am fundamentally an optimist." After 27 years of unjust imprisonment, he had every reason to turn to pessimism. Being optimistic about 2013 is hard work, no doubt, considering everything that needs improvement. But liberals are optimists who never shy away from the hard work of making the world a better place.

And here's one last bit of good news: Right here in my hometown of Northampton, Massachusetts, one of the most liberal places in the country with pockets of old New England conservatism, our most progressive candidates swept every city council election for the first time in years. If that's not reason to celebrate, I don't know what is.

When Fringe Becomes Mainstream

November 2013

Two guys recently set up posters on a local street corner showing President Obama with a Hitler moustache. They yelled at passing cars that President Obama was a foreign, Nazi, mass-murdering terrorist who should be impeached and sent to prison. Between shouts, they pushed flyers at glaring pedestrians.

I walked up and politely asked what evidence they had for their claims. "It's all in here," one guy said, shoving a flyer toward me.

"I'm asking you as one human being to another," I replied. "When did the president commit mass murder?"

I looked into his face until he finally made eye-contact. He couldn't answer my question—literally couldn't answer. Both guys actually stopped talking and looked embarrassed, suddenly more interested in studying the sidewalk than talking with me.

Because I didn't know the next time I'd be face-to-face with people voicing such ridiculous views, I asked some common-sense follow-up questions: "Where did you get your information? Do you know that I found five factual errors in just a ten-second skim of your flyer? Who's paying you to be here? Are you trained to ignore people who ask reasonable questions? Do you really believe this stuff, or is this just performance art?"

But they turned their backs and resumed yelling their nonsense with slightly less gusto. Either they were ashamed of what they were saying or they were ashamed of their inability to defend their accusations.

Our nation is full of people who inhabit the fringe of public opinion. Unfortunately, many aren't limited to yelling on street corners. Radio host Alex Jones rants about the Aurora and Newtown shootings being "false flags" staged by the government. Glenn Beck spins tales of impending government concentration camps. Rush Limbaugh—well, everything he says is a farcical froth of belligerent misinformation.

Lunacy exists, and I suppose it always has. When I was a kid, some crackpots claimed that Blacks and Jews would come from the city to our farms and imprison or kill us. Back then, though, most of those people didn't have powerful microphones. They just whispered their crazy theories in church basements to people too polite to tell them to screw off.

Unfortunately, there's little daylight between those street-corner guys yelling about Obama and many "mainstream" Republicans today. They sound too much like the church-basement whisperers of my youth. Prominent Republicans make frequent guest appearances for Jones, Beck, and Limbaugh as if they're on the nightly news and not legitimizing unhinged ignorance.

Many current Republican positions are so absurd that they're hard to take seriously. Tax cuts for the wealthy trickle down to the middle class. Poor people are lazy. More guns leads to fewer gun crimes. Government is evil. Smaller government is always better—unless you're gay or pregnant, in which case government must be big enough to invade your most private places.

And then there's the litany of lies about the Affordable Care Act, aka Obamacare. One after another—from death panels to socialism to the IRS carting us off to jail—these lies all get debunked. That doesn't stop Republicans from repeating them and creating more.

Republican representative Joe Barton said in a Congressional hearing that a secret message in the Obamacare website strips Americans of their medical privacy. Louisiana Governor Bobby Jindal, who once said Republicans should stop being "the stupid party," recently told six lies about Obamacare in less than a minute on national television. In his defense, he never claimed that Republicans shouldn't be "the lying party."

Republican are now led by far-right reality deniers like shutdown champion Ted Cruz and serial-plagiarist Rand Paul. They spread their lies on propaganda-enabling Fox News and are rarely challenged by sloppy journalists in the mainstream corporate media. Long-time conservatives get primaried out of office by Tea Party neo-confederates who campaign on birther jokes and gun conspiracies. Twenty-seven Senate Republicans recently voted to condemn their two-week-old votes to avoid a debt default, denouncing even their own temporary spasm of sanity.

Some of my Republican friends on Facebook post charts to prove that Obama caused the recession in 2008. When I point out that Obama took office in 2009, they reply, "spoken like a true liberal," as if they've made a winning persuasive point. They use "liberal" as a safe word to make me stop hurting them with sadistic facts. Then they tell me that God will punish me, but their cringe-worthy spelling would make any higher power blush.

Some Republicans compare liberals to Saul Alinsky (repeating a name they probably don't know but have heard their right-wing media role models use), or they just accuse us of being crazy or dishonest when we cite facts. I generally ask them to look up "projection" in a dictionary of psychological terms. They don't get the joke. As my father once said, "Some people should flush the B.S. in their own toilet before they start sniffing around their neighbor's bathroom."

We live in a free country where we can all voice our views—but freedom requires responsibility. The jerks with the Obama-as-Hitler poster couldn't answer basic questions. Members of Congress blather about secret computer codes. Facebook friends post obvious falsehoods and flail against facts.

When people abuse freedom of speech with ignorance and outright lies, they just look like fools. Our country deserves better.

Why Republicans Actually Hate Obamacare

October 2013

My *Daily Hampshire Gazette* columnist colleague, conservative Jay Fleitman, recently published a column titled, "Why Republicans Hate Obamacare," Like most of what Fleitman writes, this one has more inaccuracies than New England has pumpkins this time of year. Like pumpkins, Fleitman's claims rot with prolonged exposure to sunlight. Let's shed a few rays on his blatant misinformation.

To begin, Fleitman is wrong about the process of passing the Affordable Care Act. Fleitman claims that Democrats "crammed" the law past Republicans, thus creating "enduring bitterness." Hogwash. In reality, Republicans chose to obstruct the law at every turn instead of working to fix aspects they didn't like or proposing a viable alternative.

We all remember the protest signs depicting Obama as Hitler or a witch doctor, town-hall screaming fits, outright lies about "death panels," and shouts of "You lie!" at the president and "Baby killer!" at Democrats in Congress. Fleitman apparently doesn't remember, but those displays of bitterness and incivility mostly predated the actual legislative process of passing the law.

Republicans had plenty of opportunity for input as the law took shape, despite Fleitman's revisionist history. In fact, many aspects of the law were originally Republican ideas that they disowned when President Obama endorsed them. The "individual mandate," for example, was first proposed by the conservative Heritage Foundation as a personal responsibility provision. Republicans now act as though their own idea is pure tyranny from a dictatorial Obama. As Republicans obstructed, Democrats compromised on single-payer, public option, and even contraceptive coverage, but Republicans refused to budge o help the American people.

Fleitman also makes false claims about the law itself. Is the law leading to more part-time workers? No, the Bush recession years before the Affordable Care Act caused that. Is the law causing higher insurance premiums? No, premiums are rising at modest rates, and premiums on the Affordable Care Act exchanges are lower than expected. Does the law disproportionately hurt young adults? No, unless new opportunities for young adults to buy affordable, comprehensive health insurance is somehow harmful.

Basic facts such as these are easy to find. The nonpartisan FactCheck.org and PolitiFact.com have debunked many Republican claims about the Affordable Care Act. Of course, finding reliable facts about the law requires filtering out the biased right-wing sources in the corporate media that

Fleitman seems to have relied on for his skewed column.

By far Fleitman's most inaccurate statement is calling the Affordable Care Act an "intrusion of central government into the economic and personal lives of Americans, an action contrary to … the nature of American society." That's just absurd.

If the Affordable Care Act were actually an example of "central government," then it would include at least a public option if not actual government-provided insurance or healthcare. Fleitman simply uses slightly modified language to recycle the lie that the Affordable Care Act is socialism. It isn't. Fleitman's socialist boogeyman exists only in dark corners of the right-wing mind.

Fleitman also seems confused about "the nature of American society." At our best, this nation has a liberal, progressive tradition of government being a force for good in the lives of American citizens. The Affordable Care Act is squarely in the tradition of Social Security, Medicare, and Medicaid—other instances where "we the people" care for one another. One fundamental tenant of American society is that we are all in this together, even if some Republicans need to be dragged kicking and screaming into the American tradition of community.

The Affordable Care Act isn't perfect, but it grows from the view that all of us—citizens, elected leaders, and the people of the private insurance industry—can partner to serve the public good. That's not tyranny or socialism or the end of America or any other hair-on-fire attacks the right has launched against the law. Basically, the law is an attempt at good government, a concept many of today's Republican saboteurs have trouble grasping as they cheer on their shutdown and default disasters.

The core of the Affordable Care Act is a method to help uninsured Americans get affordable health insurance. And the law is funded in a way that reduces the federal budget deficit by hundreds of billions of dollars over the first decade without raising middle-class taxes. Republicans never seem to acknowledge that fact.

In addition, already insured people benefit from many other common-sense aspects of the Affordable Care Act that Fleitman ignores: keeping kids on parents' insurance until age 26; not being denied coverage for pre-existing conditions; not having annual or lifetime benefit caps; requiring that insurance companies spend the vast majority of premiums on actual health care; eliminating insurance coverage discrimination against women; making it illegal to offer substandard coverage or to cut off coverage when people get sick; expanding mental health care.

Fleitman's column purports to answer the question, "Why do Republicans hate Obamacare?" He fails miserably.

The truth about why Republicans hate Obamacare is three-fold: First, many Republicans "hate" Obama and have made no secret of it. They seem more motivated by their obstruction of the "Obama" part of the law to notice that it has a lot of "care" for American citizens. Second, as Fleitman's column shows, many Republicans "hate" facts. They are woefully misinformed about the law and frequently pass on their bias-affirming misinformation. Most important, many of today's Republicans "hate" effective government. They are terrified that the law will work. That would affirm the deepest fear in the Republican mind, the truth that government can work to help the American people.

Choose Choice

September 2013

Republican-controlled state legislatures across the country have been proposing restrictions on abortion at an astonishing rate since the 2010 elections, even accelerating their anti-choice efforts during the recent summer months.

Texas Governor Rick Perry called two special legislative sessions specifically to ram through anti-choice legislation. Ohio Republicans attached eleventh-hour anti-choice laws to the state budget in order to avoid debate. And North Carolina Republicans held a master class in craven foolishness when they attached abortion laws onto motorcycle-safety bills and even a ridiculous anti-Sharia-law bill.

Fortunately, several Republican anti-choice laws have already been ruled unconstitutional, and more will follow as new laws continue to be challenged.

Lost in the frantic Republican stampede to one-up each other's quest to restrict women's reproductive rights is the actual difference of opinion on the overall abortion issue. That primary difference has to do with the who gets to decide the exact point at which the mass of living cells inside a pregnant woman becomes a human being. Most, perhaps all, pro-choice people don't have a rigid, all-encompassing answer to that question. Our viewpoint is that each pregnant woman has the right to make her own decision. No one is "pro-abortion." No one wants to force anyone to have an abortion if she chooses not to. Pro-choice people are not against women choosing not to have an abortion. We are against others taking the right to make that choice away.

Many Republican abortion restrictions seem to be prefaced on the idea that women who have abortions do so impulsively, as if a pregnant woman simply hasn't considered her choice seriously enough. That view simply shows no common sense about human beings. I've known many women who experienced an unwanted pregnancy at some point in their lives. Some were young, some middle-aged, some alone, some with a dedicated family and man in their life. Some look back with relief that they made the right choice, some with regret. None faced their choice with a cavalier attitude. All brought their full hearts and minds to their agonizing choice.

At the core of our argument, pro-choice people believe that no government has the right to take away such an important personal decision. Our disagreement is not with people who believe they know exactly when a pregnancy can be defined as a human being. We acknowledge that every individual has the right to make that choice.

What pro-choice people object to is the insistence that government force the decisions of some onto everyone else. We object to the legislation of views that others may not share but would be forced to obey. We object to government trying to make decisions for other American citizens by enacting laws that take away choice. Anti-choice laws aren't about morality. Morality involves making choices, not eliminating choice.

Even if abortion becomes illegal, many women will still choose to get an abortion, so pro-choice people support legal and safe access to abortion. Before Roe v. Wade, wealthy women could afford relatively safe, illegal abortions. Poor and middle-class women were far too often endangered by unsafe "back-alley" abortions. We can't go back to the dark days of putting these women at risk simply because their economic circumstances conflict with someone's else's desire to impose their own views on other people. Putting women's lives at risk is not a "pro-life" position.

Most important, pro-choice people support efforts that can make a difference in preventing unplanned pregnancy, such as comprehensive sex education about the physical and emotional components and consequences of sexual activity. Republican "abstinence only" programs are ridiculously unrealistic and simply not effective at preventing unplanned pregnancy. Promoting reproductive ignorance rather than knowledge is not "pro-life."

We also support public policy that improves the quality of life for parents and children. Republicans, by contrast, have been attacking food stamp funding, a large percentage of which actually goes to families with young children. There is nothing "pro-life" about cutting food for children. Republicans also attacked the Affordable Care Act (aka, Obamacare) in part because they saw it as somehow promoting abortion. The truth is that the law's provisions promoting birth control, prenatal care, and women's health have been shown to reduce the number of unwanted pregnancies and abortions.

Fewer abortions and better life for parents and children—aren't these "pro-life" values?

Wrapped in Extremism

August 2013

Back in 2009, a friend saw a Tea Party rally on Fox News and asked me, "Where did these crazy people come from, the John Birch Society?" She was joking, but, like many the best jokes, this one was grounded in reality.

Wrapped in the Flag, a new book by Claire Conner, chronicles her life as the daughter of parents who were immersed in extreme right-wing politics as founding members of the John Birch Society in the 1950s to the present.

Connor combines her insider perspective and detailed research to illuminate the "Birchers," as they were known. The organization was founded in 1958, when Connor was a teenager, and grew directly from Joe McCarthy's paranoid accusations that Communists were infiltrating the United States government. Birchers focused not on the reality of Communism in the world, but on fabricating Communism where it didn't exist. Most famously (and most ridiculously), they accused moderate Republican President Dwight Eisenhower of being a Communist sympathizer.

In addition to seeing Communists lurking everywhere, Birchers were virulently opposed to immigration, homosexuality, civil rights, Social Security, public education, and pretty much any government action to help American citizens. They espoused devout Christianity and adherence to the Constitution (or their twisted versions of Christianity and the Constitution). They revered big business and the wealthy while dismissing unemployed and poor people as victims of their own laziness. And they believed that the constitutional concept of "we the people" applied primarily to white male property owners.

When Connor saw the Tea Party reaction to the election of President Obama, she immediately recognized the same forces that propelled the John Birch Society and their related right-wing compatriots. History repeats itself—a cliché to be sure, but an accurate one. Unfortunately, in American politics, people have trouble remembering the last administration, let alone events five decades ago, so Connor's book is particularly welcome.

As a memoir, *Wrapped in the Flag* combines coming-of-age and dysfunctional-family motifs. Connor traces her own life from childhood to maturity as she reacts to what can only be described as her parents' political insanity. These parents make her both a pariah in school and a frustrated adult who tries her best to care for them as they age, despite their continuing tone-deaf attempts to convert her to their extremist views as they accuse her of being a brainless liberal. Connor also presents own political journey from dipping a toe into supporting right-wing candidates to anti-abortion activism and anti-gay leanings to a left-of-center moderate whose views ultimately grow from her personal experiences as a parent herself.

As a work of political history, *Wrapped in the Flag* is at its best. She takes us on a true-life expedition into the fever swamp world of wingnuttery. Extreme views seem to go hand-in-hand with extreme personalities, and her parents definitely are extreme personalities—as are the many other Bircher family friends whom Connor writes about, including such infamous figures as Birch founder Robert Welch, white supremacist Revilo Oliver, anti-feminist Phyllis Schlafly, and failed presidential candidate John Schmitz. She's even privy to some certified gun nuts and stunning "family values" sex scandals, showing how little the world of right-wing politics has changed in fifty years.

Most important, Connor does her readers the essential service of showing the connections between the John Birch Society and today's equally extreme right-wingers, many of whom have wiggled their way into the mainstream of American politics far more than their Bircher antecedents. People like Glenn Beck, Sean Hannity, Rush Limbaugh, Ron and Rand Paul, Sarah Palin, Ted Cruz, and just about everyone on Fox News would be welcome at the Connor's living room Birch meetings to wail about the impending destruction of America at the hands of those filthy liberals.

And, of course, there's the Tea Party. From its founding, the Tea Party has been confused at best, much like the John Birch Society. Their movement is named after an event protesting government-corporate connections, but their own funding is largely from corporate front groups. And their claim to be "taxed enough already" falls flat in light of the fact that the Obama's American Recovery Act they hated so much included an extensive middle-class tax cut. They claim to be against government control, but most of their membership also advocates for Bircher-like theological influence on government, and they are perfectly happy to have government regulate personal behavior such as reproductive choice and marriage. The Tea Party assertion that America is at the point of imminent destruction unless we "take our country back" particularly resonates Bircher views.

Demographic and policy analysis has revealed that the Tea Party is basically a rebranding of the most far-right factions of the Republican Party. Look at the members of Congress and state governments around the nation who have identified with the Tea Party. Their focus has been on protecting tax cuts for the wealthy and corporations, enacting anti-choice legislation, opposing financial regulation, stopping immigration reform, restricting voting rights, cutting aid to our most needy citizens who were victimized by the economic downturn, praising the supremacy of corporate capitalism, and basically sabotaging government in general. Robert Welch and Revilo Oliver would feel right at home. Phyllis Schlafly still does.

Ultimately, American common sense prevailed over the Birchers and other extremists of that era. *Wrapped in the Flag* is a cautionary tale that warns us to follow suit and reject the Tea Partiers who would lead our nation on a painful rightward lurch.

Let's Light Candles, not Torches, for Obama

July 2013

The Huffington Post recently ran a photograph of the merged faces of Presidents Obama and Bush with the caption "George W. Obama." That's pretty strong stuff for a supposedly liberal publication. Considering the recent news reports about government surveillance, is it fair to say that Obama has become as bad as Bush?

Reasonable people can debate whether surveillance helps keep us safe or is a needless intrusion, but anybody who thinks Obama invented surveillance has a very short memory. Bush's surveillance was widely reported in 2006 and dates back even further. And anyone who claims Obama is as bad as Bush or the Republican Party is ignoring many basic facts.

The Obama administration's surveillance is primarily "data mining" to discover possible crime or terrorism. Michael Hayden, Bush's Director of the Nation Security Agency, has noted that Obama is "more transparent" about surveillance than Bush was. Also, despite media distortions, there is no evidence that the Obama administration has engaged in the far more invasive practice of wiretapping. Bush definitely wiretapped, and did so with, at best, questionable legal authority.

In other aspects of foreign policy and nation security, Obama has proven to be far more effective and in line with liberal American values than Bush was.

Let's begin with 9-11. Obama didn't allow the worst terrorist attack in American history—Bush did. Obama didn't start two "Bush Doctrine" pre-emptive wars for bad reasons—Bush did. Obama didn't mismanage those wars—Bush did. Obama ended one war and is winding down the other. Obama got Osama bin Laden—Bush couldn't. Obama saved lives and helped oust a dictator in Libya while avoiding the full-scale war that Bush probably would have started. Obama didn't start wars with Iran or North Korea, among other places. Bush (or McCain or Romney) probably would have.

Bush and Congressional Republicans created the Patriot Act in 2001 and spearheaded its renewal in 2006 and 2011. Obama didn't dream it up and mainly signed the renewal in 2011 because Republicans (along with too many go-along Democrats) would have overridden a veto for the sake of looking tough on terrorism.

Obama immediately banned torture and ordered the closing of the Guantanamo prison (which is being blocked by Congress). Bush, by contrast, approved torture and founded Guantanamo, sending hundreds of detainees there. Obama hasn't sent anyone new there and has been steadily extraditing prisoners out of Guantanamo.

Obama has increased the use of drone strikes begun by Bush, and those strikes are definitely not perfect. But Obama is moving the program from the CIA to the Defense Department for better oversight. Most important, targeted and limited drone strikes are far less destructive and costly than Bush's full-out wars.

Obama didn't cut taxes during wartime, which Bush did. Bush had terrible "Neocon" foreign policy advisors (Paul Wolfowitz and Dick Cheney) while Obama seeks sensible counsel (Hillary Clinton and John Kerry). Bush persecuted military members under Don't-Ask-Don't-Tell. Obama oversaw the DADT repeal.

Some of my fellow liberals may call me an "Obamabot" for daring to believe that Obama is far better than Bush, but that's okay. Along with being factually wrong, equating Bush and Obama is bad politics for liberals. This view feeds the false-equivalency argument that all politicians are bad, causing many Americans, especially independents and liberals, to disengage from politics and stop voting. When turnout is low, Republicans almost always do better. Too many independents and liberals skipped the 2010 "Tea Party" elections, and the 2014 midterms could have the same sad outcome. Criticizing Obama from the left hurts all Democrats at the ballot box. Nothing improves with Republicans controlling Congress—or, worse yet, with a Republican president in 2016.

Of course, we liberals want Obama to move leftward. But "George W. Obama" attacks are ineffective and counterproductive. We're still learning the basics about the surveillance program. As more facts emerge, the differences between Obama and Bush will become clearer, just as emerging facts about the fake IRS scandal show that Obama is nobody's Nixon. Moving forward, we're better off tempering our criticism, focusing on common sense and facts over exaggerations, and voicing our objections in reasoned tones rather than snarled attacks.

Elected leaders don't pay much attention to mobs carrying pitchforks and torches, but they welcome friends with candles to light the way.

Local Override Combats National Mistakes

June 2013

Teachers are often hailed as heroes during times of crisis. News reports praise the teachers who shielded our children in the face of the recent Oklahoma tornado or the Sandy Hook shooting, for example. By the next news cycle, however, the idea of teaching as a noble profession gets blown away faster than the school roof during that tornado. Without any concept of irony, many in the media cast teachers as "union thugs" holding children hostage for pay raises while blaming teachers' contracts for crashing the economy.

When government has a chance to help fund education, that funding often comes at the cost of teachers' dignity and value. The 2009 American Recovery Act (known as the stimulus) was inaccurately labeled a failure or a giveaway to liberal teacher unions instead of what it actually was—government action that saved millions of jobs, many of them in education. When President Obama proposed the American Jobs Act in 2011, it was criticized as "Stimulus II" and blocked by Republicans who ignored the fact that the act would have saved thousands more teachers from layoffs.

In several states, most notably Wisconsin, Republican governors and state legislators have attacked teachers' collective-bargaining rights, claiming to be simply responding to budget shortfalls while conveniently ignoring the fact that corporate tax giveaways often led to those budget problems. Their priorities are clear: teachers are valued less than corporate campaign donors.

Here in Northampton, we might easily blame the misguided scapegoatting of teachers by faraway extremist Republicans and Fox News pundits who snarl and smirk through fact-free accounts depicting teachers as overpaid and underworked. Unfortunately, the attacks on education from outside our town have more impact on us than we may think.

The connections are clear. First, the wrong-headed fetish for budget cuts in Washington affects everyone across the country. The last decade proved that wealth doesn't "trickle down"—but budget cuts do. Less federal funding to states means less state funding to towns, which means less funding available for schools. Second, Republican tax cuts made the budgets even worse, like demanding that your boss cut your pay even as your bills pile up. And third, the economic crash at the end of the Bush administration led to even less tax income for the government, further stressing everyone's budget.

Our nation is a connected community, not a set of isolated islands. To extend Tip O'Neill, all politics is just as national as local. The right-wing policies embraced in other states affect us here in Northampton where vast majorities would outvote those policies.

Northampton's budget gap isn't the result of overspending, as Fox

News might assert. The same budget-slashing trends that affect Florida and Pennsylvania and Kansas and Mississippi hit us as well. When Texas representatives vote for education cuts and tax giveaways for the wealthy, the "Butterfly Effect" causes us to suffer right along with the Texas teachers who get laid off.

Unlike most Texans, however, we can do something about it. On June 25, we can vote yes on the proposed budget override as a common-sense local response to the unreasonable wave of right-wing national politics that has led to a decade of strained local funding. The override will provide funds for a four-year plan that will save the jobs of many Northampton teachers and school staff, those professionals we know are heroes in more than just times of danger and disaster. Their everyday heroics include connecting our children with music and art, providing psychological support and learning enhancement, and helping our community's young people realize their personal and intellectual potential.

The funding would come from a modest increase in property taxes, an option that places the burden primarily on those of us who can most afford it—homeowners, myself included. I believe what Oliver Wendell Holmes said: "Taxes are what we pay for civilized society." I chose to own a home in Northampton because this is a civilized place, and I can prioritize my own family budget to help preserve the local civilization that makes Northampton a great place to live.

Unfortunately, given the regressive and counterproductive Republican policies enacted across the nation, no solution is perfect. But the override isn't a stopgap measure like the self-inflicted crisis governing practiced by Congressional Republicans. It's a responsible, long-term plan meant to avoid more crises in the future.

One of the most important aspects of this town is also one of the best qualities in our national character: we value education. Unfortunately, in some parts of the United States, extremist politicians who pay lips-service to the concept of education have forgotten to value actual educators. Here in Northampton, we have an opportunity to support education in concept and in reality. We can vote yes on the override on June 25.

Update: The override passed.

Celebrate the Helpers

May 2013

In the aftermath of the Boston Marathon bombing, many people used social media to share a lovely common-sense quote from children's television legend Mr. Rogers in an effort find comfort as the devastating and confusing events unfolded:

"When I was a boy and would see scary things in the news, my mother would say to me, look for the helpers. You will always find people who are helping."

These words exemplify a simple but profound way of looking at the world: We're either helping or we're not helping. The vast majority of people want to help, of course, and many wonderful helpers stepped up after the bombing.

Our public servants, especially Boston area police, many of whom had worked straight through the night before, reacted immediately to protect people, not knowing if more bombs would explode and any moment. (Several days later, one officer lost his life and another was seriously wounded in pursuit of the suspects.) Many everyday citizens rushed to offer any help they could immediately after the explosions. With their ears still ringing from the blast, dozens of runners, race observers, and bystanders ran to the wounded, often reacting before they considered their own safety. Ambulances filled with emergency workers flooded the scene before the smoke had even cleared.

To the brave officers and citizens and medical personnel at the Boylston Street finish line and beyond, thank you for your help.

Governor Deval Patrick brought a calm voice and level head as he shared whatever scant information was available. The local, state, and national officials investigating the crime also kept us as informed as they could when we hungered for any news about the terrible events. President Barack Obama addressed the nation several times in the subsequent days and brought a combination of reassurance, resolve, and compassion to help us deal with an event that seemed devoid of reason.

To the president, the governor, all the officials who faced the burden of publically making sense of this terrible crime, thank you for your help.

Helpers also emerged in some unexpected ways.

Red Sox star David Ortiz took to the Fenway Park microphone and dropped the F-bomb in rallying the crowd. While public profanity is usually nothing to celebrate, the slugger captured the much-hyped resilience of the Boston spirit and personified the rich strength of the city's immigrant diversity. Julius Genachowski, chair of the sometimes touchy Federal

Communications Commission, responded to Ortiz's salty language with a surprising tweet: "David Ortiz spoke from the heart at today's Red Sox game. I stand with Big Papi and the people of Boston."

To Big Papi and Big 'Chowski, thank you for your help.

We heard the term "shelter in place" many times during the daylong search for the second suspect, but I'm happy that someone invented such a nurturing term to take the place of "stay the hell inside." After the capture, someone uploaded a photo of the boat where the suspect hid, adding the caption, "worst getaway vehicle ever."

To the people who coined the unexpected term and produced the unexpected laugh during a sad and frightening time, thank you for your help.

Unfortunately, a loud minority of nonhelpers got involved as well. Some media outlets pumped out unsubstantiated reports of a Saudi suspect who was actually a victim of the bombings. The rest of the corporate media repeated those false claims, and then compounded their errors by later announcing a premature arrest with salacious claims of a "dark-skinned" suspect.

Some bigoted pundits reacted to the bombings by condemning all Muslims as terrorists, one even calling for all Muslims to be killed. Other crazies took to their self-published online shows to declare that the bombing was staged as a "false flag" by a corrupt government bent on power and control. One famously insane pundit actually went back to the clearly debunked Saudi suspect story and demanded President Obama's impeachment for hiding the truth.

Some members of Congress politicized the bombing, linking it to their opposition to immigration, calling for increased profiling of Muslims, even recommending torture for the captured suspect, as if America hasn't learned the previous decade's painful lesson that torture is immoral and ineffective.

To the rush-to-misjudgment media, to the reality-impaired pundits, to the confused members of Congress, thanks for nothing. You definitely didn't help.

Overall, the good news is that we saw far more helpers than nonhelpers after the bombing, people who spanned a range from everyday citizens all the way to the highest levels of government. Thanks again. Mr. Rogers would be happy to have you in our neighborhood.

Marriage Equality's Constitutional Trump Card

April 2013

Last month, the Supreme Court heard arguments about marriage equality, and Facebook lit up with countless supportive posts from a wide range of my friends: long-time liberals, curmudgeonly contrarians, independents, and a pleasant variety of good-hearted and open-minded people.

Of course, social media is never a place for universal agreement. None of my friends posted any "Adam and Eve, not Adam and Steve" nonsense, mostly because anti-gay ideology is now being called out for what it is: bigotry. But I was surprised by one specific response. My sister Pam posted a graphic reading, "This person supports love" with an arrow pointing to her profile picture. Go Pam! "No one could be against love," I thought.

I was wrong. One of Pam's conservative friends commented that Pam's post was "insulting," and he launched an extended attack on marriage equality from a religious perspective. Here's a summary of his view: God is against homosexuality, so it's morally wrong because it says so in the Bible and because God is life, and homosexuals can't have kids, so they will lead to the death of the human race, but it's rude for people to call me a bigot because of my beliefs.

The idea that anyone knows God's viewpoint has proven pretty arbitrary over the years. Long ago, some people cited the Bible to advocate for slavery. In recent history, people argued for outlawing interracial marriage based on religious grounds. Those embarrassing aspects of American history are eerily similar to the current religious argument against marriage equality.

Generally, the folks who claim that they know what God wants are hijacking God as an involuntary character reference while voicing what they want—slavery and racial segregation, for example. But even if they seriously have God's best intentions in mind, Christianity has so much more to offer than narrow-minded condemnation of homosexuality. My friend Wayne notes that the King James Bible has 788,280 words, but only 338 of them touch on homosexuality. That's a whopping 0.042%. And the founder of Christianity, Jesus himself, referenced homosexuality exactly never. Commentator John Fugelsang adds that the Bible has about seven verses directly referencing homosexuality but more than 4,000 relating to helping the poor. Common sense tells us that an anti-gay focus isn't just questionable morality—it's questionable Christianity.

The current Christian right's obsession with homosexuality remains a mystery. If being gay is a "sin," it's certainly not the only sin identified in the Bible. I have some questions for Pam's Bible-condemns-homosexuality friend. Did he bring a ham to his Church's Easter potluck dinner? The Bible forbids eating ham. (Leviticus 11:7-8). What if the weather had turned warm and he brought a chilled shrimp platter instead? The Bible says eating shellfish is an abomination (Leviticus 11:10). What if he wore a tank top and showed off that tattoo he got as a rebellious teenager long ago? Another abomination (Leviticus 19:28). And if that tank top was made of a poly-blend fabric? Hellbound! (Leviticus 19:19). What if someone there spoke up about some religious issue and happened to be a woman? Bam—big sin! (1 Corinthians 14:34-35). And what if he had been called into work and couldn't attend the potluck? Working on the Sabbath—yet another sin! (Exodus 31:14-15).

I'm not ridiculing Christianity—just the pick-and-choose believers trying to pass themselves off as the only true Christians. Why doesn't anyone rant about the evils of shrimp and take polyester cases to the Supreme Court? The answer is that there's usually no emotional, visceral bigotry against food or synthetic fabric. Pam's conservative friend says he's not a bigot. But how can "homosexuals will lead to the death of the human race" be interpreted as anything other than bigotry? He conveniently ignores the fact that gay people are perfectly capable of bringing life into the world and being parents, either by birth or by adoption. As Justice Elana Kagan pointed out, we don't prevent anyone too old to reproduce from marrying, so preventing gay people from marrying is nothing more than bigoted discrimination.

Most important, whatever people think of the flimsy religious case against marriage equality is irrelevant. The United States is a nation of civil laws, not religious doctrine. If the law permits me to marry my wife Betsy, then it can't simultaneously prevent my friends Jim and Paul from marrying each other. We have laws related to marriage, and those laws can treat some people as second-class citizens. The Constitutional application is simple: the Fourteenth Amendment specifically says that all citizens have "equal protection of the laws," and the First Amendment tells us that religious beliefs don't trump legal equality for all American citizens, no matter their sexual identity. Why is that such a difficult concept?

Debunking Extremist Gun Arguments

March 2013

Reactions to mass shootings in the United States have followed a depressing pattern in recent years. People become outraged when a member of Congress is shot in the head, or when twenty-nine people are killed in a Colorado movie theater. But gun advocates always manage to silence the discussion. "It would disrespect the victims to politicize this tragedy," they say with mock sincerity, failing to note that not discussing gun-safety reforms politicizes the tragedy to their advantage.

Within weeks, outrage morphs into fascination with celebrity drug relapses or the next "storm of the century." Then gun-related tragedy strikes again, and the pattern recycles.

But the December Newtown school children shooting has been different. Outrage hasn't given way to short attention spans. A National Rifle Association spokesperson callously said gun-rights advocates should wait for the "Connecticut effect" to dissolve. But it hasn't—at least not yet. For now, our outrage has turned us around to the obvious fact that our laws aren't helping to prevent these tragedies. Numerous polls show that Americans are now strongly in favor of common-sense gun-safety reforms.

Unfortunately, a small minority of gun fetishists has a disproportionately loud voice in the current debate. These are well-paid lobbyists for the gun-manufacturing industry (Wayne LaPierre), media figures whose radicalism attracts far more attention than their talent (Ted Nugent, Alex Jones), or everyday folks who have become convinced by fear-mongering lobbyists and media extremists that imaginary roving bands of criminals are at their doorstep (the sad souls on Facebook posting "Obama can take my gun muzzle first!").

Many of these everyday folks mean well. They don't want to see government micromanaging private citizens, and they certainly don't want to see people killed in mass shootings. Unfortunately, they accept and repeat seriously wrong-headed views on gun-related issues.

Ignoring extremists should be our first choice, but, unfortunately, much of the media gun-safety discussion gets filtered through these radical views. Responsible people have to meet these distractions and distortions with clear, reality-based rebuttals.

So here goes—basic facts to answer extremist gun claims.

"Obama is coming for our guns. If Obama can't pass laws to take away our guns, then he's going to use executive actions, just like a dictator would."

During Obama's first term, he actually expanded gun rights. The actual executive orders he issued recently are mostly advisory or focused on enforcing already established law. That's pretty far from a dictatorial gun grab by any reasonable measure.

"Obama is just like Hitler. Hitler's first act was to take people's guns. If German Jews had access to guns, the Holocaust never would have happened."

Comparing Obama to Hitler is a favorite tactic of the extreme right wing, and it's just as inaccurate and silly when it comes to gun reform as it is in every other instance. Hitler actually deregulated gun laws overall while restricting gun ownership by Jews, just one of his many discriminatory actions against Jews. Even Jews who were armed, such as in the 1943 Warsaw Ghetto Uprising, fell victim to genocide.

"Obama started the strictest gun control in the country when he ran Chicago, and that city has the worst crime anywhere."

Obama was a state senator who represented one part of Chicago, but he was never involved in city government, let alone in charge. Blaming gun control laws for violence in an urban area such as Chicago ignores common sense and critical thinking. City gun control laws didn't prevent the flow of guns into Chicago from many surrounding areas with lax gun laws. The strictest of Chicago's gun laws, a handgun ban, was overturned by the Supreme Court in 2010, and gun violence has increased since then. Even so, Chicago ranks as only the 79th most violent place to live in the United States. Yet gun lovers continue to chant their Chicago mantra long after it has been proven to be a myth.

"We need guns for self-protection."

The Supreme Court ruled the 2008 Heller case for the first time in American history that the Second Amendment grants citizens the right to own guns for protection. Although that ruling has very little basis in the actual Second Amendment, it is now considered accepted law. No one has proposed banning guns for self-protection. But it's important to note that studies show having a gun at home greatly increases the odds of people living in that home becoming victims of gun violence.

Too many people act as if the world is about to come to a violent end, and they either need guns to prevent that end or to protect themselves when that inevitable end happens. Republican Senator Lindsey Graham recently ranted about "armed gangs roaming around neighborhoods" in the event of a natural disaster as a reason for owning an AR-15 rifle. Disaster paranoia has existed throughout human history, yet we've somehow always managed to go on despite the fearmongering. In the real world, the zombie apocalypse is just an entertaining fiction, not a preview of coming events.

"The Second Amendment says guns can't be regulated."

The Second Amendment actually includes the word "regulated," and the Supreme Court's Heller ruling establishes that the government has the right to regulate dangerous weapons. Ultra-conservative Justice Antonin Scalia himself wrote in that decision, "We also recognize another important limitation on the right to keep and carry arms. … prohibiting the carrying of "dangerous and unusual weapons.""

"The Second Amendment was established so that citizens could have guns to protect themselves from a tyrannical government."

No clear or informed reading of the Second Amendment in the context of the entire Constitution suggests an anti-tyranny or anti-government conclusion. This theory is mainly advanced by gun advocates as a way to vent their frustrations with not getting their way in elections or the legislative process. But bullets are not the same thing as votes, not in the United States, at least.

Former Chief Justice of the Supreme Court Warren Burger (a Republican-appointed conservative) accurately called this anti-tyranny viewpoint a "fraud." In addition, the government has nuclear weapons, so owning a few shotguns isn't going to offer much protection to any gun advocates who launch an insurrection against the American government.

"The term 'assault weapon' is just a scary name for a regular rifle used for hunting or protection that happens to be painted black and have some military features."

Legal analysis finds that Supreme Court rulings show that military-style rifles are, in Justice Scalia's words, "dangerous and unusual" weapons and are subject to stricter regulation than basic hunting or self-protection firearms. The emphasis on the name of the gun is irrelevant. Military-style automatic and semiautomatic "assault" weapons are absolutely not the same as basic rifles.

"The previous assault weapons ban clearly didn't work."

Responsible, nonpartisan fact-checkers have concluded that the previous assault weapons ban showed, at worst, mixed results. Although the law had far too many loopholes and wasn't in place long enough to have full impact, there's plenty of evidence that it helped hold down the number of mass shootings while not depriving responsible gun owners of weapons for hunting or self-protection. In basic numbers, research by The Century Foundation found that there were 1.5 mass shooting per year during the 1994-2004 assault weapons ban. Since then, there have been 3.5 per year.

"Killers will find a way to kill people even if we ban assault weapons or high-capacity magazines."

Bans on the kinds of weapons most commonly used in mass shooting (semi-automatics, assault weapons, and high-capacity magazines) won't stop all mass shootings. But bans on underage drinking don't stop all underage drinking. The point of such bans is the same as any other ban on dangerous items or activities: to make them more difficult, less devastating, and less frequent. If absolute prevention is the measure of any law, then all laws fail. But if the standard is reduction, then bans on assault weapons and high-capacity magazines can be successful.

"Hardly anyone is killed with assault weapons, so there's no reason to have special laws to ban them."

True, rifles account for only a small percentage of gun deaths, but rifles are far from the only kinds of guns used to kill people. And, as noted above, mass shootings frequently use "assault weapons." These are the worst crimes our society experiences, and the psychological damage they do to the victims' families and our nation as a whole far outweighs the actual number of deaths. Would any reasonable person advise us not to worry because "only" twenty children were killed in Newtown?

"Criminals have assault weapons like AR-15 rifles, so law-abiding citizens need similar weapons to protect themselves."

Weapons experts agree that handguns or shotguns, not assault rifles, are the best firearms for home protection.

"We just need to enforce current gun laws, not make new ones."

Current laws have many loopholes, largely thanks to NRA lobbying, that they are ineffective in many ways—stopping mass shootings, for example, where a majority of mass-murderers got their guns legally.

"Guns don't kill people; people kill people."

This is one of the most common gun-related myths. Why anyone would embrace such an obviously flawed statement is a mystery. On its face, it's absurd. A person without a gun pointing a finger and saying "bang" isn't going to kill anyone. Having a gun makes a big difference in that equation.

Gun advocates have told me that the "guns don't kill people" statement signifies the fact that guns are merely tools, and how people use these tools is what really matters. Okay, let's explore that line of thought. Substitute any other tool into the equation too see if the overall idea makes sense:

"Umbrellas don't block the rain. People block the rain."

"Bread Knives don't cut bread. People cut bread."

"Hammers don't pound nails. People pound nails."

Do any of these statements make any kind of sense? You could use your hands to block the rain, but that wouldn't keep you very dry. You could cut bread with your hands, but you'd make more crumbs than neat slices. You could pound nails with your hands, but you'd probably end up with a hospital visit and very little carpentry work done.

Just as umbrellas, bread knives, and hammers do their intended tasks far better than our bare hands, so too do guns fulfill their purposes better than bare hands. The reason groups of people have never been strangled in large numbers or killed efficiently is that guns are the tool of choice for the horrible task of mass murder.

In the United States, 30,000 people a year are killed with guns. More than 60% of all homicides in the United States are committed with guns. Umbrellas block the rain. Bread knives slice bread. Hammers pound nails. Guns kill people. This is not a difficult concept to understand—even for people who desperately want to blame gun deaths on everything except guns.

Guns make it more likely that conflicts will result in violence, and that more people will be killed as a result of those conflicts. States with more gun ownership and laxer gun laws have a higher gun death rate than areas with lower gun ownership and tougher gun laws. States with more gun safety regulations have fewer gun deaths. The overall evidence shows that more guns leads to more crime. In short, guns are dangerous weapons that help people kill people, which is why they need to be strictly regulated.

"Cars kill more people than guns, and we don't ban cars, so banning guns would be crazy."

No one is talking about banning guns—just regulating them because guns, like cars are undeniably dangerous. Cars are heavily regulated because they're dangerous, but when used as designed, cars deliver people to desired locations. Guns, when used as designed, deliver lethal force to a target. Anyone who doesn't know the difference between guns and cars has no business operating either one. (By the way, trends show that gun deaths are predicted to surpass auto deaths in the United States in the near future.)

"Criminals won't obey gun laws anyway."

This defeatist slogan is a very common comment whenever someone says that we need to have better gun-safety laws. But it clearly makes no sense. No law concerning any kind of criminal activity prevents all crime—yet we still have laws because we live in a civilization where laws identify our values. No one would say we shouldn't have strong laws against child molestation because molesters won't obey those laws anyway. Strong gun-safety laws can make it harder for criminals to get gun, which can save lives.

All criminals, by definition, don't obey laws. But that's no reason to abandon the rule of law. Laws can reduce crime, and a civilized society still has laws even when they don't prevent all crime. And it's interesting that many folks who say gun laws won't stop people from getting guns also insist we need tougher abortion laws to stop people from getting abortions.

"Background checks are just a slippery-slope that leads to gun registration, which is a slippery-slope to gun confiscation."

The "slippery-slope" argument is an example of a classic logical fallacy that relies on sloppy thinking rather than facts and common sense. When gun advocates actually use the term "slippery slope," they're showing deep ignorance of the issues as well as poor critical thinking skills. Just because some unlikely event could possibly happen, that doesn't mean that we should expect it to happen. The United States has universal car registration, for example, and that hasn't led to auto confiscations.

"Violent video games and movies are the real problem, not guns."

Many countries play violent video games and watch violent movies and still manage to have far less gun violence that the United States because those countries have stricter gun laws than we do.

"Mental health is the real problem, not guns."

Access to mental health care is an important issue in the United States. But the same politicians who oppose common-sense gun regulations have also opposed funding for increased access to mental health care. For example, Republicans in Congress have voted more scores of times to repeal Obamacare, which includes many provisions for improving mental health access. And Ronald Reagan, the guiding light of the contemporary Republican Party, set in place the budget policies and social priorities that led to the current lack of comprehensive mental health care.

In addition, the rate of mental illness in the U.S. is roughly the same as the rest of the world, but we have far more gun deaths than the rest of the world.

"The only thing that stops a bad guy with a gun is a good guy with a gun."

Reasonable people would agree with this statement if it had been made with trained police officers or soldiers in mind. Unfortunately, NRA lobbyist Wayne LaPierre was thinking of armed citizens who would use their weapons to stop mass shootings when he said this. But there hasn't been a single case of an armed citizen stopping a mass shooting in at least three decades. Gun advocates love to present what they call "examples" of good guys with guns stopping would-be mass murderers, but simple analysis of those examples show they aren't true. On the other hand, an unarmed, 61-year-old woman stopped the 2011 Tucson Gabby Giffords shooting, while an armed person in the crowd almost shot a bystander whom he mistook for the shooter.

"The Newtown shooting was staged by the government to drum up support for gun control. A video on the internet proves it."

This desperate and shameful claim echoes a similar one that surfaced after the shootings in Aurora, Colorado. To use a technical term, these conspiracy theories are full of crap. The video in question is filled with inaccuracies, innuendo, and easily debunked misinformation. Even conspiracy-theorist Glenn Beck's *The Blaze* website debunks the Newtown-staged theory. When crap-master Beck thinks you're full of crap, that's a pretty damning indictment.

Anyone wondering where the term "gun nut" comes from doesn't need to look further than claims about the government staging shootings. They should try making this claim to the parents who lost children in the Newtown shooting or to those who lost loved ones in Aurora. More than anything else, this terrible claim shows that some gun advocates need to get over their irrational fear, grow out of this insecure and paranoid phase, and join the real world.

Of course, gun fetishists will dispute these points and dig up questionable sources friendly to their cause as "evidence." But common sense and the vast majority of reliable data contradict their extremist talking points and supports gun-safety reform. Extremists will never see reason as they try to block progress and wait out the "Connecticut effect." But, as responsible citizens, we need to debunk the extremists and focus on reality-based discussions to make our country safer.

Downton Liberals

February 2013

Many of us here in Northampton, Massachusetts, proudly embrace the liberal nature of our town. A Mitt Romney bumper sticker is about as popular around here as a flu epidemic. I'm happy to call Northampton by the same name as my favorite political podcast, "The Liberal Oasis," which originates right here in our town.

My liberal friends and I were glued to coverage of President Obama's second inauguration with the same dedication that we usually reserve for the PBS hit *Downton Abbey*. So I got a big laugh when I heard Fox News pundit Stuart Varney say that my liberal friends and I should be worried about *Downton Abbey*.

"The politics of *Downton* are very important, and it's important that they are popular in America today," Varney said to the charmless hosts of *Fox and Friends*. "Rich people, powerful people, in America today, are reviled. They're dismissed as fat cats ... Yet, along comes this show *Downton Abbey*—rich people prominently featured, and they're generous; they're nice people; they create jobs, for heaven's sake; they're classy; they've got style and we love 'em ... That show is wildly popular, which poses a threat to the left, doesn't it?"

Varney, as usual, seems as far from common sense as the distance between Northampton and Varney's native England. First of all, the show doesn't focus exclusively on the wealthy Grantham family of the titular mansion. On the contrary—the working class is equally represented in the persons of the household staff: butlers, footmen, cooks, maids, chauffeurs, etc. For every moment of drama, heartache, resentment, courage, and devotion "upstairs," the "downstairs" residents experience the same breadth of human experience and emotion. That's a notion squarely in the liberal camp: that we are all equal human beings despite our level of birth, breeding, or wealth.

Varney praises the Granthams as "generous job creators" while lamenting that liberals "revile" the rich in America today. The distinction that seems to evade Varney's grasp is that the Granthams understand that the primary purpose of their wealth is to create jobs for members of their community. Yes, they have fancy meals and parties because they enjoy them—but they also do so to create jobs for cooks, servers, cleaners, farmers, and a host of others around them. In contrast, the wealthy in America today, our corporate elite, have regained all of the profits they lost in the crash of 2008, but they have been hoarding their wealth and cutting jobs, pay, and benefits rather than hiring at a rate commensurate with their income.

When Lord Grantham experiences post-war financial problems that put the estate at risk, he's just as worried about all the people in his employ losing their livelihood as he is about the possibility of his family moving to a smaller home. Here in present day America, most of those few unelected individuals sitting on vast corporate wealth have shown no such concern. The "job creators" that Varney and his colleagues at Fox News love so much don't seem to understand the societal obligation of employing their fellow Americans. They don't even understand that true "job creators" are actually hard-working middle-class citizens whose paycheck purchasing power provides the demand that leads to new jobs. The Granthams understand the liberal proposition that we are all in this life together, so wealth exists mainly to benefit as many fellow human beings as possible, not just an elite few.

Varney is right about one thing: we certainly "love" the Grantham family. But they are not presented as flawless royalty. One daughter has a sexual scandal in her recent past, and even stuffy Lord Grantham himself is tempted to near-adultery by a vulnerable new maid. We liberal viewers don't love the Granthams because they're wealthy, as Varney implies. We love them because they're human, just as we love the equally flawed house staff with their own history of imperfections. Loving all people equally for their whole selves, warts and all, is a decidedly liberal perspective.

My liberal friends and I will continue to tune into *Downton Abbey*, not because the show sends some "love the rich" message, as Varney would have us believe. No, we'll return for the excellent acting, well-rounded characters, historical context, beautiful sets and scenery, and dramatic (if occasionally melodramatic) plot developments.

And we'll keep watching in part because liberals don't revile rich people. We revile the greedy and admire those who understand a French phrase that can be well applied to this British television show: *"Noblesse oblige,"* the sense that vast wealth implies an equally vast sense of community responsibility. But there is a television phenomenon that we'll definitely tune out: Fox News pundit Stuart Varney and his whole propaganda network.

Update: I was pleased that my first regular column for the *Daily Hampshire Gazette*, "Downton Liberals" spurred the *Gazette's* resident conservative columnist Jay Fleitman to respond a few weeks later with, "Downton Abbey Conservatives," perhaps his best-written column in years. It's a strange testament to "Downton Abbey" that people at disparate points on the political spectrum can claim loyalty to the show's message. Unfortunately, like the wrong-headed Fox News punditry that inspired my column, Fleitiman's response has as many obvious distortions as the Downton mansion has rooms—and more than a few insults for me. Welcome to the columnist's club, I guess.

The inaccurate talking points that Fleitman tries to pass off as truisms litter his column like husks at harvest time: liberals don't understand business or hard work, liberals hate capitalism, Obamacare is a burden, Obama is divisive, the Federal Reserve is a conspiracy, Medicare and Social Security are near bankruptcy. All of these claims are untrue and misleading— not to mention mostly irrelevant to the subject of "Downton Abbey." Thankfully, the public roundly rejected these right-wing views in the 2012 election, favoring the common sense of Democrats in the House, Senate, and Presidency by millions of votes.

Liberals aren't anti-work, as Fleitman has implied in this and some previous columns. Hard work is a fundamental American value shared by liberals and conservatives alike. Liberals also aren't anti-capitalism, anti-business, or anti-wealth—as my column makes quite clear. But we are against the corporate greed that has contributed to current income inequality greater even than the upstairs/downstairs differences of Downton Abbey. The economic crash of 2008 didn't happen because the wealthy were working hard to advance the good of humanity in the style of the Grantham family. The crash happened because too many corporate executives, bankers, and stock traders indulged in un-Grantham-like greed and disregard for community responsibility.

Fleitman's claim that businesses aren't investing in the U.S. because they're over-regulated is simply untrue on two factual fronts. First, Obama hasn't increased regulations, despite right-wing media repetition of that erroneous talking point. Second, surveys of business leaders themselves show that their greatest concern is the lack of consumer demand in our economy, not regulation. Any company that bases its decisions solely on misinterpretations of the regulatory environment would be out of business quicker than a Dowager Countess wisecrack.

On one point, Fleitman is correct: government mismanagement has led to the federal debt. But Fleitman seems to believe that American history began the day that Barack Obama took office. He fails to note that much of our national debt has been brought on by Republican mismanagement: unfunded wars, corporate welfare, bloated defense industry spending, and tax cuts favoring the wealthy. Lord Grantham's mismanagement is analogous to the previous presidential administration and current Republican members of Congress, not to the Obama administration. Young Matthew compares far more closely to President Obama as the voice of reform breaking with the previous practices that caused the problems in the first place. Matthew grew up working class (like Obama) and actually came into his wealth somewhat reluctantly. And he certainly didn't propose laying off the household staff or outsourcing their jobs overseas.

Finally, Fleitman's conclusion distorts my column into saying that liberals believe the wealthy and conservatives are inhuman, heartless monsters—which I did not say. A fair reading of my column shows that I noted that the Granthams are "human" as opposed to "flawless," not that I called the wealthy or conservatives something less than human. That inference is so out of context, surprising, inflammatory, and reductive that it should have no place in civil discourse. Such a context-free interpretation of my column, however, would be right at home on Fox News where pundits are paid millions for their propaganda. Sometimes, strangely, that propaganda gets repeated for free by folks like Fleitman. That's a shame.

The Parable of Right-Wing Milk and Cookies

January 2013

Note: A brief parable buzzed around the Internet in 2011, at the height of the Wisconsin protests against the Republican attacks on unions. I loved the common sense of this parable and immediately posted it to my own Facebook page. But it took some detective work to figure out where the parable originated. The author seems to be Jennifer Brunner, the former Ohio Secretary of State. I decided it would be fun to extend the very brief Facebook post into an allegory because it still applies today, nearly two years later. Here's the original parable, followed by my allegory:

> *A dozen cookies are put down in front of a C.E.O., a union member, and a Tea Partier. The C.E.O. takes 11. Then he says to the Tea Partier, "That union guy wants yours."*

Three people sit at a kitchen table: a corporate CEO, a Tea Partier, and a unionized teacher. There are twelve large cookies and two small ones on the table, along with a gallon of milk and three glasses. The CEO looks confident and powerful. The Tea Partier looks a bit dazed. The unionized teacher is hard at work grading student papers. A Republican politician stands beside the CEO.

The CEO points to the Republican politician and says, "See this person? I've hired him to divide up our treats." The Tea Partier nods and rubs his eyes in relief. The unionized teacher moves on to the next student paper. The Republican politician says, "Yes, sir," to the CEO.

The Republican politician places a very large goblet in front of the CEO and fills it to the top with fresh, whole milk. He places two small juice glasses in front of the Tea Partier and the unionized teacher and splashes about an inch of milk in each. The Republican politician then heaps the twelve large cookies onto the CEO's gold-plated china and drops one crumbling little cookie onto a napkin in front of the Tea Partier and another in front of the unionized teacher.

As the CEO happily dips a big cookie into his milk goblet and munches away, the Tea Partier stares at him longingly and asks, "What about me? Why am I stuck with this one little crappy cookie and hardly any milk?"

The CEO laughs and says, "Don't look at me! I earned my cookies!" And then he leans toward the Tea Partier and whispers, "See that unionized teacher sitting there? I think her cookie is bigger than yours, much bigger, and she doesn't deserve her cookie nearly as much as you do."

The Tea Partier looks at the unionized teacher's meager cookie and splash of milk. In reality, her cookie isn't any bigger than his own, but it suddenly looks so much bigger. After all, why would the CEO lie to the Tea Partier?

"Your cookie is bigger than mine," the Tea Partier says to the unionized teacher.

The unionized teacher looks up from a stack of student papers she has been grading and glances from her cookie to the Tea Partier's cookie. "They look the same size to me," she says before going back to her work.

The Tea Partier flushes with anger and shame because he remembers doing very poorly in school and blaming the teacher rather than studying harder.

Just then the Republican politician switches on a television. An angry, red-faced man on Fox News is shouting: "Unions have the biggest cookies of all despite the well-known fact that union members don't do any actual work!" The angry man turns to an attractive blond woman who agrees and says in a seductive voice, "And these lazy liberal union members want to take cookies away from all the real hard-working, red-blooded Americans out there."

The Tea Partier looks at the CEO, who says "It's true," milk dripping from the corner of his mouth. "By the way, that socialist Obama wants to tax your cookie but not hers."

The Tea Partier looks at the Republican politician, who nods seriously and then sneaks a wink at the CEO. The Tea Partier glares at the unionized teacher and bangs his fist on the table. "I want a bigger cookie than hers!" he shouts.

The unionized teacher closes one folder and opens another. "I have papers to grade, classes to prepare, and studying to do so that I can maintain my certification," she says. "I teach summer school and moonlight at the local community college so I can pay back my student loans. All I want to do right now is take a few nibbles from my cookie and sip a little milk while I get my work done."

The tea partier sneers at the unionized teacher and says, "Intellectual elite! You think you better than me, don't you?"

The unionized teacher ignores him as she makes a list of schools supplies she'll have to buy herself because of another round of budget cuts.

"Can I do anything else for you?" the Republican politician asks the CEO.

"Yes!" the CEO replies in a confident voice. "More cookies! I'll start with that greedy unionized teacher's cookie."

The Republican politician breaks off half of the unionized teacher's cookie and places it on the CEO's plate. The tea partier nods approval and says, "You've got my vote!" The unionized teacher sighs. On the television, Fox News shows film of her sipping her milk. The angry male commentator says, "It looks like those union thugs are about to riot!" The attractive female commentator says, "They should all be forced to get real jobs!"

The CEO thinks for a moment and then says to the Republican politician, "You know, I've decided that one of my corporations should start making these cookies."

The Republican politician says, "Well, sir, you are a job creator."

The CEO continues, "I want you to see to it that the evil government won't interfere with me closing down the local cookie producers or creating cheap labor cookie jobs overseas or hiring illegal immigrants to make cookies for me. None of that minimum wage nonsense, either! And if I hear one word about cookie-safety regulations or cookie taxes, I'll be very angry with you!"

"Yes, sir!" the Republican politician replies. "Umm, also sir—about my campaign contributions?"

"Oh, yes, yes, of course," the CEO says, reaching into his pocked for his checkbook. "We'll launder this through the usual anonymous channels, just like the Supreme Court said we could."

"The constitution guarantees your money freedom of expression, sir," the Republican politician says as he slips the CEO's check into his pocket.

The tea partier glances longingly at the unionized teacher's remaining cookie crumbs while she works on her lesson plans.

"One more thing," the CEO says, lowering his voice to a whisper, "If this idiot teabagger asks for more cookies, make up some ridiculous story about how Obama stole all his cookies and gave them to those terrible gays, blacks, Muslims, and Mexicans. This dumbass will believe anything!"

"Yes, sir!" calls out the Republican politician, snapping to attention. "I'll get right on that!"

Underpants Voters

December 2012

Leading up to the 2012 election, popular pastor Rick Warren said that American Christians should vote "for a Christian worldview which stands up for the sanctity of life, the sanctity of sex, and the sanctity of marriage." No offense to Pastor Warren, but common sense should tell us that reducing Christianity and American civic engagement to the things that happen in our underpants is terrible Christianity and even worse citizenship. Warren's reductive marching orders to American Christians hit three hot social issues from this year's presidential campaign: abortion, birth control, and marriage equality. I've been told that I'm belittling Christianity with the term "underpants voters," but isn't presenting these sex-based issues as if they are the only issues that should be important about Christianity in America simply an insult that belittles American Christians?

Conservatives too often equate "the sanctity of life" with making sure that government imposes a narrow set of dogma on a woman's pregnancy, regardless of her own thoughts, feelings, or needs. People in America (including Christians) honestly disagree about the exact point at which the mass of living cells inside a pregnant woman becomes a human being. But there is no disagreement that an actual child is a human being. Shouldn't the "sanctity of life" continue once a baby is born? Welfare, social-service programs, and public education are designed primarily to benefit children, to keep them fed, clothed, protected, healthy, and smart. But Republicans rail against these programs. Where is the "sanctity of life" in claiming to protect fetuses while ignoring the needs of children?

The debate about access to birth control burst into the American political scene in ... well, sometime in the 19th Century. The issue was pretty much settled among most Americans about four decades ago. But the Republican Party, spurred on by the Christian right, brought the issue back this year. Why? Apparently because they consider birth control, in the words of far-right presidential candidate Rick Santorum, "a license to do things in the sexual realm that is counter to how things are supposed to be. They're supposed to be within marriage." Santorum doesn't seem to understand that contraception is often used to treat medical conditions, and that most married women use birth control at one time or another, including most Christian women. Is sex really only "sanctified" when it results in a child? Do conservative Christians know that birth control is the main tool we have to prevent unwanted pregnancies and, consequently, abortions? Where is the "sanctity" in making laws that invade our bedrooms and increase the number of abortions?

On the subject of marriage equality, American public opinion has reversed in recent years. More people now endorse marriage equity than oppose it, and an increasing number of states have overturned legal restrictions on who we love, our most personal of human freedoms. President Obama himself has come out in favor of marriage equality, much to the scorn of conservative Christians. They love to quote the Old Testament verses calling male-to-male homosexuality an abomination. At the same time, they conveniently ignore similar verses that condemn eating shellfish and pork, wearing poly-blend fabric, and planting different crops in the same field. Even worse, many also tend to ignore the countless biblical references to loving one another. Where is the "sanctity" in ignoring many Bible verses while obsessing about a few that support a desire to discriminate against people who love each other and want to express their love publically and legally?

The Constitution of the United States doesn't mention God and only brings up religion to prevent the government from establishing theology into law. Of course, Jesus himself never said a word about abortion, birth control, or marriage equality. His teachings went far beyond what happens inside our underpants and focused on our minds, hearts, and souls. Maybe all Americans, Christian or not, should follow that example when we step into the voting booth.

Breathe In, Breathe Out ... In ... Out ... *Good*

November 2012

To all the people ranting that Obama voters are crazy idiots who have ruined the country by reelecting the president ... Please take a long, slow, deep breath. The country hasn't been ruined.

I awoke each morning through 20 years of Reagan/Bush I/Bush II worried that they would destroy our nation. The election nights of 1980, '84, '88, '00, and '04 were long, dark, and cold. In particular, the reelection of George W. Bush was a punch in the gut. Remember that? ... a sitting president re-elected when he won Ohio ... hmmm, that sounds familiar. But if President Obama's approval rating reaches the upper 20% range at the end of his second term, as Bush's did, I'll shave my gray hair from my middle-aged head and eat it for breakfast with a little milk and sugar.

I eventually discovered that America is much stronger than presidents I don't agree with. Reagan, Bush I, and Bush II tried to walk us backward, but the country moved forward anyway. We lurched and staggered through those years when I hoped for a steady jog—but it was still forward motion, however unsteady. Those presidents certainly slowed American progress, but they couldn't stop our nation from growing and improving.

Those presidents also taught me that America is much bigger than any president, and American history is a far wider span than any four-year term. The best minds and hands and voices of the American people always keep this country on the forward path. Not everyone will embrace progress as it opens its arms to us, but progress will draw us into its bear hug anyway. And I recognize that people who disagree with me still love America, and I expect the same common sense consideration in return.

Obama's reelection must be a shock to anyone whose echo-chamber of Obama-bashing news sources has been assuring you for four years that everyone hates the America-apologizing-Kenyan-usurper-anointed-one who grovels to foreign leaders and steals your paycheck. The fact that a majority of Americans don't share your views must be a terrible burden, but it's a fact as clear as the perpetual scowl on Sean Hannity's sweaty mug. Your shock, however, is no excuse for disparaging that majority of Americans who swept Obama back to the White House for four more years.

As an Obama voter, I'm being accused of some wildly ridiculous things right now. But I didn't vote for Obama because I'm crazy or an idiot or a socialist or a communist or any other silly label. I don't want a bunch of stuff from the government, not even an Obamaphone, whatever the hell made-up thing that is. I'm not rubbing my hands together with maniacal glee as I envision America in flames. I'm not trying to wrestle away your freedom or pry your guns from your cold dead fingers. I don't hate America. I haven't spit on the flag. I haven't thrown Israel under the Iranian nuclear bus. I don't want America to become a third-world country. I'm not shoving us down the greasy path to becoming Greece. I'm not trying to crush anyone's children or grandchildren under mountains of debt. I don't support the Muslim Brotherhood or the New Black Panthers or any other phantom menaces. I don't sympathize with terrorists or demean our troops. I don't shake my fist at God. I'm not causing hurricanes by sending a wedding gift to Robert and Brian. I don't want to kill babies or destroy marriages and families. I don't want to steal your money and give it to lazy drug addicts who are too stoned to work for themselves. I don't want to take anyone's job and give it to an illegal alien from Mexico or from Mars. I don't want to force food stamps into anybody's wallet or health care reform down anyone's throat.

Here's a news flash: President Obama doesn't want any of those things either. That's the truth, no matter what you may have heard from Fox Fake News or Rush or Beck or your crazy uncle who runs his own end-times website from his mother's basement.

I don't accept the lies that are being hurled at President Obama and, by extension, about me as an Obama voter. Reasonable Republicans also accept that Obama doesn't hold any radical, anti-American ideas either. Reasonable Republicans (those few lonely ones who haven't been chased off by the fringe elements in their party) recognize that Obama is working to improve America, even if they don't agree with him on all policies and positions. When you strip away the right-wing propaganda, here's what Obama actually stands for—and the actual reasons I voted for him:

- We believe that government shares a role with the private sector in creating good jobs for middle-class Americans.

- We believe that government has a major role in helping our most vulnerable citizens, especially in bad economic times.

- We believe that health insurance should be affordable and available to all Americans.

- We believe that Social Security, Medicare, and Medicaid are great programs that should be kept and strengthened.

- We believe that Wall Street should be strongly regulated to prevent another economic collapse.

- We believe that long-term deficit reduction can't be accomplished by simply cutting government programs that help poor and middle-class Americans.

- We believe that corporations do not have the same rights as people, and the wealthy should pay their fair share in taxes.

- We believe that money does not equal speech, and the influence of secret money from wealthy sources should not control our elections or our government.

- We believe that every citizen should have the right to vote without restrictive laws designed to suppress turnout and manipulate the results of elections.

- We believe that education is the key to keeping America great, and our taxes have no higher purpose than supporting qualified students.

- We believe that America is a member of the world community with every right to defend ourselves but no right to force our views on the rest of the world.

- We believe that sensible immigration reform is far better than xenophobia for both immigrants and native-born citizens.

- We believe that America is a diverse nation of different faiths, ethnicities, races, genders, and identities where we all deserve respect from one another.

- We believe that government should not control personal choices about your body or who you love.

These are core American values that make our nation great—not symptoms of idiocy or insanity. American history was at its worst only when we have veered from these values. I hold these values sacred because they help define who I am as an American and as a human being. I share them with the president, and I'll resist anyone who attacks these values—but I'm happy to work side-by-side with anyone who shares these core American values to keep our country moving forward. These values are the basis of *good* government, not big government—a *responsive* state, not a nanny state. These values represent government as *we the people*.

My advice to all the people who think America is somehow going to hell because Obama got re-elected is this: Calm down, unbunch your undies, be still and quiet for a few moments, and search for your faith in America and in humanity. Even if Obama were the goblin that you've been told he is, he couldn't ruin our nation. The American people are far stronger than that, and our founding system of laws and government is far smarter than that. Don't move to Canada (there are lots of liberals there too) or secede from the union or go to Colorado and stay high for the next four years.

My advice is simple: The next time you hear a talking head in the media rant about Obama as some threat to your way of life, press the "power off" button on the remote control. When you click on the next link, delete any website that throws knee-jerk comments about our "socialist" or "communist" president. When you're at work or the local bar, walk away from any person who calls our president an enemy of America or any Obama voter an insane idiot. Learn to "just say no" to mindless Obama-bashing. Your feelings of disappointment are real, but your sources of information spurring those feelings are deeply flawed. Learn the difference between facts and opinions, history and revisionism, concern and hysteria, news and propaganda.

You'll survive ... and maybe even thrive. America will too.

Romney Fails Commander-in-Chief Test Yet Again in the Presidential Debate

October 2012

Moderator Candy Crowley fact-checked just one of Mitt Romney's many distortions during last night's debate when she correctly affirmed that President had indeed called the recent Libyan consulate attack an "act of terror" during a Rose Garden speech the next day. When Romney questioned Obama's honesty, saying he wanted to get the president's comment "for the record," Obama, fed up with years of Romney's lies, responded, "Get the transcript." Crowley somewhat reluctantly set Romney straight, saying, "He did call it an act of terror."

Some Romney supporters are attacking Crowley today for unfairly showing a "liberal bias." Some even say that she helped Obama win the debate. Nothing could be farther from the truth. Obama won the debate by passionately defending his many accomplishments and not letting Romney get away with his multiple lies. Crowley was fair and truthful, and Romney lost the debate all on his own, thanks in no small part to his dishonest failure on the Libya issue.

The reality is that Romney's lie about the president's reaction to the Libya attack was so blatant, with Romney himself calling so much attention to it at that moment, that Crowley had no choice but to state a clear fact. Romney was in the middle of losing the debate, and he obviously thought he had caught the president in a "gotcha" moment that would make a sparkling sound-bite to distract from his overall debate loss. But Romney simply revealed more of his dishonesty, arrogance, and ignorance. Crowley may have actually done him the favor of not letting him dig his hole any deeper.

For more than a month, Romney has twisted the facts on the Libya tragedy in a quest for cheap political points. Instead of trying to unite the country in a crisis, Romney has done everything in his power to use the Libya attack to divide the nation. On the day of the attack, before even the basic details of the events were known, Romney falsely claimed that Obama's first response was to "sympathize with those who waged the attacks." Both the rapid nature and inaccurate content of Romney's attacks were unprecedented for a presidential candidate, and he was widely criticized by members of both parties for his rash and ignorant response.

Romney hasn't waited judiciously as the facts about these complex events continue to gradually unfold as anyone with basic common sense would. Instead, he charged in blindly and took every opportunity to criticize the president without having full knowledge of what really happened. Such rashness is not a good quality for someone who aspires to be the leader of the free world. And Romney has offered very little constructive criticism, choosing instead to simply attack.

Worst of all, Romney so shamelessly used these American deaths that the father of slain Ambassador Christopher Stevens called politicizing the events "abhorrent." The mother of former Navy SEAL Glen Doherty, killed in the Libya attack, was more specific in her criticism of how Romney was using her family tragedy for his own gain: "I don't trust Romney. He shouldn't make my son's death part of his political agenda. It's wrong to use these brave young men, who wanted freedom for all, to degrade Obama."

Romney is fond of invoking former president Ronald Reagan, but Romney's response to the Libya attacks has been far different from Reagan's response to the 1980 Iran hostage crisis during Jimmy Carter's presidency. In contrast to Romney's injudicious attacks on Obama, Reagan called for national unity when he was a candidate for president running to unseat Carter. Reagan criticized Carter's foreign policy in general during the campaign, but he didn't attack Carter on the hostage crisis—*even when the issue came up during their presidential debate.* Romney had a similar opportunity to call for national unity during a time of crisis, but he chose to attack and divide America instead.

The third presidential debate next week will focus on foreign affairs, but Romney has already exposed himself as unqualified to lead our country in the world. Romney seems to think that organizing the Olympics and outsourcing American jobs to China makes him qualified on foreign policy issues. Even before his Libya missteps, Romney's embarrassing European tour showed that he is a terrible representative of our nation as he displayed profound ignorance of world affairs and the arrogance to offend even our closest allies.

Romney's incompetence and divergence from mainstream American views on foreign policy has been on display throughout the presidential campaign. He was against President Obama's decision to end the war in Iraq, and he has postured for going to war in Iran. He has largely ignored the war in Afghanistan (including not even mentioning it in his acceptance speech at the Republican convention). When he does actually mention it, he gives contradictory statements about how he would handle that war, an inconsistency amplified by his running mate Paul Ryan's naïve and confusing answers to questions about Afghanistan in the vice presidential debate last week.

Today many Romney supporters are blaming Candy Crowley for Romney's colossal "gotcha" debate failure. The party that loves to talk about "personal responsibility" is trying to shift responsibility from Romney to Crowley, and they look just as pathetic as Romney did at that moment in the debate.

Last night Romney punctuated what has been campaign with ample evidence that he would be even worse than George W. Bush in foreign affairs. Romney has been an abject failure each time he has weighed in on situations he might face as Commander in Chief. No amount of Republican spin can cover that fact.

President Obama perfectly summed up Romney's response to the Libyan attacks last night with just one word: "offensive." He's absolutely right, and Mitt Romney is absolutely wrong for the presidency.

Are We Better Off?

September 2012

I have a Republican colleague who keeps asking anyone he bumps into at work, "Hey, are you better off than you were four years ago?" Before they can answer, he jumps in for himself: "I'm not. Obama's done nothing for me. My salary is down, I can barely fill my gas tank, and I still have to work for a living while half the country goofs off and lives off of my taxes!"

Republicans have resurrected this leftover Reagan campaign "are-you-better-off" mantra, trying to use it to lay the blame for any current national woes on President Obama. Even setting aside the selfish notion of measuring a president by what he does just for "you" rather than the country as a whole, the whole claim that my Republican friend is worse off because of president Obama is a boatload of crap.

First of all, my Republican friend and I work at the same place, so I know that he got a salary increase. So did I. I'm not sure why he feels compelled to lie about it, but dishonesty has become a basic strategy of Republican campaigning. Those people he claims are "living off his taxes" (the 47% of Americans who paid no federal income tax in 2009, the people Mitt Romney erroneously labeled as "irresponsible") are actually the elderly, the working poor, students, combat veterans, and the disabled—hardly a collection of "goof-offs."

In fact, my Republican friend and I both work at a state institution, so we actually get paid with other people's tax money. For me, working for the public is a blessing and motivation to do the best job I can in service to my fellow human beings. For my Republican friend, the reality that taxes fund his salary is just an inconvenient fact he never acknowledges. In addition, a big chunk of Obama's stimulus funds wound up in our state and kept the pressure off the state budget, which probably contributed to saving our jobs.

My friend likes to point out that gas prices have doubled since Obama took office, but he omits the crucial detail that the price per gallon dropped by half during the economic crash at the end of the Bush administration. Gas prices during Obama's term have averaged out about the same as they did before the crash, and they rise and fall based on factors outside the control of any president (except when it comes to starting wars in the Middle East or setting the stage for a major financial crisis, as Bush did), so blaming Obama is just more dishonesty.

But the key words in my friend's Obama-bashing question and response are "you," "I," and "me." Republicans seem to be more self-centered these days than ever. Sure, politics is personal, but why have Republicans made everything about isolated personal greed and blaming others? We live in the United States of America, not the Individualized Singularities of America. We are all in this together.

"Are *we* better off?" is a far more appropriate question for anyone hoping to bring common sense to current electoral politics. How is the nation as a whole doing? Things aren't perfect, of course, and many people are still suffering from the economic downturn brought on by the financial crisis. But President Obama was still just running for president in 2008 when the economy hit the skids. American history didn't begin when Obama took the oath of office in January 2009 as my Republican friend wants everyone to believe. When we sort through the right-wing propaganda nonsense of blaming Obama for everything and look at reality, we can clearly see that the country has turned the corner in the past few years.

The president's stimulus plan saved millions of jobs and gave tax relief to the middle class and small businesses. The nation didn't fall into another Great Depression thanks to Obama's economic policies. The American auto industry is alive. Reforms of Wall Street, credit cards, and college financial aid have helped middle-class pocketbooks and wallets. Health care reform will literally save thousands of lives and billions of dollars a year. The Supreme Court has two new members who aren't ideological extremists.

One misguided war that never should have started has ended, and the other is winding down. Even better, we didn't get into a third misguided war with Iran. Obama's leadership has regained much of the international respect that Bush squandered and Romney threatens to decimate. There hasn't been a repeat of the massive terrorist attack that began the Bush administration or the financial crisis that ended it. Bin Laden is no longer a threat to America, and Al Qaeda has been decimated.

The stock market has doubled and corporate profits have completely recovered. And the main reason conditions haven't gotten even better for the middle class is that corporations are hoarding rather than hiring, Republicans in Congress are obstructing the president's job-creating legislation at an unprecedented rate, and state-level Republicans have slashed public sector jobs as well.

All of these points are verifiable facts that are pretty easy to find using that evil liberal tool known as research. My Republican friend thinks "research" involves skimming conspiracy websites, listening to right-wing talk radio, and, of course, watching Fox News. If a Republican president did all the things that Obama has in his first term, Fox News would campaign to put him on Mt. Rushmore.

Besides, I thought Republicans were the party of "personal responsibility." No offense, but if my friend honestly believes he's worse off than he was four years ago, shouldn't he look in the mirror instead of whining about President Obama?

What's Wrong with Drug Tests for Welfare Recipients? Plenty.

August 2012

Thank you Florida, Kentucky, and Missouri, which are the first states that will require drug testing when applying for welfare. Some people are crying and calling this unconstitutional. How is this unconstitutional??? It's OK to drug test people who work for their money, but not for those who don't? ... Re-post this if you'd like to see this done in all 50 states. If you can afford to buy drugs and extra illegal things then you can afford your own groceries.

Once or twice a week, I see someone post a version of the message above on Facebook. These posts are usually images that have been conveniently created so that re-posters don't even have to retype the message or think about its meaning. And this pre-packaged bit of "common sense" is designed to push lots of the superficial outrage buttons.

Aren't we all at least a little "sick and tired" of something these days? But where should we project our frustration? Posts like the one above give people an easy scapegoat. Oh, yeah, it must be those people on welfare! They're the problem, the post asserts between the lines, especially because so many of them are on drugs! If only life were that simple.

Yes, it's common sense that people on welfare shouldn't abuse drugs. But neither should wealthy people—or the middle-class—or anyone. And, as with many things that seem to make sense at first glance, the reality is that mandatory drug tests for welfare recipients is anything but common sense.

In the United States, true common sense begins with the Constitution. Here's the Fourth Amendment to that Constitution:

"The right of the people to be secure in their persons, houses, papers, and effects, against unreasonable searches and seizures, shall not be violated, and no Warrants shall issue, but upon probable cause, supported by Oath or affirmation, and particularly describing the place to be searched, and the persons or things to be seized."

Oh, that pesky Constitution. Being a nation founded on the rule of law can be so annoying when someone has a great idea that just happens to be a clear violation of our most basic legal document.

People who claim to revere our Constitution usually tell me that the Fourth Amendment has nothing to do with drug tests for welfare recipients, that I'm somehow comparing apples to oranges. But the application of the Fourth Amendment is really pretty simple:

1. The government can't search citizens or seize anything from them without

probable cause that they have committed a crime.

2. Drug tests involve a form of search and seizure of bodily fluids.

3. Receiving government benefits doesn't show probable cause that someone is on drugs.

4. Therefore, the government can't drug test people simply because they receive government benefits.

This isn't some crazy, bleeding-heart, liberal theory I'm tossing out here. This is a basic reading of the Constitution. I'm glad we have actual judges to interpret the Constitution and not a gang of Facebook users. "Unreasonable searches and seizures ... warrants ... probable cause" ... those aren't just empty words. Those words are from the founding legal document of our nation, and they don't get violated just because somebody incorrectly thinks a little unwarranted search and seizure of bodily fluids without probable cause would be good policy.

Of course, the folks who support drug tests for welfare recipients could always start a national movement to get the Fourth Amendment repealed. I wish them luck with that impossible and misguided task. Or they could move somewhere with a Constitution that they like better than ours. The government of North Korea, for example, provides very little for the welfare of its citizens and would probably be happy to search just about anybody it chooses.

Here in the United States, the Fourth Amendment applies to what the government does, not private employers. Yes, private American employers can require employee drug tests under certain specific conditions. That's because employers have liability issues related to what their employees do while working for a company. If a truck driver crashes into a van load of elementary school kids while under the influence of alcohol or cocaine, for example, the trucking company that employs the driver could be subjected to a significant lawsuit. Welfare recipients, on the other hand, pose no such liability. No one is going to sue any American citizens for paying the taxes that funded welfare in the unlikely event that a direct link can be established between welfare payments and drug abuse that led to an accident.

The primary outrage about "welfare" relies on the misguided theory that poor people are only poor because of some personal character flaw—that it's their own fault. Of course, much of welfare funding goes to benefit children, senior citizens, and disabled people—and those demographic qualities are not exactly "character flaws." Setting aside the facts about welfare recipients, it's popular these days to say that people on government benefits are simply too lazy to get a job. I've never understood why people assume that there is some epidemic of laziness in America. My parents were great role models who taught me that hard work is one of the core values of this nation. Every day, hundreds of millions of Americans put in an honest day's work. I personally see far more people heading off to work than sleeping on the couch all day. Sure, there are some goof-offs out there, but they are the exception, not the rule, at my place of employment. No one at my job is napping rather than working.

Paul Ryan, the Republican nominee for Vice President, once said that the government-funded social safety net is in danger of becoming a "hammock," implying that those lazy people receiving government benefits would rather lounge and sleep than work. Of course, Ryan himself got government-funded social safety net cash in the form of Social Security payments after the untimely death of his father when Ryan was sixteen years old. Rather than refuse that money and get a job on moral grounds, Ryan used his government program benefits to help pay for going to an expensive, out-of-state university, where, presumably, he didn't have a hammock in his dorm room.

Ryan's criticisms punch my stomach more than the average misguided Republican rant because my own father passed away when I was in college. I received the same kind of support that Ryan did, although probably far less. Those modest monthly checks helped me meet the expenses that scholarships and multiple jobs didn't cover. And that funding helped ease the burden on my mother, who had to deal with her grief while still trying to support four kids in college. To hear Ryan talk about hammocks when I know how he benefitted from government assistance makes me want to climb through the television and tug on those big ears of his.

Should Ryan have been subjected to a drug test to get his benefits? How about me? I avoided any drugs stronger than caffeine while I was in college. Where do we draw the line? Should student loan recipients have to take a drug test? How about public school children? How about public-sector workers whose salaries are funded by taxpayers? (Florida tried that one and had it shot down as unconstitutional.) All Americans benefit in some way from the American government. Should everyone be forced to pee in a cup before visiting a national park or calling the fire department when their house is burning? How about drug test before reading this article when it was originally published on the internet (which, after all, was created with government funding)?

Some people like to exhort the unemployed to "get a job after you take a bath," as Newt Gingrich said during a Republican presidential debate, ignoring the fact that there have been between 3.4 and 6.7 applicants for every job opening in American during recent years, depending on which labor study you consult. In addition, many of those jobs pay federal minimum wage, $7.25 per hour, which is well below the family poverty level and which hasn't kept up with inflation, thanks to corporation-loving Republican policies that have held the minimum wage as low as possible. So getting a job isn't anywhere near as easy as welfare critics think it is, and Republicans bent on low wages have made sure that having a job isn't really such a great financial alternative either.

As if the indignity of being unable to find a job that pays a living wage isn't enough, Americans seem intent on further humiliating the poor by ridiculing them for trying to feed their families with the help of government assistance. Adding the further indignity of mandatory drug tests just to get essential government assistance feels like hitting below the belt. People like to say that if someone has nothing to hide, then he or she shouldn't object to a drug test. But the rate of false positive drug tests is 5-10%, frequent enough to give anyone pause. And do we really want to live in a society where we assume the worst of people and make them prove their virtue? Or do we want to live in a society where people are presumed innocent until proven guilty? Our Constitution makes very clear that the presumption of innocence is a founding principle of our nation. I'd like to presume that people, by and large, are not on drugs and not lazy.

Actually, the theory that poor people are lazy relies on believing *other people* are lazy. No one who is poor believes he or she is poor due to his or her own laziness. Some poor people will blame bad luck or claim false victimhood because they believe liberals give everything away to everyone else except them. To these folks, they're poor only because of Obama and his terrible Kenyan socialism somehow took their job and led their poverty— even though Obama's policies have created millions of jobs and reversed the Bush economic crash. They blame everyone else except themselves. In their minds, only *other* poor people are lazy—certainly not them. In their minds, they are the patriotic taxpayers who support all those lazy welfare recipients— even if their own income is so low that they don't pay any federal income tax at all.

Yes, actual taxpayers fund welfare programs. But one ironic fact that hardly ever gets mentioned is that welfare recipients themselves have paid into the system through their own taxes. Many people who are currently receiving government benefits previously held jobs and paid taxes. Unemployment insurance, for example, only goes to people who had been in the work force before becoming unemployed. Government benefits aren't some kind of free gift when the recipient has helped to fund the program. From my personal point of view, I paid into the system for decades and will for many more years of my working life. I would much rather have people get the benefits that I helped to fund during tough times than see them suffer or turn to crime. Only a truly mean person would want to inflict suffering during tough times, and only someone with no common sense would want to create conditions that encourage people to turn to crime to feed their families.

But paying taxes doesn't mean we each get to determine where every dollar gets spent. I've heard this line many times: "I should have a say in where my tax money gets spent, and I say we shouldn't spend it on drug-addicted welfare bums." Well, in our form of government, we actually do have a system for making our voice heard in terms of where our tax money is spent. We vote for representatives who make laws directing government spending of tax revenues. But no individual citizen gets to use his or her tax forms to explicitly direct where those taxes get allocated. In fact, there's no country on earth like that.

For example, I don't want my tax dollars going to fund the misguided and mismanaged Bush wars that have killed so many of our brave soldiers. And I certainly don't want my tax dollars going to support people in Congress who still believe that tax cuts for the wealthy leads to job creation and increased government revenue despite overwhelming evidence to the contrary. But, the funny thing is that no one said I could drug test the Bush administration officials or elected Republicans who started their pointless wars or pushed their ridiculous trickle-down theories. We live in a representative democracy where not every citizen gets the final word on every governmental decision.

Most people don't realize that "welfare" is a tiny part of the federal budget, and there are work requirements that make it not "free." Mitt Romney plays this card in his recent dishonest ads claiming that President Obama is just giving away welfare to anyone and everyone. The social safety net is an easy target for propaganda artists who just want to tap into the frustrations of economic insecurity. Romney knows how unpopular he is with people of color, so he's trying to use welfare as a target to court the misinformed white vote, which is the only way he thinks he can win the election. The ironic fact is that there are more white people on welfare than anyone else, but irony is often lost on people who assume welfare recipients are predominantly minorities.

Romney and other Republicans think it's good politics to demonize welfare because myths about welfare abound, including the cost of welfare fraud. We've all heard a third- or fourth-hand story about someone's cousin's brother-in-law who knew a family that lived next door to people who swore that they knew a guy who traded his welfare check for heroin. When I hear stories like this, I always ask the teller to prove it, to show me some evidence. They never can. Of course, that may happen one out of a million times, but this type of story has somehow become accepted wisdom from the days when Ronald Reagan told a huge lie about a fictionalized "welfare queen" driving a Cadillac and scamming the system.

Demonizing drug users is also very safe politics. Many people in America suffer with drug addiction, and there is a tremendous outcry to punish people for their drug use. It's much easier to condemn and blame drug users than it is to help them. Right-wing commentator Rush Limbaugh is a good example. Limbaugh himself called for drug abusers to be sent to jail before his own drug-related problems came to light. Unfortunately, condemnation and blame don't help anyone—not the drug abusers themselves or the loved ones around them whose lives are negatively affected. Limbaugh was able to get treatment for his addiction and seems to have gotten past his problems. He has returned to his regular job of being incredibly hypocritical, rude, and dishonest about American politics—but at least he seems to be no longer abusing drugs. Why shouldn't everyone get the same opportunity that Limbaugh got? But no person receiving government benefits would even try to get help if he or she knew that their benefits would be cut if they acknowledged having a drug problem.

Pinning down the exact percentage of welfare fraud is far more difficult than making up stories about "welfare queens," but analysis shows that fraud in government assistance programs amounts to around 2%. That translates to success rate greater than 98%, which is excellent for any endeavor.

In fact, the entire budget for social welfare programs is far less than federal spending on corporate welfare. But Exxon-Mobile isn't cashing out its EBT cards at the store down the street. While everyone claims examples of people abusing the welfare system, very few people are aware of the actual facts about the rarity of welfare fraud. And people don't seem to notice the countless times that welfare keeps people from going hungry or homeless and helps them get back on their feet after tough times. When was the last time local or national media ran a report about how government welfare programs kept children from starving or made sure that families could stay together and survive? If a private charity does something to help people, that becomes a feel-good story for the six o'clock news—and that's great. But when the government helps people again and again, millions of times over, it's a yawner that's just not sexy enough for TV.

I personally know many people who have turned their lives around due to government benefits. One friend of mine was in a car accident and couldn't return to his job as a waiter. Because he had basic health coverage (thanks to Romneycare here in Massachusetts!), he didn't go broke while recuperating. He collected unemployment benefits and applied for a government-secured small-business loan to open his own restaurant when he was well again. He's become successful, thanks to the combination of his own hard work and government benefits. And I read countless essays from community college students in my classes about how government-funded financial aid (often combined with welfare and/or unemployment benefits) enabled them to go back to college and improve their lives. Basically, not only have I read the statistics that show the need for a social safety net, but I've also seen with my own eyes how government funding can help people.

And I understand the power of government benefits in my own life. I grew up in a low-income, rural family without the resources to send me to college. But I was able to go because of a combination of jobs, scholarships, grants, and student loans—much of which came from the government. And I got that small check each month from Social Security after my father died during my junior year—much like Paul Ryan. The difference between Ryan and me is that I remember how the government helped me to help myself. Ryan has conveniently forgotten that uncomfortable fact.

I guess people tend to think that their own preconceptions about welfare abuse constitute the whole of reality rather than actual comprehensive research or first-hand experience with the subject. No politician wins elections by telling the truth about how rare welfare fraud actually is or relating a story of how government assistance changed his or her life. It's much more appealing to rail against fictional lazy people who are stealing our money to support their drug habit.

And it's also strange how the drug-testing advocates often claim to be guided by the their religious faith, saying that drug use is a sin. But what would these folks do with poor people who tested positive for drugs? Would they help these needy people, as the Bible advises? No, it's far more likely they would cut off their welfare benefits and send them on their way to deal with their poverty on their own. Would these religious types be happy that the children of poor people with drug problems would go hungry? I guess the Gospel somehow skipped over the section where Jesus asked everybody to pee in a cup before he fed the multitude.

Finally, for anyone who still wants to ignore the Bible, the Fourth Amendment, and basic common sense because they are just so sure that drug tests for welfare recipients is a wonderful idea … well, consider these two assumption-busting facts:

1. Many people wrongly assume that a high percentage of welfare recipients use illegal drugs. But, when Florida drug tested welfare recipients before the courts closed down the program, only 108 of the 4,086 people who took a drug test failed. That's 2.6%. The rate of drug use in the general population is more than three times that high, nearly 9%. So welfare recipients, in this case, were actually shown to be far less likely to use drugs than other people are.

2. Many people wrongly assume that drug tests for welfare recipients will save the taxpayers' money. But the overall "savings" to the taxpayers of Florida turned out to be negative $45,780. That means the drug tests actually cost more tax dollars than the amount saved in withheld welfare payments. (And that loss doesn't include the state's legal fees in defending the drug-testing program in court.)

So who is actually wasting tax dollars? How about the misguided Republican lawmakers who pass these drug-testing laws? Or how about the people who keep posting Facebook rants about drug tests for welfare recipients? It would be tempting to say that they're the ones who should be forced to pee in a cup—but that would be unconstitutional, ineffective, and just plain wrong.

Debunking Some Ridiculous Obamacare Lies

July 2012

A quote attributed to omnipresent irritant Donald Trump has been floating around Facebook lately, usually posted by opponents of Obamacare who say some variation of, "Wow, The Donald really nails it!"

In fact, the quote almost certainly didn't come from Trump, according to fact-checkers. Someone seemed to think that crediting the quote to Trump gave it more credibility. Let's put aside the scary idea that Trump could bring credibility to anything and look at the quote itself:

"Let me get this straight. We're going to be "gifted" with a health care plan we are forced to purchase and fined if we don't, which purportedly covers at least ten million more people without adding a single new doctor, but provides for 16,000 new IRS agents, written by a committee whose chairman says he doesn't understand it, passed by a congress that didn't read it but exempted themselves from it, and signed by a president who smokes, with funding administered by a treasury chief who didn't pay his taxes, for which we'll be taxed for four years before any benefits take effect, by a government which has already bankrupted Social Security and Medicare, all to be overseen by a surgeon general who is obese, and financed by a country that's broke! What the hell could possibly go wrong?"

Trumpius Maximus supposedly spewed these words back in February, but they didn't go viral until after the Supreme Court upheld the constitutionality of Obamacare. What amazes me is that anyone would still take Trump seriously after his amazing run of idiocy and lies. Trump may be a joke to most people, but he is an official supporter of, fundraiser for, and adviser to Republican presidential nominee Mitt Romney. Romney himself has proven to be a world-class liar, repeatedly making documented falsehoods a key aspect of his campaign. So perhaps he welcomes Trump's dishonesty. In a perfect world, no one should have to debunk this much Trump-crap, but people actually believe it—so debunk we must.

In his defense, I guess Trump would be making a good point—if anything in this quote were remotely close to the truth. In fact, the paragraph is just one lie after another. I'm not sure which of Trump's ghostwriters came up with this turd party wrapped up in a crap festival, but it's a complete sewer system. I counted twelve violations of the Ninth Commandment just at first glance. That's a lot of false witness!

The good news is that evil liberal web browsers like mine come with a search feature. The truth about Obamacare is actually pretty easy to find. This will be a fairly long post compared with much of what we see on Twitter and Facebook, but Trump gives us quite a few lies to deal with.

Let's take the lies one at a time:

1) No one is forced to purchase "Obamacare." (Obamacare is a set of common sense regulations of the health insurance industry. It's not some separate product that anyone has to buy.) The individual mandate "fine" would only be levied against people who can afford health insurance but purposely don't buy it because they want to gamble that they won't get sick but then freeload off the rest of us when they do get sick. People who are too poor to afford health insurance on their own can get subsidies to help purchase insurance, or they can get Medicaid.

2) Obamacare actually makes health insurance available to more than 30 million uninsured people (not 10 million, a number Trump must have pulled out of his famously weird hair), ensuring that nearly everyone in America will have affordable access to health care for the first time in history.

3) The legislation actually does have provisions and funding for training new doctors.

4) The 16,000 new IRS agents will mostly work to hand out tax *credits* to approximately 16 million Americans covered under Obamacare and to advise individuals and businesses—not be some sinister army to enforce Obamacare.

5) There's no evidence that any congressional committee chair ever said he didn't understand the law. And the members of Congress who voted for the law, assisted by their staff members, did actually read and understand it. That's their job. And for all the complaints about how long the bill is, the truth is that actual text of the legislation is about the same length as a *Harry Potter* children's novel and about a third the length of the Bible—which, incidentally, includes all that liberal, socialist stuff about Jesus giving away free health care.

   Trump himself either hasn't read the legislation or he has read it and is purposely lying about it because his comments bear no resemblance to the actual law. And, by the way, has Trump read every word of every legal document for each of his four bankruptcies or more than one hundred lawsuits? Of course not, but he has a staff to help him read and understand the documents that show what a multiple failure he has been in the business world.

6) Members of Congress didn't exempt themselves from the law. In fact, the law includes a provision that members of Congress are *required* to get their health insurance through Obamacare—the exact opposite of Trump's claim.

This is one of the biggest "zombie-lies" about Obamacare that has been thoroughly debunked by multiple fact-checkers. Why ignorant people continue to believe it is a complete mystery (although perhaps people like Trump getting frequent airtime on Fox News to push their lies might have something to do with it).

7) Obama quit smoking two years ago—and besides, so what? Does smoking make him unqualified to develop a plan to address the nation's health care issues? If that's the case, then human chimney John Boehner would be even less qualified for the task.

8) The Secretary of Health and Human Services has primary responsibilities for administering Obamacare, not the Treasury Secretary. That's common knowledge—although Trump seems immune to common knowledge. It's common knowledge that the president's birth certificate has been available on the internet for years, but Trump seems unable to find it.

9) Many benefits of Obamacare have already taken effect. And some of the taxes to help fund portions of Obamacare (which are all aimed at upper-income people and corporations making big profits in the health care industry—not the middle class) haven't kicked in yet.

10) Social Security and Medicare are far from bankrupt, despite the cries of right-wingers across the nation. Social Security is solvent through 2038. Medicare is solvent until 2024. In fact, Obamacare actually helps save Medicare funding.

11) The Surgeon General also doesn't oversee Obamacare, as mentioned earlier—the Secretary of Health and Human Services does. And the United States Surgeon General, Regina Benjamin, may not be as skinny as Trump's multiple wives, but, where I come from, only an obnoxious jerk would berate a woman for her weight, let alone assume that makes her unqualified as a medical person.

12) The United States isn't broke. In fact, our nation has the most resources of any nation on earth—we're just spending far too much of our government funding on folks like Trump with corporate welfare.

The caption on Trump's photo accompanying his alleged comments about Obamacare reads, "Think about it ..." Okay, I did. Based on his comments, Trump is a liar, a jerk, and an ignoramus completely devoid of common sense.

Do Spoons Make People Confused?

June 2012

This is Sarah Palin's idea of common sense: guns equal spoons. It would be easy to dismiss Palin as a right-wing fringe lunatic who has been relegated to frothing up her word salad on Fox Fake News until her contract runs out and the national embarrassment ends. But her infantile gun-spoon photo featuring a gun advocate holding a sign reading "spoons make you fat" went viral on Facebook, with more than 65,000 people reposting it in just a few days as if to prove that those silly liberals may have book learning, but they fall short on common sense. "Guns don't kill people," one commenter ranted. "People kill people. Spoons don't make you fat—that's just common sense. Next thing you know, liberals will want to ban cars or garden rakes because someone could use them to kill someone else. Those silly liberals."

Let me ask Sarah Palin and her reposting fans this question: Which item would you give to a ten-year-old child so that she could eat her chicken noodle soup, a spoon or a loaded handgun? Still think there's no difference? Still think your nonsense is any kind of common sense?

We may not always share the definition of common sense, but we do have common ground. The first idea we share is that I have no interest in taking basic guns away from reasonable, law-abiding citizens. I grew up on a farm and helped feed my family by hunting as a teenager. I also understand the concept of owning guns for self-protection. The vast majority of liberals I know share that same understanding. Only a tiny percentage of people actually want guns eliminated from America or even believe that such a thing is possible. "Liberals are trying to take everybody's guns!" is an inaccurate generalization that shouldn't be part of an honest discussion of the issues.

The bottom line is that we all grieve for the victims of the Aurora tragedy, which took place only a few days after Palin posted her gun-spoon photo—and all reasonable people want to keep guns away from people who use them irresponsibly. Without getting too far into the politics at this early stage, there is one thing we know for sure. The assault weapons ban that Republicans let expire would have either stopped Holmes (and Jared Loughner before him) from getting their guns—or at least made it much more difficult for them too obtain their murder weapons.

Common-sense laws about extremely dangerous weapons are the minimum we can do as a reasonable society, but the far-right Republican Party and the gun lobby have made it impossible even to have a grown-up conversation about gun laws. As soon as anyone talks about gun laws, the NRA board rants about how Obama is coming for everybody's guns and attacking the Second Amendment. (Guess what? Obama is the Commander in Chief of the strongest military force in the history of the planet. He's got access to plenty of firepower. He has nukes, for crying out loud—he doesn't need anybody else's guns.)

Here's a fun experiment to try with someone who thinks guns and spoons are pretty much the same thing. Ask the person to tell you what's in the Second Amendment. The likely response is that it says Americans can have any gun they want. Then show them the actual text of the Second Amendment: "A well regulated Militia, being necessary to the security of a free State, the right of people to keep and bear arms, shall not be infringed." The Second Amendment is actually about the government being able to muster a civilian fighting force at a time in our history when guns were single-shot muskets, and our young nation had no standing army.

The kind of twisted thinking that translates an amendment focused on how the government can protect the nation into a free pass for assault weapons is common among gun extremists these days. The NRA officially opposes detailed background checks to keep mentally ill people and people with violent histories from buying guns. The organization even opposes making it illegal for people on the terrorist watch list to buy guns. That would make a great bumper sticker in an alternate universe, wouldn't it? "Another Patriot in Favor of More Guns for Terrorists!"

Wayne LaPierre, the executive vice president of the NRA thinks that the fact that Obama hasn't tried to enact gun control laws is proof that he'll try to enact gun control laws in his second term. Look it up—he really said that. There are even people who think that Obama is trying to create some kind of one-world-government plot to have the U.N. take everyone's guns. And I actually heard today that some confused people are saying that the government staged the Aurora shooting to create anti-gun feelings in the public (similar to the "fast and furious" fake scandal drummed up by ignorant extremists and carried on by shameless Republicans in Congress). That's a very high level of delusional thinking.

These kinds of paranoid, reactionary responses make progress on gun safety next to impossible. The good news is that polls show large majorities of everyday gun owners and even NRA members don't agree with their extremist leaders. People who support basic, reasonable gun rights should be offended and embarrassed that their political and organizational leaders are taking such a counter-productive stance and making all gun owners look unreasonable and even crazy by association. The extremism has to change to help get what we all want—guns as far as possible from the hands of irresponsible and dangerous people.

Another kind of delusional thinking involves the ideas that laws that limit access to dangerous guns are the problem, that less restrictive gun laws could have actually prevented the Aurora tragedy. Some people believe that everything would have turned out better if only there had been more guns in that theater, more armed citizens, more good guys with guns to stop the bad guy. On a simplistic level, I can understand why some people might think that way. We all want to believe that we can make a difference and do good in the world, and sometimes that impulse for doing good morphs into a hero complex.

Unfortunately, many of these people seem to have had their most meaningful life experiences while playing video games or watching action movies. They don't understand real life. In a video game or action movie, the good guy pulls his gun and takes out the bad guy, just the way God intended. But the harsh reality is that the more likely outcome finds that the good guy with the gun would shoot innocent bystanders instead of the perp, or another good guy with a gun would shoot the first armed good guy because he thought he was the bad guy. (That almost happened at the scene of the Gabby Giffords shooting when the only armed citizen came a fraction of a second from shooting the unarmed man who had taken Loughner's gun.)

Considering Holmes was wearing body armor, and the Aurora theater was dark, loud, filled with teargas, and crowded with fleeing people, more guns would have just made things far, far worse.

No matter how pure the motives or brave the heart, real life is not a video game or action movie. I, for one, don't want to live in a hair-trigger country where everybody carries guns and thinks they're going to be some kind of hero—where bullets could fly at the slightest provocation, and the difference between the good guys and the bad guys isn't anywhere near as clear as we wish it could be.

One effort that actually might help in determining who has the potential for committing acts of atrocity like the Aurora shooting is mental health assessment. If proper mental health care were as readily available in America as guns are, we'd be a far better place. Perhaps Holmes would have been flagged by the system early enough to prevent his crime. Holmes was already identified as showing signs of a mental problem by the owner of a gun range where Holmes applied for membership just a month before the tragedy. If a psychological layman such as a gun range owner spotted red flags, then a psychological professional certainly would have as well.

A friend told me today that gun laws wouldn't have stopped Holmes, so we should just abandon gun laws and focus exclusively on mental health assessment. I can understand that impulse considering how the extreme right has made gun laws almost a forbidden subject for discussion—even in the wake of gun tragedy.

My friend may be right that restrictive assault weapons laws wouldn't have stopped Holmes. He may have used his explosives to kill people in that theater if he couldn't get guns (although he had the explosives and chose the guns for what he did in the theater). He may have illegally obtained his assault weapon even if the assault weapon ban hadn't been allowed to expire by

Republicans in Congress (although the ban would have certainly made it harder for him to get his assault weapon).

Of course, no precaution is perfect. Door locks don't keep out all intruders, yet we still lock our doors because that keeps out most would-be intruders. Sunblock doesn't prevent every fraction of damage from ultra-violet radiation, yet we slather it on our kids all summer long because it helps to protect them as much as we can.

Likewise, no law is perfect. No law, including gun restrictions, would ever stop all gun crimes. I don't think any reasonable person would ever say that any law is 100% effective. People jay-walk all the time despite anti-jay-walking laws. But our laws help to protect us. And our laws do more than simply control behavior. Our laws reflect the values of our society.

Drug laws are a good subject for comparison. The fact that heroin is illegal doesn't mean that no one can get heroin. But no one suggests legalizing heroin (except Ron Paul, who sometimes seems like a good candidate for that mental health assessment mentioned above). We continue to make heroin illegal for two reasons: 1) The fact that it is against the law does actually prevent some people from trying to get heroin. 2) Our society values keeping people away from dangerous drugs, and making heroin against the law reflects that value.

Research has shown that minimal common-sense gun laws (such as the assault weapons ban) do help prevent violence by making assault weapons harder to obtain. But, more importantly, common-sense gun laws reflect the societal value that guns can be dangerous things that need to be handled responsibly for the good of everyone. Isn't that a common-sense value we all share?

Despite the antics of the NRA and what we hear in the mainstream media, polls show that most Americans want common-sense gun laws. If events like the Aurora and Giffords shootings don't facilitate an adult conversation about enacting those common-sense gun laws, then what will? If people are misguided enough to compare a gun with a spoon and not recognize that such a comparison is obviously insane, then how can we ever prevent guns from falling into the hands of people who will become the next terrible news story?

Ron Paul is Far from a Liberal Alternative

May 2012

The supposed liberal dissatisfaction with President Obama has been greatly exaggerated in the mainstream media. Unfortunately, that exaggeration has led to speculation that Republican Ron Paul could be an alternative candidate for liberals who might be disappointed in the president. In reality, nothing could be further from the truth.

Paul has inspired people to get involved in the political process, which is great. He opposed the Iraq War and the Patriot Act, and he favors marijuana legalization. Those are appealing positions to liberals, no doubt. And he projects a certain "grumpy-grandpa" image that liberals admire in fighters like Senator Bernie Sanders. But when you look deeper, most of Paul's views are antithetical to the liberal perspective and simply terrible for America.

Paul's actual anti-war views aren't really liberal because he supports military action based on his narrow view of American economic interests. Many liberals support the moral use of military force to protect innocent people. Paul is against the United States assisting citizens of other countries defend themselves against cruel dictators. For example, Paul opposed the recent successful intervention in Libya, skillfully and reasonably orchestrated by President Obama, which saved countless lives.

Paul is certainly no liberal on social issues. He wants to end Social Security, Medicare, Medicaid, and unemployment insurance, progressive programs that have protected millions of people from poverty and suffering. His solution to rising health care costs is for the uninsured to rely on the charity of doctors and churches. He wants to abolish the federal departments of education, environmental protection, and energy (among others), agencies that help keep Americans productive and safe. Just like all the other science-denying Republicans running for president, Paul calls climate change a hoax. He even wants to abolish FEMA because he says that it's "immoral" for the government to help victims of natural disasters. That's not exactly a liberal view of "morality."

In addition to legalizing marijuana, Paul supports legalizing truly dangerous drugs such as heroin and cocaine. His advice to victims of sexual harassment is that they should quit their jobs. Even though he claims to be against government intrusion, he believes the government should control women's reproductive rights and tell us all whom we can and can't marry. He's also against any form of gun control. Do any of those positions sound remotely liberal?

Paul is militantly anti-immigrant and has ties to white supremacist organizations (not to mention a long history of racist, homophobic, and anti-semitic comments in his newsletters and other sources). He opposes the Civil Rights Act of 1964 and voted repeatedly against the Martin Luther King holiday. While he may not personally be bigoted, his public policy views are clearly far to the right of mainstream American perspective on race. He calls himself a Christian, but he's a longtime devotee of the completely anti-Christian Ayn Rand philosophy that selfishness is a virtue.

On economic issues, Paul is even farther right than the already extreme Republican Party. He's against all forms of government consumer protection and financial regulation—even after unregulated Wall Street abuses crashed the economy. He claims that taxes are a form of immoral theft, but he doesn't explain how government could fund essential services without taxation—except through vague "fees" that would radically shift the burden from the wealthy onto the backs of the middle-class and the poor. He often rants against "the FED" and American monetary policy, but experts on the subject consider him a confused conspiracy theorist.

If America ever adopted Paul's extremist agenda, our nation would become a cut-throat, self-centered, trample-the-weak type of place that would favor the already super-rich and plunge everyone else into poverty and danger. That's not a liberal utopia by any means.

Yet the inexplicable rumblings persist that Paul is a liberal alternative, defying all common sense. Of course, President Obama hasn't been perfect. He hasn't done everything liberals want to correct the Bush administration failures. No president could. But Obama has overseen steady progress in the face of relentless right-wing obstruction. The reasonable liberal alternative to the president's difficult first term is reelection with a renewed Democratic Congress to accelerate the progress already begun. Paul, on the other hand, would be a regressive disaster that liberals would deeply regret.

A Shining Beacon for Slackers Everywhere

April 2012

Supreme Court Justice Antonin Scalia complained last week about reading the Affordable Care Act, stating directly that he didn't plan to read it and derisively invoking the Eighth Amendment to the Constitution that bans "cruel and unusual punishment."

Get it? Reading is punishment. Ha, ha. That might be cutesy coming from a third grader who didn't finish the assignment and doesn't know any better, but from a Supreme Court Justice? Not exactly "supreme."

Scalia's comments sound more like something we'd hear from a dropout who would rather party or play video games than crack open a textbook. He reminds me of the guy who sneaks off to the far corner of the warehouse to take a nap on company time rather than unload that truck backed up to the loading dock.

Yes, the Affordable Care Act is long. Complex legislation is not usually written on an index card. But Scalia is a grown man with a law degree from Harvard, an extensive staff, and all the resources of the United States Supreme Court at his disposal. He's not some ten-year-old telling his mommy that he wants to play instead or doing his homework. *Reading the Affordable Care Act is his job. If he's not up to that job, he should retire.*

When Justice Elena Kagan made the common-sense suggestion that Scalia's law clerks could easily read the bill, Scalia replied, "I don't care whether it's easy for my clerks—I care whether it's easy for me."

Scalia isn't exactly the kind of role model young people in American need. Here we have a Supreme Court Justice who whines about how hard it is to do his required reading and who brags about being too lazy to do his job effectively. How can one of the nine people deciding the most important legal cases in our nation think, talk, and behave this way on the bench? It must be nice to have a lifetime appointment with no consequences for being blatantly terrible at your job.

Scalia has been parroting right-wing talking points about the Affordable Care Act rather than even bothering to give the appearance of impartiality. Scalia has even appeared at fundraisers (with fellow conservative Supreme Court Justice Clarence Thomas) for the anti-health-care-reform Koch brothers, which is a clear conflict of interest that should have led both judges to recuse themselves from this case. So Scalia's vote in this case is hardly in doubt. Partisanship will guide him far more than actual judicial thought.

Scalia is a case-study example of the current Republican Party, the party that used to be known for emphasizing personal responsibility—which is the core concept of the health-care reform mandate opposed by Republicans and currently being debated by the Supreme Court. Today's G.O.P. has evolved into the party of complaints, laziness, and ethical conflict.

Canada Enacts Harsh and Misguided Anti-American Immigration Law

March 2012

Warning: This essay is satire, of course. Canada hasn't enacted any such law. For some states in the U.S., unfortunately, satire has become reality.

Due to a perceived influx of illegal immigrants from the United States, the Legislative Assembly of the Canadian province of Alberta recently passed Canada's toughest immigration law ever, know as "Bill 1070." The new law requires police officers to stop and question any persons they suspect of being an illegal alien from the United States.

According to Percy Moose, a Conservative Party member of the Alberta assembly, "We can't have these Yankee hosers sneaking across our border and ruining our great nation. They're taking our jobs and bringing down the general quality of life. A Canadian citizen should be able to walk down the street and not have to worry about being accosted by some lowlife illegal American."

When asked to present evidence that illegal immigrants were raising the crime rate or taking jobs from Canadians, Moose ended the interview without comment.

Not all Canadians are simply blaming Americans. Many point to the bad U.S. economy for the increase in illegal immigration northward into Canada. These dismal economic conditions in the United States are widely considered by Canadian authorities to be the result of nearly a decade of ultra-conservative economic policies on the part of former President George W. Bush and his Republican allies in congress.

"President Obama is working very hard and doing everything he can, and conditions are beginning to turn around," says University of Lethbridge economics professor Annabelle Bergeron, "but former President Bush left him a mountain of manure to dig out from under, if you'll pardon my harsh language. It's easy to understand why anyone stuck in that economy would want to come here."

The explosion of illegal American immigration has had some unintended consequences. According to a Ponoka mother of three who spoke on the condition of anonymity, "Our nanny is an undocumented American. She has a master's degree in education, but they've laid off so many teachers in the lower forty-eight that she can't find work. It's sad, but we're happy to have a nanny with a master's degree who we pay in cash. My neighbors' gardener was a telecommunications specialist in the United States for twenty years until his job was outsourced to India."

Dr. Gary Hunter, a general practitioner at Calgary Hospital sees some signs of immigration relief in changes recently approved in America: "At least now, thanks to President Obama and the Democrats in their Congress, they have a minimal kind of universal health care at long last. Hopefully, Americans will have less need to come north to Canada for basic medical services."

Bill 1070 is being applauded by right-wing Canadian politicians, and some opinion polls show a majority of Canadians support the measure—although these same polls show most respondents know almost nothing about the new law. Unfortunately, despite Bill 1070's popularity, the new immigration law is full of problems.

The new law takes the focus away from the main reason Americans enter Canada illegally: because they want to work. Big Canadian corporations are exploiting the bad U.S. economy by using these illegal American immigrants as cheap labor for industry. Existing Canadian laws, such as fines for companies that hire undocumented workers, aren't being enforced. Immigration experts are saying that stricter laws against corporations and strict enforcement of existing laws would do far more to curb illegal immigration than the misguided Bill 1070.

"Most of the Conservative Party is in the pocket of these corporations," says one Alberta legislator on the condition of anonymity. "But if you say anything against their illegal hiring practices, they'll target you for defeat in the next election."

Bill 1070 requires Canadian Mounties to stop anyone who might appear to be undocumented and demand these people show documentation to prove they are in Canada legally. Of course, authorities will be looking for people of "American" origin, which usually means people who exhibit impolite behavior or who can't discuss the rules of hockey. That's profiling, which has been shown to be an ineffective law-enforcement technique, both in Canada and the United States.

This law profiles people based on their appearance, which sounds a lot like other ineffective profiling techniques that are sometimes used in the United States against African-Americans ("driving while black") and Arab-Americans ("flying while Arab"). This new Canadian law could be called "breathing while American." According to Milk River police chief Raymond Gangne, whose town borders the United States, "Profiling is lazy police work. Canadians don't look for the easy way to do something if the easy way doesn't work. We're Canadians, after all, not Americans."

The idea of having police officers demanding, "Show me your papers!" to people on the street doesn't sound very democratic. It sounds more like something done in a dictatorship, not a nation with a rich history of democracy such as Canada.

The way that Bill 1070 targets American immigrants has come under questioning. Besides Americans, there are thousands of undocumented people who have entered Canada illegally, including people from Asia, Africa, and Central America. This new law doesn't address these people, instead singling out Americans based entirely on their nationality, as if they are the only sources of immigration problems. "That sounds bigoted to me," says Dominick Sandarski, a Redwater restaurant owner and critic of Bill 1070.

Nearly a third of Alberta's residents have some family history in the United States, and the vast majority of these people are legal residents or Canadian citizens. But Bill 1070 will subject them to questioning from police simply because of their national origin. "My ex-husband lives down in Butte, Montana, now," says Two Hills resident Haruhi Shizaki. "Are they going to try to kick my kids and me out because he's living in the U.S.? That's discrimination."

Many Canadian Mounties themselves are against the new law because it requires them to focus so much time and effort on potential undocumented Americans that they won't be able to focus on protecting law-abiding people from crime. In the words of Constable Benton Fraser, "We have real police work to do to keep our citizens safe. Thank you very kindly, but no, Bill 1070 doesn't help us at all."

Many province and city officials are against Bill 1070 as well because it has already lead to boycotts of Alberta tourism and products by Canadians and Americans, as well as lawsuits by legal residents who are improperly arrested and detained under this law. These boycotts and lawsuits could potentially have a terrible effect on a province already suffering due to the global economic downturn.

"If we lose the Yank tourist, we might as well close up shop," says Sylvan Lake mayor Gordon Pinsent. "That's two-thirds of the town's economy."

The new law has social consequences as well. Bill 1070 could drive undocumented Americans in Alberta "underground" and cause many of them to leave their productive jobs in farming, labor, and the service industry and take up ways to support themselves and their families that are much more harmful to Canadian society (organized crime and the drug trade, for example).

In addition, the mass deportations of Americans back to the United States that Bill 1070 could lead to are very expensive for the province, squandering tight government funds during difficult economic times. "We just don't have the resources to move that many people," says Jan Brewer of the Medicine Hat town council. "No one up in the assembly thought about the cost of holding and transporting all those illegal Americans. Where do they expect us to get the money for all those transport vans, not to mention feeding and housing these folks while they're in custody?"

Families may also suffer due do Bill 1070. Children born in Canada to undocumented parents are Canadian citizens under the Canadian Citizenship Act of 1946, just as children born in the United States are American citizens under the Fourteenth Amendment to the U.S. Constitution. Consequently, another problem with the new law is that arresting, detaining, and deporting parents under Bill 1070 would separate them from their dependent children, breaking up families and leaving a generation of Canadian citizens without parents.

In addition, Bill 1070 could lead to undocumented American workers pulling their children out of school or not taking them for treatment when they are sick, fearing discovery and arrest, leading to a dangerous lack of education and health care as well.

"The Conservative Party has long been known for espousing 'family values,' but what value is there in breaking up families or endangering health and education under Bill 1070?" says Green Party representative Landon Gordon-Smyth. Taking their anti-family stance one step further, some ultra-conservative Canadian politicians have even proposed altering the Canadian Citizenship Act to do away with what has been derisively called the "anchor baby" aspect of Canadian law.

The new law has any number of unintended consequences, according to legal experts. For example, anyone who has a disagreement or dispute with a neighbor, coworker, or acquaintance of American descent (or who is simply "Yank-looking") could harass that person anonymously by telling authorities that these people are undocumented Americans—even if they are perfectly legal residents or Canadian citizens.

Additionally any legal resident or Canadian citizen questioned by the police who doesn't have his or her "papers" can be charged with a crime under Bill 1070, meaning that it is illegal for legal residents and Canadian citizens not to have their birth certificate with them at all times.

Ultimately, Bill 1070 may not be around long. The Canadian constitution gives the federal government the power to regulate immigration, not the provinces, much the same as the United States Constitution establishes immigration enforcement as federal, not state purview. "Not to cause a kerfuffle, but any kid in school should know that," according to Whitecourt High School civics teacher Gwen Two Arrows. "If they don't, they don't now their own Constitution, and they're not very good citizens." Ultimately, the Alberta law will be struck down as unconstitutional for that reason alone. Until then, unfortunately, it will damage and ruin the lives of many innocent people.

The Canadian federal government hasn't done anything substantive to curb illegal immigration from the United States because Conservatives in the Canadian Parliament have blocked any serious efforts for more than a decade. "They haven't worked with us to find a solution because they are beholding to their corporate donors who benefit from the cheap American labor," according to Liberal Party Member of Parliament Donald O'Shea of Toronto. "It's no wonder the right-wing xenophobic types in the Alberta assembly pass such a silly law when the conservatives haven't done anything productive concerning immigration."

Around the world, observers of Bill 1070 have been appalled by its many problems, not the least of which is its blatant discrimination—a quality not usually associated with Canadians. Fair-minded Americans can only hope that cooler and more common sense viewpoints prevail, and the new Alberta law gets repealed. In addition, people in the United States should be watchful that right-wing extremists in an American border state (North Dakota, perhaps, or even Arizona to the south) aren't ignorant enough to push through anything as counterproductive as Alberta's Bill 1070.

That would be downright crazy, eh.

Is a Little Common Sense too Much to Ask?

February 2012

A social media posting making the rounds lately presents the following comparison: "If a single living cell was found on a distant planet, scientists would exclaim that we had found life elsewhere in the universe. So why is a single living cell found in the womb of a pregnant woman not considered life?" For visual appeal, the words are superimposed on a pretty lavender photo of what seems to be a cell. Thousands of people have tweeted or reposted this meme and made supportive comments about the wonderful sentiment expressed. Unfortunately, this comparison is a glaring sign of the lack of common sense that goes into important issues these days.

Let's begin with a look at the basic use of language and how this comparison twists definitions so much that the words become meaningless.

No one who would consider a "single living cell" on a distant planet to be "life," wouldn't also consider a "single living cell" in a womb of a pregnant woman to be "life"? A cell is a cell; life is life—no matter where it is. The animal or vegetable we ate for dinner last night contained many "living cells" at one time, yet we still ate dinner. Living cells inhabit the world all around us, and we destroy millions of them on any given day without even thinking about it.

Why does this comparison rely so heavily on an obvious "straw man" argument that no one believes? Who exactly is saying that living cells inside a pregnant woman aren't considered life? I honestly don't think anyone would be so irrational that they would make the case that a cell's location somehow determines whether or not it could be defined as "life."

Obviously, the comparison assumes people with pro-choice views somehow hold the view that there is no "life" inside a pregnant woman. I'm pro-choice, and I certainly don't believe that the womb of a pregnant woman is "lifeless." I know many other pro-choice people, and none of them would make such an indefensible claim. The assumption that pro-choice people don't believe "a living cell" is "life" is completely ridiculous. The pro-choice side of the abortion debate simply doesn't hold that position, and anyone who says we do is blatantly distorting reality.

The difference between the two basic sides in the abortion debate has to do in part with the exact point at which the mass of living cells inside a pregnant woman becomes a human being. I don't make any claim to special knowledge on that subject. Most pro-choice people share my lack of a rigid, all-encompassing position on that question. Our viewpoint is that each individual person should make that personal, moral decision when faced with a possible pregnancy.

Most important, pro-choice people believe that no government or religion has the right to force its will on that decision. Our argument is not with people who believe they know exactly when a pregnancy can be defined as a human being. We acknowledge that every individual has the right to make that choice.

What pro-choice people object to is the insistence that government force the decisions of some onto everyone. We object to the legislation of religious beliefs that we may not share but that we would be forced to obey. We object to other people trying to make decisions for us by enacting laws that take away our choice. Anti-choice laws aren't about morality. Morality involves making choices. Anti-choice laws are immoral because they take away our right to make our own choice and to follow our own individual beliefs and values.

I'm not trying to be argumentative or offend anyone, and I understand the emotional appeal of the pretty purple photo and the over-simplified and purposely misleading comparison. The appeal is to the heart, especially the heart of people who value religious beliefs. I've seen this post being applauded on many Facebook pages today, mostly by people who self-identify as religious.

But shouldn't religious faith come from our brains as well as our hearts? As theologian James Luther Adams said, "An unexamined faith is not worth having, for it can be true only by accident. A faith worth having is a faith worth discussing and testing." Shouldn't we examine, discuss, and test our faith rather than simply swallowing obvious distortions? Shouldn't we be clear about our definition of "life" and "living cells" rather than make comparisons that no rational person would actually believe? No one believes that a "single living cell" on a distant planet is more valuable than a viable human life.

Shouldn't we resist the temptation to cheer emotional appeals that have no basis in common sense or critical thinking about this important issue? And even if the people who applaud the pretty purple picture and its obvious distortions refuse to think sensibly, shouldn't they at least be held to a minimal standard of honesty?

The Republican Hall of Shame

I've been accused many times of being too hard on Republicans. If reporting what Republicans do and quoting what they say constitutes the crime of being too hard on them, well, then I plead guilty.

In the Age of Confusion that has befallen our country, we too easily forget exactly how far from common sense the Republican Party has drifted. Republicans actually count on Americans losing interest in what they say and do—in fact, they actively work to annoy everyday Americans so that we pay as little attention to them as possible. But now, more than ever, we need to chronicle their public statements and actions to make sure that they can't escape down the memory hole.

That's why I started the Republican Hall of Shame. This is only a small sample of the misdeeds of those in power on the right from 2012 to 2016, but it's enough to remind us all that today's Republican politicians do not deserve our allegiance—much less our votes.

* * *

Republicans claimed that Joe Biden was rude during the Vice Presidential debate. But Republican role models include some of the rudest people in the world: Rush Limbaugh Ann Coulter, Bill O'Reilly, Michelle Malkin, Sean Hannity, Sarah Palin, Joe Walsh, and Allen West, to name just a few. Republicans have no credibility on the issue of civil discourse.

* * *

The Republican health care plan calls for tossing senior citizens out of traditional Medicare and having them wander about in the complicated private health insurance market to find their own coverage. To help sell this scheme, Republicans sent out a celebrity senior citizen, Clint Eastwood, at their party's convention during prime time television coverage and let him ramble incoherently at an empty chair for eleven agonizing minutes. Yes, what could possible go wrong with the Republican health care plan that forces senior citizens to navigate the open market and make complicated decisions?

* * *

After Hurricane Sandy struck the east coast just before the 2012 presidential election, America got to see the stark contract between the Democratic and Republican responses to disasters. President Obama worked closely with both Democratic and Republican governors, called off campaign appearances to travel to hurricane-damaged areas, and praised the great work of FEMA first-responders. Mitt Romney called only Republican governors, held a campaign rally with a photo-op featuring staged donations that Red Cross officials said they didn't want, and ducked questions about his proposals to cut or privatize FEMA. It's pretty clear who is better at leading our nation in tough times.

* * *

Representative Allen West (R-FL) baselessly claimed that "78-81" Congressional Democrats are Communists. Most of them got re-elected in 2012. He didn't. That's justice.

* * *

Representative Allen West (R-FL) said this about Representative Tammy Duckworth (D-IL): "I just don't know where her loyalties lie." Reality: Duckworth is an authentic war hero who lost both legs in Iraq. West was kicked out of the Army for torturing a captive and voted out of Congress after just one term.

* * *

Representative Michelle Bachman (R-MN) told President Obama that he should bomb Iran … *while she was attending the White House Christmas party!* Merry Christmas! Let's celebrate the birth of Christ by killing thousands of people!

* * *

Representative Michelle Bachman (R-MN) criticized President Obama by saying that 70% of food stamp benefits went to "bureaucrats in Washington." The actual amount is about 5% at most. Hey, she was only off by more than $100 billion, but that's how Republican math works. Bachmann has been called a "national treasure" by right-wingers. Thank goodness she's not the "national treasurer."

* * *

Ken Cuccinelli, Virginia's Republican Attorney General and candidate for Governor, tried to outlaw consensual oral sex in the state of Virginia. Most

Republicans are content with cutting jobs. Cuccinelli wants to cut blow jobs.

* * *

Do the voices inside Sarah Palin's head sound as annoying as her outside voice?

* * *

Speaker of the House John Boehner quoted Abraham Lincoln about the dangers of government debt. But he left out the fact that Lincoln was talking about the dangers of not raising taxes to deal with the government debt related to fighting the Civil War. A lie of omission is still a lie.

* * *

John Boehner said that Congress "should be judged not by how many new laws we create. Congress ought to be judged on how many laws we repeal." Okay. The Republican led Congress has repealed exactly zero laws. Boehner can't even meet his own fake standard.

* * *

John Boehner said that unemployed Americans would "rather just sit around" than work. Then he gave himself and the rest of the House of Representatives the next two months off.

* * *

John Boehner recently tweeted, "Frivolous lawsuits drive up the cost of everything Americans do." This was after he had filed a frivolous lawsuit against President Obama.

* * *

When Kansas Governor Sam Brownback was asked why people were dissatisfied with Kansas Republicans, he said, "I think a big part of it is Barack Obama." Seriously? Brownback is yet another member of the alleged "party of personal responsibility" who jumps to blame someone else for his own incompetence.

* * *

Scott Brown campaigned by driving his pick-up truck around Massachusetts, pretending to be a "regular guy." The next time Brown or any other Republican tries to pass himself off as a regular guy, check the back of his truck for a big load of BS.

* * *

As Scott Brown ran for the Senate in New Hampshire in 2014, he tried to present himself as an expert on border security. He neglected to mention that he skipped every border security hearing when he was previously a short-term Senator from Massachusetts. I guess all those Fox News softball interviews were his first priority.

* * *

While he was in the Senate, Scott Brown claimed that he had, "secret meetings with kings and queens and prime ministers ... every single day." Elizabeth Warren did Brown (and all of us) a favor when she beat him for that Senate seat, allowing Brown to continue having his imaginary tea parties with far-away royalty whenever he wants, unburdened by the realities of being a United States Senator. When Brown was running for the Senate in New Hampshire, he summed up his own candidacy perfectly: "Do I have the best credentials? Probably not. Cause, you know, whatever." Even in 2014, a big Republican year, Brown lost. A few months later, he was trying to drum up business for a weight-loss pills, and then he endorsed Donald Trump for president. There's no pill in all the world's medicine cabinets strong enough to give Brown a basic level of common sense.

* * *

Representative Eric Cantor (R-VA) says that the federal government needs to cut spending and "learn to live within its means." Meanwhile, Cantor himself has reported more than $1 million in personal debt.

* * *

Former Arkansas Governor and Republican presidential candidate Mike Huckabee recently ranted about Democrats who support mandatory health insurance coverage for women's contraceptives. Huckabee also claims that women who want their contraceptives covered by health insurance can't control their libidos and want "Uncle Sugar" to pay for their sexual activities. But back in 2005, as governor of Arkansas, Huckabee signed a bill requiring—guess what?—mandatory health insurance coverage of women's contraceptives. I guess Uncle Sugar is actually Uncle Huck.

* * *

Mike Huckabee claims he has gay friends. He just doesn't want those gay friends to have the same rights that he does. That's called being a terrible friend.

* * *

Mike Huckabee likes to accuse President Obama of character flaws. But Huckabee recently appeared on evangelist Jim Bakker's television show. Yes, that would be Jim Bakker of "Jim and Tammy Faye" fame. He was imprisoned on 24 counts of fraud and conspiracy, caught in a major sex/rape scandal, and still owes millions in back taxes. Huckabee also criticized the president's parenting skills, but the Huckster's son was fired from a camp counselor job at age 17 for killing a stray dog. Mike Huckabee doesn't have anywhere near the moral authority to criticize President Obama on any subject.

* * *

Mike Huckabee advised Americans not to join the military while President Obama is in office. "I'd wait a couple of years until we get a new commander-in-chief," he said. Can you imagine the fake outrage on Fox News if President Obama advised Americans not to join the military while Republicans control Congress? Huckabee is just another fake-patriotic Republican who hates Obama more than he loves America.

* * *

In 2013, former vice president Dick Cheney admitted to a shocking lack of gratitude and curiosity about the donor of his transplanted heart. "It's my new heart, not someone else's old heart," Cheney said. "I don't spend time wondering who had it." It's tempting to say that Dick Cheney never had a heart in the first place—but that would be a cliché. Of course, the real shock is that this man was once Vice President of the United States. The fact that he spent eight years only "a heartbeat away" from the presidency is enough to stop the heart of anyone who longs for American leaders who represent basic American values.

* * *

Marco Rubio (R-FL) once equated liberals with "freeloaders." Hey Marco … getting paid $174,000 per year from taxpayer's money to insult Americans like me makes you the freeloader.

* * *

Maine's Republican Governor Paul LePage tried to roll back child labor laws. Yet another "family values" Republican at work.

* * *

New Jersey's Republican Governor Chris Christie vetoed a bill that would have banned a specific form of pig torture used in meat manufacturing. Seriously. He's courting the pro-pig-torture vote.

* * *

Some people think that Chris Christie is a moderate or even a secret liberal because he doesn't seem as extreme as most right-wingers or because he worked with President Obama during Hurricane Sandy when his state was literally under water. Please keep in mind that Christie bashes unions, has cut education and social services, vetoed early voting and marriage equality, campaigned for Mitt Romney, and used his office to exact political revenge on people who crossed him. Republican is as Republican does.

* * *

Representative Matt Salmon (R-AZ) criticized President Obama in 2014 that he would "give my right arm to have him [Bill Clinton] back right now." But back in 1997, Salmon voted to impeach Bill Clinton. I guess he's hoping our memories only go back to about 1998.

* * *

Senator Tom Coburn (R-OK) blocked a bipartisan bill to help prevent military veteran suicides. That was his last major act before retiring from the Senate in 2015. Nice job leaving office on a positive note.

* * *

This exchange between then Senator John Kerry (D-MA) and Senator Ron Johnson (R-WI) at Kerry's Secretary of State hearing sums up Republican hypocrisy on the subject of Benghazi:

Kerry: "Were you at the briefing?"

Johnson: "No."

Kerry: "Well, there was a briefing ... those of us who went to it."

If Republicans can't even be bothered to do their jobs and show up for official briefings on Benghazi, then they aren't entitled to make up their own fantasy version of events.

* * *

I just got a Romney robocall that told me seven lies in less than a minute. Now I know how President Obama felt during the debates.

* * *

Mitt Romney didn't mention the war in Afghanistan during his convention speech and didn't mention veterans during the foreign policy debate. But Republicans threw a hissy-fit because President Obama said "acts of terror" instead of "terrorism" about the Benghazi attack. That deserves a special certificate of advance hypocrisy.

* * *

Michael Wolf, a Kansas Tea Party Republican running for the Senate, compared President Obama to Hitler and other dictators. Wolf used his family connections to gain notoriety leading up to his Senate campaign. *He's President Obama's cousin.* I'll bet those Hitler comparisons make for a fun family reunion.

* * *

Republican Debbie Dunnegan, the Jefferson County Missouri Recorder of Deeds, called President Obama a "domestic enemy" and encouraged members of the military to remove him from office. Later, she said that she "meant no ill intent" toward the president with her "innocent" statement. What do you think she says when she actually means "ill intent" toward someone?

* * *

Mitt Romney said that President Obama won the election because he promised voters, "extraordinary gifts." Yes, affordable access to health insurance, fair tax rates, reproductive choice, protection from Wall Street abuses, smart foreign policies, and getting us out of unnecessary wars are "extraordinary gifts" for the American people. Thanks, Obama!

* * *

Representative Jack Kingston (R-GA) used an Obama impersonator's voice in an ad for his Senate campaign without revealing that the voice was fake. Republicans like campaigning against a made-up Obama far more than the real one.

* * *

Indiana Governor Mike Pence said that cutting food stamps would "ennoble" poor people. In reality, cutting food stamps will "enhunger" poor people.

* * *

Representative Phil Gingrey (R-GA) complained that his congressional salary wasn't as much as a lobbyist's income: "I'm stuck here making $172,000 a year." Gingrey's new worth is approximately $3 million, and his congressional salary is more than three times the median American family income. Georgia voters should get Greedy Gingrey unstuck from his job in Congress and cut his taxpayer-funded salary to $0.

* * *

Back in 2010, Republicans insisted that members of Congress give up their previous health insurance plans and enroll in Obamacare exchange policies. They thought Democrats would recoil in horror and abandon health care reform, but Democrats embraced the idea and passed the Affordable Care Act. When the Affordable Care Act was implemented in 2014, Representative Louie Gohmert (R-TX) chose to go without health insurance and pay the fine rather than get a policy through Obamacare. Then he blatantly lied about the reasons for his idiotic decision. Gohmert loves playing the victim, even though he could get a perfectly fine insurance policy through the Obamacare exchanges. This level of delusion is pathetic. When he gets sick and doesn't go to a doctor because he has no insurance, that'll really show Obama who's boss. Nose. Spite. Face.

* * *

While arguing against Obamacare, Utah Republican state legislator Mike Kennedy claimed that access to health care can be "damaging and dangerous." Kennedy is a medical doctor. It's more accurate to say that access to Mike Kennedy can be "damaging and dangerous."

* * *

Representative Darrell Issa has lied about his military career, been arrested for car theft and weapons charges, and been accused of arson at this own company. This is the guy Republicans put in charge of investigating Benghazi. Seriously, why is this person allowed to investigate anyone, let alone the President of the United States?

* * *

Louisiana Governor Bobby Jindal has been lying about Obamacare, claiming the law is bad for disabled people. Health care experts say he's completely wrong, and Jindal himself accepted $82 million in Obamacare funding that specifically helps disabled people. Guess what? A Republican is lying about Obamacare again. And in other news, water is wet. If Obamacare is as bad as Republicans claim it is, then why do they need to lie about it so much?

* * *

Louisiana Republican Governor Bobby Jindal signed into law a bill called "The Unsafe Abortion Act," a law that, ironically, makes getting an abortion far more dangerous. Welcome to Republicanland.

* * *

In 2013, Republicans in Kansas passed a law allowing teachers to carry guns in schools. The state's schools promptly lost their insurance coverage. Risk-management professionals know the truth that gun fanatics keep trying to hide: Guns in the hands of untrained civilians make an environment more dangerous.

* * *

After the Newtown shooting, Senator Lamar Alexander (R-TN) said, "You know, I think video games is a bigger problem than guns, because video games affect people." Perhaps Senator Alexander should ask the parents of the Sandy Hook shooting victims if guns affect people.

* * *

The Republican-led Louisiana House voted to reaffirm a law that outlaws consensual oral and anal sex—a law ruled unconstitutional more than a decade ago. That's what Republicans do best: Micromanage our private lives and violate the Constitution.

* * *

Representative Louie Gohmert (R-TX) has flirted with "birtherism," railed against "terror babies," doesn't believe Americans should elect their own Senators, and thinks members of Congress should come to work armed (among other extreme views). Gohmert was the only member of Congress to vote against removing the outdated term "lunatic" from federal laws. Hits a little too close to home, eh Louie?

* * *

Senator Marco Rubio (R-FL) was featured on the cover of *Time* with the caption, "The Republican Savior." Rubio co-sponsored a bill to allow employers to deny birth control insurance coverage to employees, voted against renewing the Violence Against Women Act, recorded robocalls for an anti-gay group, is a climate-change denier, politicized the debt-ceiling vote, signed the destructive Grover Norquist tax pledge, backed Florida Republicans' vote-rigging purge scheme, was fined for breaking campaign laws, was implicated in a political credit card scandal, has had huge personal debt problems, and lied about his family history. The supposed Republican "savior" is no different from the same old crop of "Republican "sinners."

* * *

Who did Congressional Republicans turn to for expertise on the computer-related aspects of Obamacare? John McAfee, admitted drug abuser, sexual braggart, accused murderer, and all-around crazy person. That's really the best expert Republicans could find? John McAfee invented the computer security software that bears his name. Then he lost his mind. But he opposes Obamacare, so Republicans in Congress trotted him out as an "expert" and pretended he's not insane. The bottom line is that if Charles Manson had something bad to say about Obama, then he'd be on Fox News live from his prison cell ten times a day.

* * *

At a town hall meeting, Senator John McCain (R-AZ) got yelled at by an angry, misinformed, old man. Did it sting to look in the mirror, Senator McCain?

* * *

Senator Mitch McConnell (R-KY) made a wisecrack about Hillary Clinton's age. *McConnell is more than five years older than Clinton.*

* * *

Senator Mitch McConnell (R-KY) once actually filibustered his own bill in the Senate. I guess his mother never told him that if he does that too often, he could go blind.

* * *

Senator Mitch McConnell (R-KY) made the absurd claim that Kentucky's state Obamacare exchange is just a website and not really Obamacare. McConnell has given up even trying to hide his Obamacare lies.

* * *

Senator Mitch McConnell (R-KY) claimed that Obamacare abolished the student loan program. In fact, a law passed along with Obamacare eliminated private banks as unnecessary middlemen for federal student loans, saving taxpayers billions of dollars in wasteful kickbacks to McConnell's big bank buddies.

* * *

North Carolina Republican Governor Pat McCrory promised during his campaign for office that he wouldn't enact any new abortion restrictions. Within a year of assuming office, he signed new abortion restrictions into law.

* * *

Georgia Republican legislators used taxpayer money to fund a presentation about how President Obama uses mind-control techniques to take away our freedoms and give sovereignty of the United States over to a United Nations dictatorship. So, seriously, if Georgia Republicans want to secede from the union, then please proceed.

* * *

Sometimes we have to wonder what planet Republicans live on. Case in point: Reince Priebus, their party chair said that 2012 voters thought Romney would make a better president than Obama. His exact words were that Romney "won on the question of, 'Who do you actually think would make a better president?'" Actually, no. Meanwhile, back on planet Earth, President Obama won the 2012 election by more than 5 million votes. I wonder how the Romney administration is doing on Planet Priebus?

* * *

North Carolina Republican State Senator Bob Rucho tweeted that Obamacare is worse than "Nazis, Soviets, and terrorists combined." Meanwhile, Nazis, Soviets, and terrorists were probably thinking, "That's a load of crap!"

* * *

In 2013, Former Speaker of the House Newt Gingrich said that future historians would look back at yet another meaningless House of Representatives vote to repeal the Affordable Care Act's individual mandate as the "the beginning of the end for Obamacare." Of course, Obamacare has been going strong ever since. Future historians will look back on Newt Gingrich and ask, "Who?"

* * *

During the 2014 Ebola not-a-crisis, Nick Muzin, the deputy chief of staff for Senator and presidential candidate Ted Cruz (R-TX), tweeted that "Before Obamacare, there had never been a confirmed case of Ebola in the U.S." Of course, before Obamacare, Ted Cruz was a little-known Texas state functionary. Now he's one of the biggest jerks in Congress, despised by Democrats and Republicans alike. Coincidence?

* * *

Senator and presidential candidate Rand Paul (R-KY) released a "secret" tape of Hillary Clinton talking with Jeb Bush. Of course, the tape was a fake. Paul thinks running for President of the United States is like running for president of the eighth grade.

* * *

Rand Paul (R-KY) claims that it's perfectly consistent for him to be a Libertarian and a Christian, which proves he doesn't understand Libertarianism or Christianity.

* * *

In 2013, after Republicans had taken nearly 50 votes trying to overturn Obamacare, Rand Paul (R-KY) said, "We haven't had a big debate on Obamacare." Seriously? Is this guy even paying attention?

* * *

Rand Paul (R-KY) has proposed lifting the ban on guns in post offices. Does he really not know where the term "going postal" comes from?

* * *

Rand Paul (R-KY) doesn't believe in "gay rights." According to Paul, "I don't think I've ever used the word 'gay rights,' because I don't really believe in rights based on your behavior." Does Paul believe that his own heterosexuality is just a "behavior" and not a part of his identity? I doubt it. And I guess Paul doesn't believe in any aspect of the First Amendment because it protects several different types of "behaviors": religion, speech, assembly, etc.

* * *

After the Obama administration negotiated the release of POW Beau Bergdahl, Rand Paul (R-KY) joked about trading Democrats to the Taliban. Paul skipped the classified briefing about the Bergdahl case.

* * *

Senator Rand Paul got caught plagiarizing from Wikipedia in 2013. Seriously? Plagiarizing from Wikipedia? Dude, you can like totally flunk 9th-grade English for that. Paul shows how low the standards are for being a United States Senator from the Republican Party. No wonder they often threaten to get rid of the Department of Education. How did Paul react to the people who caught him plagiarizing? He threatened gun violence: "… if dueling were legal in Kentucky, you know, it'd be a dueling challenge." Yeah, let's elect Rand Paul to the office of President. What could possibly go wrong?

* * *

Douglas MacKinnon, a former advisor to Republican President Ronald Reagan, called for southern states to secede from the union over opposition to gay rights and name their new nation "Reagan." This is a serious proposal frroomm a perhioo dkfma kkkga … Sorry about the typos, but it's hard to type during fits of laughter.

* * *

At a recent political event, Republican Party officials sold buttons that read, "KFC Hillary Special: 2 Fat Thighs, 2 Small Breasts, Left Wing." The party of Lincoln has devolved into the party of 12-year-old boys.

* * *

Imagine a government program that saves you and your family money and improves your health insurance coverage. Now imagine taking advantage of that government program but not wanting other people to have the same opportunity. Now you're thinking like a Republican. Case in point: Fergus Cullen, the former chair of the New Hampshire Republican Party is getting better insurance coverage for his family and saving big money thanks to Obamacare. Guess what? He still doesn't approve of Obamacare, proving once again that no matter what the facts might be, if a policy is connected with President Obama, Republicans will hate it.

* * *

Senator Bob Portman (R-OH) dropped his opposition to marriage equality because his own son came out to him. Wouldn't it be great if more Republican politicians' kids cam out to them? Even better, wouldn't it be great if more Republican politicians just automatically saw all people as equal human beings?

* * *

The bigoted *Duck Dynasty* television star, Phil Robertson, spoke at the Republican Leadership Conference. "I guess the GOP may be more desperate than I thought to call somebody like me," Robertson said at the event on May 29, 2014, the day that the Republican Party officially became a joke.

* * *

In 2013, Representative Paul Ryan said, "I'm focused on poverty these days." Just days earlier, Ryan voted against the Farm Bill because it didn't cut Food Stamps enough for his taste. Yes, Ryan is focused on poverty. He's focused on making it worse.

* * *

Republicans in South Carolina elected Mark Sanford to Congress. Yes, that Mark Sanford. The one who, when he was governor of the state, disappeared from his family on Father's Day, claimed he was hiking the Appalachian Trail while he was actually shacking up with his mistress in Argentina at taxpayers' expense, got booted out of the house by his wife, violated court-ordered child support, and then trespassed in her home. Republicans would vote for the devil himself if he had an "R" beside his name.

* * *

Representative Steve King (R-IW) bragged about supporting the Violence Against Women Act. Earlier that same day, he had actually voted against the Violence Against Women Act.

* * *

In 2013, Republicans in the House of Representatives voted to delay the Obamacare employer mandate. In 2014, Republicans in the House of Representatives voted to sue President Obama because he delayed the Obamacare employer mandate.

* * *

Representative Mo Brooks (R-AL) claimed that Democrats and President Obama are waging a "war on whites" by addressing issues such as immigration reform. Brooks himself seems to be waging a war on sanity and common sense.

* * *

Former Florida Governor and Republican Presidential candidate Jeb Bush claims that he wants to be the "technology president." But he released e-mails from his time as governor, many of which contained personal information from thousands of private citizens, and he hired a technology director with a history of publishing racist, sexist, and homophobic statements in social media. Let's hope Bush doesn't get the chance to do for America what he has done for technology.

* * *

Senator Tom Cotton (R-AR) is worried that Iran controls Tehran, *that nation's own capital city.* Meanwhile, the rest of us are worried that Cotton and his fellow Republicans control our capital city, Washington, DC.

* * *

Senator Tom Cotton (R-AR) says that discriminating against gay people in the United States isn't such a big problem because Iran executes gay people. Somebody should explain to Cotton that discrimination and execution aren't the only options for how we should treat our fellow citizens. Republicans enjoy pointing out that Muslims are harder on gay people than Republicans are. These Republicans are ignoring a very important fact. Muslims in general don't want to hang gay people. Only the right-wing Muslims do. Moderate and liberal Muslims around the world have no more problem with gay people than moderate and liberal Christians do. If right-wingers like Tom Cotton had been born Muslim, they'd be the ones calling for the execution of gay people.

* * *

Republican Senator and presidential candidate Ted Cruz's campaign logo resembles a burning American flag, as well as the Cuban flag. It's not surprising that Cruz is incompetent at graphic design considering he has proven to be one of the most incompetent government workers in American history.

* * *

Ted Cruz has only ever earned one "true" rating from the nonpartisan fact checking service PoltiFact.com. His true statement was about toilets.

* * *

Ted Cruz picked the fifth anniversary of the Affordable Care Act to announce his presidential campaign—a campaign that includes a promise to repeal the Affordable Care Act, which would result in taking health insurance away from millions of Americans. One day after vowing to repeal "every word" of the Affordable Care Act, Cruz announced that he would be getting his own health insurance through the Affordable Care Act exchanges. Cruz sees no irony in that blatant hypocrisy.

* * *

Republican Florida Governor Rick Scott banned state officials from using the terms "climate change" and "global warming," as if that would make the issue go away, even as climate change has already begun to have a negative effect on his own state's environment. That's an excellent strategy! Let's ban the word "Republican" and see if they'll go away.

* * *

State Senator Thomas Corbin (R-SC) said that God made women from Adam's rib, which Corbin called "a lesser cut of meat." Corbin seems to have forgotten Genesis 2:7, which tells us that God made men like him from dirt.

* * *

Mitt Romney criticized Hillary Clinton for using a personal e-mail address. Romney neglected to mention that he spent nearly $100,000 in taxpayer money to hide his computer and e-mail records, even going so far as having computers destroyed, when he left office as governor of Massachusetts.

* * *

Even after leaving Congress, Republican Michele Bachmann can't stop embarrassing herself. She posted this message on her Facebook page, comparing President Obama to the mentally ill German pilot who purposely crashed his jet, killing everyone on board: "With his Iran deal, Barack Obama is for the 300 million souls of the United States what Andreas Lubitz was for the 150 souls on the German Wings flight—a deranged pilot flying his entire nation into the rocks. After the fact, among the smoldering remains of American cities, the shocked survivors will ask, why did he do it?" Bachmann's own mental health remains in question. Experts agree that the Iran deal gives us the best chance to avoid a horrible war. Anyone who believes that the president's peace efforts are in any way similar to mass murder should be considered a danger to everyone around her.

* * *

Rand Paul (R-KY) misspelled "education" on the education section of his presidential website, apparently trying to appeal to the anti-spelling base of the Republican Party. Yes, Rand Paul would make a wnoderflu persidnet.

* * *

Marco Rubio said he would attend a gay wedding even though he "disagrees" with the "choices" of gay people. Rubio opposes marriage equality, employment and immigration protections for LGBT people, and LGBT adoption. He believes businesses should be allowed to discriminate by not serving LGBT people, and he opposed the repeal of the military's Don't Ask Don't Tell policy. Scott Walker said he wouldn't attend a gay wedding, but he did once attend the gay reception after the gay wedding. Three words come to mind: freeloader, crasher, and homophobe. I hate to break it to you fellas, but no one will be inviting you to any gay weddings any time soon.

* * *

Republican New Jersey Governor Chris Christie's family income is $700,000 a year, more than 13 times the median income for American families, but he claims that he's "not wealthy by current standards." How much more wealthy than average Americans does Christie need to consider himself wealthy? The bottom line is that Christie is yet another out-of-touch Republican who would make a terrible president.

* * *

Republican Wisconsin Governor Scott Walker celebrated Earth Day 2015 by sending layoff notices to 57 employees of the Wisconsin Department of Natural Resources. This isn't satire.

* * *

George W. Bush recently criticized Obama's foreign policy. That's not an *Onion* headline. Let me get this straight … The guy who allowed 9-11 to happen on his watch and then started and mismanaged two dumb wars in Iraq and Afghanistan has the nerve to criticize the guy who's working for a nuclear disarmament deal with Iran? Hell, no!

* * *

Here's what Mike Huckabee tweeted after the Supreme Court's marriage equality ruling: "My thoughts on the SCOTUS ruling that determined that same sex marriage is okay: 'Jesus wept.'" If Jesus himself had a Twitter account, I can imagine him sending out this tweet to Huckabee: "Read your New Testament, Hucklebigot. I never said anything against being gay. So shut your stoopid pie hole before I give you something to weep about." Yes, Jesus gets to use more than 140 characters. He's Jesus, after all.

* * *

Ted Cruz is a professional hypocrite. Case in point: In 2013, he voted against federal funding for Hurricane Sandy, calling such disaster funding "pork." In 2015, he begged for federal funding during flooding in his home state of Texas. "Cruz" is a Cuban-Canadian word meaning, "jerk."

* * *

Ted Cruz was upset because people he doesn't like got marriage rights and health insurance. Here's how you can tell that June 25 and 26, 2015 (when the Supreme Court upheld Obamacare and struck down marriage equality bans) were great days for America: Cruz said, "Today is some of the darkest 24 hours in our nation's history." Awww ... Teddy haz a sad.

* * *

State Representative Randy Boehning (R-ND) voted against gay rights, but then got caught posting x-rated photos of himself on a gay dating website. Another anti-gay Republican got caught in a gay sex scandal—how shockingly not shocking.

* * *

Representative Michael Burgress (R-TX), who is an OB/GYN physician, says he's against abortion because he has seen male fetuses masturbate in the womb. Oh my God, even Republican *doctors* are a whacky as the rest of them! Rand Paul's and Ben Carson's jibberish in their presidential campaigns isn't helping to disabuse that notion.

* * *

Rand Paul (R-KY) claims that the Baltimore civil unrest is a result of "the breakdown in family structure, the lack of fathers." Paul's own son has been arrested on alcohol-related charges three times. But thanks for the lecture on fatherhood, Randy.

* * *

Ben Carson said that he could ignore Supreme Court rulings about marriage equality of he were elected president. Imagine the outrage from Republicans if President Obama said that he could ignore the Supreme Court.

* * *

Jeb Bush said he would have invaded Iraq in 2003, just as his brother George did, even knowing what we now know about that tragic mistake. One day later, Jeb changed his tune: "I don't know what that decision would have been. That's a hypothetical." Jeb Bush on Iraq: Wrong on Monday, flip-flopper on Tuesday. What will Wednesday bring?

* * *

Representative Marsha Blackburn recently claimed that Christians in the U.S. are being persecuted. When asked to give a specific example of even one case in which Christians in the United States were being persecuted, she couldn't. Blackburn failed a basic critical thinking task: providing specific examples to support general claims. The reason she failed? Because Christians aren't actually being persecuted in the United States ... obviously.

* * *

Ted Cruz made an insulting joke about Vice President Joe Biden just days after Biden's son died of brain cancer. Every day, Ted Cruz gives us more evidence that the only way he should ever enter the White House is when he pays for a tour.

* * *

Long after he lost the presidential election, Mitt Romney proved again that he has absolutely no self-awareness. Romney criticized Hillary Clinton after one of her first big campaign speeches in June 2015 when he made this bizarre comment: "She's smiling with her mouth, but her eyes are saying, 'Where's my latte?'" Romney was a famously wooden campaigner who frequently had trouble connecting with everyday voters. When Romney smiles, his eyes are saying, "My paid handlers told me to smile now."

* * *

Here's what Rand Paul said about the Charleston shooting: "There's something terribly wrong, but it isn't going to be fixed by your government." Translations: Want to make sure government is as useless as possible, no matter how serious the situation? Vote for Rand Paul.

* * *

After the Supreme Court again upheld Obamacare in the summer of 2015, Senator John Cornyn (R-TX) said that Republicans will "continue to fight tooth and nail" to repeal the Affordable Care Act. Lucky for Cornyn,

Obamacare covers missing teeth and nails.

* * *

Many Republicans were happy to accept donations from the Council of Concerned Citizens, the Charleston shooter's favorite racist hate group, and they only said they would return the money after the shooting. Here's a list of prominent Republicans who accepted donations from the Council of Concerned Citizens: George W. Bush, Dick Cheney, Mitt Romney, Ted Cruz, Rand Paul,, Steve King, Tom Cotton, Jeff Flake, Michele Bachman, Sharon Angle, Ken Buck, Rob Portman, Ron Johnson, Louie Gohmert, Dean Heller, Linda McMahon, George Allen, Richard Murdock, Todd Akin, Pete Koekstra, Allen West, Mia Love, Joni Ernst, Thom Tillis, Nen Sasse, Tom Emmer, Mark Sanford, and Paul Broun. Here are some important questions: Why did Republicans think it was okay to accept money from a racist group before the shooting? How many other Republicans have taken donations from other racist hate groups? Why do racist hate groups support Republicans?

* * *

Rand Paul met with racist deadbeat criminal Cliven Bundy while Paul was running for president. Why would Rand Paul meet privately Cliven Bundy? What do they have in common? A lot, if you ask the racist deadbeat criminal. After the meeting, Bundy said, "In general, I think we're in tune with each other."

* * *

President Obama didn't say the word "God" in his 2015 July Fourth address to the nation, so, naturally, right-wingers lost their minds. One lunatic even tweeted that the president is "an atheist with Muslim tendencies." And this was mere days after the president sang "Amazing Grace" while delivering the eulogies for the Charleston shooting victims. Once again, childish Republicans forgot the Constitution and threw a hissy fit. "... no religious test shall ever be required as a qualification to any office or public trust under the United States." Article VI, paragraph 3, United States Constitution Should we tell these right-wingnuts that the Constitution doesn't say the word "God"? I'm not sure their fragile minds could take that fact.

* * *

Throughout history, great philosophers have asked, "What is the cost of ignorance?" Now we know the answer. The *Sarah Palin Channel* is available to online subscribers for $9.95 per month.

* * *

Donald Trump actually said, "I will win the Latino vote." Ha, ha, ha, ha, ha, ha, ha, ha, ha, ha, ha, ha, ha, ha, ha, ha, ha, ha, ha, ha, ha, ha, ha, ha, ha, ha, ha, ha, ha, ha, ha, ha, ha, ha, ha, ha, ha, ha, ha, ha, ha, ha, ha, ha, ha, ha, ha, ha, ha, ha, ha, ha, ha, ha, ha, ha, ha, ha, ha, ha, ha, ha, ha, ha, ha, ha. No.

* * *

Americans are working harder than ever, but Jeb Bush, a man born with a silver foot in his mouth, who never had to work a day in his life, actually said that everyone else "needs to work more." If you're reading this, then Jeb Bush thinks you're not working enough.

* * *

Republicans are outraged that Donald Trump attacked John McCain's war record. But they had no problem attacking John Kerry's war record in 2004. Does "Swift Boating" ring a bell? Trump got his nasty attack strategy straight from the Republican playbook.

* * *

A PAC supporting Senator Ron Johnson (R-WI) ran an ad with a fake photoshopped picture of President Obama shaking hands with the Iranian president to stoke fear about the Iranian nuclear deal. Johnson's campaign denied they had photoshopped it, and then they quietly removed it from their ad with no comment. It would be nice if Republicans would stop attacking the fake Obama so much and try working with the real Obama instead.

* * *

Mike Huckabee compared the Iranian nuclear deal with the Holocaust. It wasn't easy, but we finally found something nice to say about Mike Huckabee: At least he's not a Holocaust denier.

* * *

Representative Steve King (R-IA) said that marriage equality will lead to people marrying their lawnmowers. Marrying lawnmowers? WTF!? Seriously, what kind of mind comes up with the idea of marrying a lawnmower?

* * *

"Oh my gosh, we had no idea Donald Trump was sexist!" said no reasonable person ever.

* * *

The smartest nuclear scientists in America approve of Obama's Iran nuclear deal. So, of course, Republicans must oppose it. Republicans have never been very good at science.

* * *

Ben Carson said that he wants to defund Planned Parenthood because the organization facilitates donation of aborted fetal tissue for medical research. But Carson himself used aborted fetal tissue in his own medical research. Then he defended his obvious hypocrisy by claiming that Planned Parenthood founder Margaret Sanger supported eugenics against Black people, a claim that has been thoroughly debunked by nonpartisan fact-checkers. Why are Republican doctors as fact-impaired as Republican high school dropouts?

* * *

Linguistic analysis of Donald Trump's speeches shows that he speaks to America at a fourth-grade level. Now we know why he's leading the Republican field: Trump talks down to America, which means he talks directly to the Republican base.

* * *

For Republicans, e-mail is the new birth certificate. They hypocritically attack Hillary Clinton for doing the same things many other Republicans did. Scott Walker, Marco Rubio, Christ Christie, Rick Perry, and Bobby Jindal all used private e-mail for official government business. In addition, Colin Powell and the staff of Condoleezza Rice also used private e-mail accounts as Secretary of State. George W. Bush used an RNC e-mail account and destroyed those messages. Mitt Romney even destroyed government computers at the end of his term as Massachusetts governor. Clearly, Republicans have a double standard when it comes to Hillary Clinton's e-mail.

* * *

All of the Republican candidates for president are against abortion. All but one are men who can never be pregnant.

* * *

You can tell how wonderful the next Republican presidency would be based on how often the current Republican candidates brag about how great things were under the last Republican president, George "Where's Waldo" Bush. Here's a hint: never.

* * *

Jeb Bush tried to explain away his use of the derogatory term "anchor baby" by claiming that he was talking about Asians, not Hispanics. How exactly does that make it better?

* * *

I support building Trump's wall … as long as it's soundproof and he's on the other side.

* * *

Dear World: Donald Trump represents only the craziest third of our craziest political party and 99% of our sensationalism-obsessed media. Please don't blame the rest of us for him. Sincerely, The Reasonable American Majority.

* * *

Trump is a complete con artist. Trump swindled millions of dollars from people who enrolled in his fake "Trump University." The court found Trump liable for operating a for-profit school without the required license, and Trump is being sued by victims who spent thousands of dollars only to discover that the "university" was a sham. Trump's latest scam is running for president.

* * *

The next time a Republican claims that President Obama is wrong about something, please remind him or her that the leaders of the Republican Party have been wrong about almost everything. We only need to look into the recent past to see how wrong Republicans can be. For example, back in 2012, Republican Presidential candidate Newt Gingrich published a book about how Republicans were the only ones who could possibly get gas down to $2.50 per gallon. Now it's well under $2 per gallon, and Obama is still president. Republicans: wrong then, wrong now, always wrong.

* * *

Republicans claim Obama hates Christianity. The top Christian in the world disagrees. The Pope supports Obama's Iran nuclear agreement.

* * *

Jeb Bush said in a Republican debate that his brother kept America safe. Did he mean Neil or Marvin? Because it sure as hell wasn't George!

* * *

Jeb Bush admitted smoking pot, perhaps as a ploy to win over Trump supporters because you'd have to be high to vote for either one of them.

* * *

The three most right-wing Supreme Court justices (Scalia, Thomas, and Alito) all skipped the Pope's address to Congress. All three are Catholic. What do you suppose they were afraid of?

* * *

Donald Trump: Born on third base. Brags that he hit a triple.

* * *

Remember how Ted Cruz led the government shutdown? What if an inexperienced middle-manager tried to shut down your workplace because he didn't like a few company policies? Would you want him to get promoted to company president? Or would you want that jerk fired?

* * *

Marco Rubio said, "You can't live on $11 an hour." But Rubio opposes raising the $7.25 federal minimum wage. Rubio has some problems with the minimum wage. And math. And reality.

* * *

Representative Mo Brooks (R-AL) was already talking about impeaching Hillary Clinton more than a year before the damned election! Republicans seem intent on inventing a time machine to go back and blame Obama for Bush's screw-ups and to go into the future to impeach Hillary because e-mail and Benghazi and flapjacks and ponies and whatever the hell they're ranting about this time.

* * *

Even the Republicans who try to pass themselves off as a sane alternative are just as bad as the rest. Ohio Republican Governor John Kasich, for example, used a fake Abraham Lincoln quote and lied about Lincoln's views on progressive taxation to support his own regressive tax policies. Kasich also signed a bill cutting funding for Planned Parenthood.

* * *

Donald Trump recently said that "wages are too high." He didn't whisper it at a secret, back-room meeting with other billionaires. He said it in a nationally televised presidential debate. He said it to everyone in America. He said it directly to all of us. Basically, he just told us that we're getting paid too much. And then he went on national television the following morning and said it again. Can you imagine the freak-out if a Democrat had said that American's "wages are too high"? Yet the leading Republican presidential candidate said those exact words in a nationally televised debate, and Republicans don't even notice.

* * *

Chris Christie (R NJ) recently vetoed two bills in New Jersey: One would keep guns away from people convicted of domestic violence, and the other would expand voting rights. But it's all okay because he also signed a bill outlawing sex with animals. Your Republican tax dollars at work, ladies and gentlemen.

* * *

In response to the fact that the San Bernardino murderers possessed bombs but used only guns, Marco Rubio said, "I don't hear anyone talking about bomb control." Does Rubio know that we already have bomb control? Does he know that bombs are illegal?

* * *

Today's Republican Party resembles a poorly run day care. Donald Trump is an angry toddler trying to convince confused infants to vote for him.

* * *

In the year 2050, somewhere in her secret bunker, an octogenarian Sarah Palin will still be waiting for Obama to come for her guns.

* * *

Seriously, congratulations to Sarah Palin on the birth of another abstinence-only grandchild.

* * *

People who shout, "Black Lives Matter!" at Donald Trump rallies get insulted, threatened, and dragged out. People who shout, "White power!" are welcome to stay. Draw your own conclusions.

* * *

Rand Paul said Obama should have resigned during the State of the Union address. Pretty big talk from a guy who can't seem to get above 2% in the Republican presidential polls.

* * *

Sarah Palin endorsed Donald Trump. Honey Boo Boo loves Chucky Doll.

* * *

Donald Trump opposes marriage equality. That's not a big surprise considering he opposes pretty much every other form of equality.

* * *

Iowa Republicans can be proud of Ted Cruz the same way they're proud of their other recent caucus winners, Presidents Huckabee and Santorum.

* * *

Chris Christie left the presidential race right after a terrible showing in the New Hampshire primary. Goodbye, Christie! You were almost as rude as Trump, almost as clueless as Carson, almost as dishonest as Fiorina, almost as much of a corporate toady as Bush, and almost as big a warmonger as Cruz. Now go home. But thanks for pointing out that Marco Rubio is an unqualified, scripted, robot!

* * *

"Trump" is British slang for "fart." Thank you, Great Britain!

* * *

Holy crap! Did you see that vicious Democratic attack add on television? Oh, man, they made those Republican candidates look like complete morons! Wait, what? That was another Republican debate? Oh, sweet baby Jesus, please save the United States of America from that unholy horde!

* * *

The most clueless people in the world are Republicans who are surprised that Trump is a sexist jerk who hates women. Haven't they been paying attention for the past forty years?

* * *

All the talk about the "size" of Republican presidential candidates reminds me of a 2009 headline: "Republicans Turned off by the Size of Obama's Package." As usual, Republicans don't measure up to the president.

* * *

Donald Trump recently said, "I know nothing about white supremacists." Here's a hint, Donald: White supremacists are evil racists who support your campaign. Any questions?

* * *

Donald Trump claimed that "Islam hates us," and that 27% of Muslims are terrorists. 100% of Donald Trump is an ignorant bigot.

* * *

Trump's Secret Service code name should be "Jellyfish" because a jellyfish's mouth also functions as its anus.

* * *

I recently heard Donald Trump described as the student who didn't do his homework or read the assignment, but who then tries to wing it when the teacher asks for discussion. That's a pretty apt description of Trump's rambling, off-topic, confused rants. But the analogy doesn't go far enough. I've seen hundreds if not thousands of unprepared students during my teaching career. Most of them have the minimal moral sense to be embarrassed about not being prepared for class. Trump, on the other hand, is proud of his ignorance. He thinks his lack of knowledge makes him superior to the students who actually completed the reading assignment and did the homework. Trump thinks other students don't even belong in the same classroom that he inhabits. He thinks they should just be silent or go away. In fact, Trump thinks he can fire the instructor and teach the class himself. Trump thinks everyone should pay tuition directly to him. His teaching method is fact-free lecturing with no discussion or assignments beyond his pontification. If the students have questions about what he's teaching, then Trump thinks he has the right to have them tossed out of the classroom or out of the country.

* * *

What just happened in North Carolina tells us everything we need to know about today's Republicans. When a state political party convenes a special session of the legislature to micromanage which bathroom people can use and to overturn a local law that protects LGBT people from discrimination, it's no longer a political party. It's a goon squad.

Brief Glimpses into the Age of Confusion

2012-2016

Sometimes I go on and on. If you've made it this far in this book, I don't need to tell you that fact twice. But there are only so many hours in my day considering I have a full time job beyond trying to scribble some common sense in response to often confusing current events. So the rest of this book consists of "short takes"—brief pieces that often appeared with images on my Facebook page named after my previous book, *Tales of a Real American Liberal*. Enjoy these little tales as you recover from digesting the longer essays that fill this book.

* * *

Ann Coulter said that Michelle Obama wanted to go home with Mitt Romney after their first presidential debate. Just because Ann Coulter would go home with a rich older guy who lies to her for two hours doesn't mean that Michelle Obama would.

* * *

Anyone who doesn't understand that the economy is a moral issue doesn't understand the words "economy" or "moral."

* * *

Sometimes Republicans git so made about all the forniers in Americia that wont learn Engilsh that thay cant spel strait!

* * *

For "Small Business Saturday in 2012, President Obama took his daughters to an independent bookstore where they bought 15 books to give as Christmas presents. Our president is a reader, a supporter of small businesses, a great father, and a role model for every American.

* * *

The Republican Party's worse nightmare is President Obama signing laws that help the American people.

This is why bipartisanship is difficult in America today: Democrats say, "2 + 2 = 4." Republicans say, "2 + 2 = 22." Centrists say, "Let's compromise and agree that 2 + 2 = 13."

* * *

Nearly half of Republicans believe ACORN stole the 2012 election for Obama, but ACORN was defunded by Republicans in Congress and went defunct in 2010. Raise your hand if you think the GOP has a reality problem.

* * *

President Obama is a life-long Christian who has attended the annual National Prayer Breakfast every year he has been in office, prays daily in private, and often prays in public with religious leaders and members of his administration. So, of course, Republicans accuse Obama of waging a "war on religion." Welcome to Republican Logic 101.

* * *

Jesus was an unmarried guy in his mid-thirties who hung out with twelve other men, never condemned homosexuality, and taught people to love each other. But, sure, Republicans are perfectly reasonable when they use his name to justify bigotry against gay people.

* * *

If guns don't kill people, then why are practice archery targets usually shaped like a series of concentric circles while practice gun targets are often shaped like a human being?

* * *

If we expect all Arab-Americans to condemn Arab extremists, then why don't we expect all Irish-Americans to condemn Bill O'Reilly and Sean Hannity?

* * *

The next time you get upset at the talking heads on Fox News who have sold their souls to lie about America every day, please remember that things could be much worse. You could be one of them.

Everything you need to know about the NRA in two quotes: The NRA surprised the world by making a sensible statement about jerks bringing guns into public places on May 30, 2014: "Using guns merely to draw attention to yourself in public not only defies common sense, it shows a lack of consideration and manners." Then they took it back less than a week later on June 3, 2014: "That was a mistake ... Our job is not to criticize the lawful behavior of fellow gun owners." So four days is the longest period that the NRA can maintain sanity.

* * *

Here's a reality check for people who complain that Obama hasn't done anything about the employment situation in this country: 1) The roots of the current job shortage lie in the financial collapse of the fall of 2008, when we had a Republican president. 2) There are three applicants for every open job in this country, so blaming unemployed people isn't exactly realistic. 3) Republicans at the federal and state levels have cut public sector jobs across the nation, contributing to unemployment. 4) Republicans have blocked Democratic job creation efforts in Congress for the past five years. Experts agree that these job creation bills would have added millions of jobs. 5) Corporations have completely recovered from the recession and are sitting on record profits but not hiring. 6) The social safety net helps people get by during tough times and does not encourage people to give up work. Most people collect benefits only for a very short time, but some need longer-term help. 7) Unemployment benefits lessen personal suffering and are usually spent immediately for basic needs, providing strong economic stimulus that can lead to new hiring. But, sure, blame Obama if that fits your political agenda.

* * *

Here's a suggestion for gun purchase background check: Question #1: Do you believe you need a gun to protect yourself from the government of the United States? If you answered "no," please proceed to question #2. If you answered "yes," please proceed to remedial history lessons and psychological counseling. No guns for people that confused.

* * *

In the real world, being frequently wrong and terrible at your job would get most people fired. But at Fox News, that's just a great résumé.

Massachusetts just expanded voting access. Red states make it harder for you to vote. Blue states make it easier for you to vote. Have you ever wondered why? Republicans want fewer people to vote because when more Americans go to the polls, Democrats are more likely to win. We are a center-left nation, despite what the corporate media might say. Republicans care more about winning than they do about Democracy.

* * *

In May 2014, President Obama walked from one meeting to another near the White House, greeting people along the way. To the amazement of Fox News addicts, people didn't throw tomatoes at him. One woman called out, "Oh my gosh, it's like the best day of my life!" while having her picture taken with the president. Despite years of dishonest right-wing attempts to demonize the president, most Americans like and respect him.

* * *

Open carry? Real men don't have to carry rifles just to go out to lunch or shop at a department store. Open-carry enthusiasts have many problems that guns won't help solve. People who cling that hard to their guns need therapy far more than they need weapons.

* * *

Tom Harkin, retiring Iowa Senator, said this about the state of education in America: "If you are a high-income, low-performing student, you have an 80% chance of going to college. But if you are a low-income, high-performing student, you have only a 20% chance of going to college. That's inexcusable." Thomas Jefferson envisioned free university education for the best American students. He would be appalled at how education has become a commodity in our country.

* * *

"Operation American Spring" was supposed to bring up to 30 million "patriots" to Washington, DC, to remove President Obama from office. When the event actually happened on May 16, 2014, Jackie Milton, one of the organizers, said, "It ain't no millions. And it ain't looking like there's going to be millions. Hundreds is more like it." They were short by about 30 million, give or take. In a time when loud, misinformed people get so much attention, the whimper that was "Operation American Spring" gives our nation hope for sanity.

* * *

Most Republicans couldn't find Benghazi on a map, let alone understand the issue.

* * *

Michael Sam isn't the first gay man to be drafted by a professional football team. He's the first *openly* man to be drafted by a professional football team. Oh my gosh, a football player just kissed another man! What's next? Players touching each other on the field? Anyone who was shocked by his televised kiss has clearly missed the obvious homoeroticism of football. I guess we need fainting couches for all the tough guys who can't handle Michael Sam kissing his boyfriend.

* * *

I tried to play a drinking game where I took a sip every time Fox News made up more crap about President Obama, but I ended up getting too drunk to finish this senten ...

* * *

May is "Teacher Appreciation Month"—or as Republican politicians like to call it, "Evil, Lazy, Overpaid, Godless, Secular, Communist, Socialist, Fascist, Union-Thug, Liberal-Agenda-Indoctrination Month."

* * *

The next Republican who suggests that African-Americans were better off under slavery than they are today should be forced to stare at those photos of slaves with deeply scarred backs from multiple whippings. It's hard to believe that we have to remind some conservatives that slavery was really, really bad. Seriously, it was. Being owned by someone else is worse than Obamacare or food stamps. So was the Holocaust. Please read a history book.

* * *

I enjoy those singing and dancing competition shows as much as anyone else, but what about the academic superstars out there? I'd be happy to watch shows like *Mathematics with the Stars*, *Chemistry Idol*, *America's Next Great Sociologist*, and *So you Think you Can Write an Essay?*

* * *

The men of Fox News were mindless propaganda puppets long before the network specialized in attractive women with blonde hair.

* * *

The Benghazi attack was a tragedy, but there is no scandal. The way that Republicans have been using the attack to try to score cheap political points is absolutely shameful. But they have a long history of shameful behavior. The Pat Tillman cover-up is a prime example—along with the lies that led us into two mismanaged wars. Republicans are counting on people forgetting about their terrible actions, but we remember.

* * *

Keystone Pipeline advocates claim that the pipeline will create thousands of jobs. What they don't tell us is that those jobs will require wearing hazmat suits.

* * *

No matter how often the Republican Party claims to be "rebranding," they're still represented by folks like Ted Cruz, Sarah Palin, Chris Christie, Cilven Bundy, Donald Sterling, Donald Trump, Pat Robertson, Ann Coulter, Sean Hannity, and Rush Limbaugh—which continues to make their party a dark and dangerous place.

* * *

Republicans have become the Bundy Party. Here are the options: A racist, freeloading, criminal gun-nut who disrespects the United States government (Cliven Bundy). A lazy, obnoxious TV character stuck in a previous decade who disrespects women (Al Bundy). A smooth-talking, murderous pretty boy who disrespects human life, especially women (Ted Bundy). Bonus Trivia Points: Serial killer Ted Bundy actually was active in Republican politics.

* * *

Renewable energy is booming, so Republicans are frightened. They are trying to use excessive taxes and fees to discourage solar energy and please their overlords in the fossil fuel industry. They'll have to pry my photovoltaic panels from my cold dead fingers.

* * *

Our friends at Fox News recently reported that solar power won't work in the United States as well as it does in Germany because Germany get more sunshine than the United States does. Seriously? Does that also explain why brain power doesn't work at Fox News?

* * *

The real "death panels" are the Republican politicians who refuse to expand Medicaid coverage in their states for political reasons. A recent study by Harvard University and the City University of New York estimates that as many as 17,000 people will die due to the lack of Medicaid expansion. The healthcare debate shouldn't be about politics—it should be about health. Thousands of Americans will die simply because Republicans are endangering people's lives to play partisan politics.

* * *

If you reject the authority of the American government just because you don't like President Obama or Democrats in Congress, then you aren't a "patriot." You're just a sore loser. I didn't like President Bush, but I didn't use that as an weak excuse to pretend the federal government had no authority. I didn't point guns at our country's law-enforcement officers as the right-wing fake patriots in Nevada did recently. I worked for change by legal and nonviolent means. I used my mind, my voice, my words, and my vote. I acted out of patriotism and love for my country, not a blind hatred of a president whose views didn't match my own.

* * *

Remember that time when the media speculated about the political impact of a male politician expecting a grandchild? No? Neither does anyone else. Get over it, sexist media. Hillary Clinton might run for president and be a grandmother at the same time. Let's congratulate her on both counts. Now let's focus on the issues.

* * *

217

The right-wing refrain, shouted in an endless loop: Obama loves terrorists! Obama's a foreigner! Obama's a Socialist! Obama's a baby killer! Obama's a Muslim! Obama's coming for our guns! Obama's a dictator! Obama hates white people! Obamacare's gonna kill us! Obama plays golf! Benghazi! Benghazi! Benghazi! All this irrational hatred for a nice guy who just wants us sell us some affordable health insurance.

* * *

Patri-idiot: (Noun) A person displaying boastful pride at having been born American but at the same time displaying profound ignorance about what makes America great. (See also Tea Party, Fox News, right-wing talk radio, NRA leadership, the Christian right, most elected Republicans, and half-term Alaska governors.)

* * *

The same people who would gladly wait in line 48 hours in terrible conditions to buy the latest video game console or cell phone and then brag about it for months scream "train wreck!" when they have to take one hour on the Obamacare website to get affordable health insurance.

* * *

News flash #1: The Obamacare website had some problems. News flash #2: It's still a good law that's helping millions of people. Republicans have done everything they can to sabotage Obamacare, but now they think we should repeal the law even though their sabotage didn't work. You can't desperately try to break something and then complain that it's not perfect. Here's a better strategy: Accept the reality that the law is a huge improvement and is helping people, and now do your job and fix the problems so that it works even better in the future.

* * *

Republicans are trying to get the nation to believe that the Obamacare website is the first piece of technology in history to ever have a problem. Of course, Republicans refused to fund Healthcare.gov adequately. In 36 states, they failed to oversee their own exchanges, overburdening Healthcare.gov. In nearly half the states, Republicans in charge declined the federally funded Medicaid expansion. Republicans warned people not to sign up for insurance under Obamacare even when they could save money and get better coverage. Republicans constantly lied about Obamacare for years, creating a completely distorted view of the law. They even made up dozens of Obamacare real people "horror stories" that were all discredited within days. As usual, Republicans seem to think Americans have no memory. They say that the government is too incompetent to set up the website. They say private industry would handle the technology much better. Sure. Like Apple Maps, for example. Good luck with that!

* * *

Republicans love to call the Obamacare website a "train wreck." When the Obamacare website allows the worst terrorist attack in American history, starts two misguided, mismanaged, and unfunded wars, presides over a devastating economic collapse, and shuts down the government … then it might approach Republican standards for a "train wreck."

* * *

Now that Obamacare has helped millions of Americans get affordable health insurance, it's important to look back and understand the biggest problem the law faced from the beginning: Republican sabotage. Imagine if Republicans had supported and improved the law instead of dishonestly obstructing it. Millions more Americans could have been helped. It's time to vote the sabotage party out of office.

* * *

Rush Limbaugh claimed that CBS has "declared war on the heartland of America" by hiring liberal comedian Stephen Colbert to replace David Letterman. Limbaugh knows as little about comedy as he does about America.

* * *

Fox News lies about climate change. And in other news, lemons are sour. A recent study showed that Fox News was inaccurate in its climate reporting 78% of the time in 2014, compared to CNN being wrong 30% of the time, and MSNBC wrong 8%. Fox actually improved to 72% wrong in 2013 after going 93% wrong in 2012. At this rate, they'll get the facts straight by the time their studios are flooded from melting polar ice caps.

* * *

Anyone whose first thought after hearing about a school stabbing is, "I guess the libtards who want gun control will try to ban knives now," is disqualified from contributing to reasonable discussions.

* * *

The next time you hear a Tea Party Republican misusing the motto, "Don't Tread On Me," remember that what they're really saying is more like, "I'm too lazy and lack the personal responsibility to understand and research the issues, so I'll just believe anything Fox News tells me."

* * *

If you claim that the President of the United States is a dictator, but you haven't disappeared yet, then you're just a con artist with a microphone.

* * *

The American people miss George W. Bush. We all misjudged Mitt Romney. Tax cuts for the wealthy create jobs for the middle class. Rand Paul is reasonable, knowledgeable, and courageous. The Republican Party is growing in popularity. That Marco Rubio fellow is full of new ideas. Global warming is still in dispute among climate scientists. Chris Christie isn't really a right-wing union hater. Jeb Bush is a perfectly viable presidential candidate. President Obama is a Socialist. Conservatives have been right about everything throughout American history. Happy April Fools' Day!

* * *

Have you noticed that many Republicans now say "Affordable Care Act" more often and "Obamacare" less often? That's because they know it's working.

* * *

That liberal Pope is really screwing with the Republican theory that liberals hate God.

* * *

Republicans love to talk about Jesus. Too bad they don't even know that Jesus was a liberal. How do we know that Jesus was a liberal? The evidence is in a little book called *The New Testament*.

* * *

Republicans claim to love the Constitution. Unfortunately, it's the kind of "love" we see most often from abusive spouses. Case in point: The Georgia State House just passed a clearly unconstitutional Obamacare "nullification" bill. In typical Republican fashion, they just wasted huge amounts of time, effort, and taxpayer money that should have been spent working to help their constituents, not violating the Constitution and trying to deny health insurance to their citizens. Instead of being ashamed of their actions, they celebrate them. It's time to vote out every Republican who disrespects the Constitution and the American people.

* * *

Republicans ranted that Putin got out of control because Obama is weak. Okay, then here's a suggestion: Obama should toss all those loud-mouthed Republicans in jail as a show of strength. By Republican logic, Putin will then magically stop misbehaving. Two birds, one stone. (Satire. Not meant to be taken literally—except maybe Hannity, Limbaugh, Coulter, and Palin. Put them in the same cell. They deserve each other.)

* * *

How a political party can lose credibility in one easy step: Republicans are so desperate to make President Obama look like a Socialist that they create dopey memes about him stealing toys from children.

* * *

Religion should be about loving our fellow human beings. But throughout history, a minority of people have tried to use their religion to justify discrimination, hate, violence, and even murder. Names like Hitler, bin Laden, KKK, and Westboro come to mind right away. They were wrong then. They're wrong now. There's a term for people who use their religion for hate instead of love. They're called false profits.

* * *

George Zimmerman recently got paid to sign autographs at a gun show. "Stand Your Ground" should be renamed "Kill the Witness."

* * *

Polls about Obamacare show a wide variety of opinions, depending on how the questions are worded. But the bottom line is that the public overwhelmingly supports the Democratic position (keep and improve the law) over the Republican position (repeal the law). You won't see that reported on Fox News.

* * *

Bill O'Reilly didn't like President Obama's humorous appearance on the comedy show *Between Two Ferns* and claimed Abraham Lincoln wouldn't have used humor to advance a policy. For a guy who supposedly wrote a book about Lincoln, O'Reilly doesn't know much about our 16th President. Lincoln's warm and gentle sense of humor is something the gruff and egotistical O'Reilly wouldn't understand. O'Reilly is about as funny as an airless whoopee cushion. The sad thing is that O'Reilly doesn't even realize that his show is broadcast on a comedy channel. Republicans are upset that President Obama has a sense of humor. Many were worried that the president's appearance on *Between Two Ferns* was somehow undignified. You know what actually is undignified? The thousands of lies Republicans have told about the president. Meanwhile, Obama's *Between Two Ferns* appearance helped get young people interested in the benefits of Obamacare. Given the choice between the president showing his humor and humanity in a very funny comedy sketch and constant Republican lies, I'll happily take the humor.

* * *

Mitt Romney and Paul Ryan, 2012 Republican presidential running-mates, met by accident at the Jacksonville, Florida, airport in the spring of 2014. Their sweet reunion should remind the nation just how fortunate we all are. It's far better that they met once by accident at an airport than on purpose at the White House every day.

* * *

Republicans held a "minority outreach" panel at the conservative CPAC conference, and almost no one showed up. The only surprise is that anyone is surprised that the party that treats anyone other than gun-owning white males like second-class citizens has largely given up on getting minority votes.

* * *

I like to leave my change in the vending machine because it's worth a few random coins to know that the next person who buys a candy bar will feel like a lottery winner for about five seconds.

* * *

For anyone who thinks Democrats and Republicans are equally bad, here's a question: Who's the liberal equivalent of Ted Nugent? Answer: No one. There is no liberal equivalent of Ted Nugent, but there are dozens of Republicans in the media and elected office who are just as bad a Nugent. Anyone paying attention knows that Republicans are far worse than Democrats.

* * *

If some people think that the government should support their bigotry against gay people, then they should go somewhere with that kind of government—because that's not what America is all about. I hear Uganda is nice this time of year, and they just made being gay a crime. Tickets for one-way flights are available now. Buh-bye!

* * *

The Republican Party has no credibility on the issue of Putin and Russia. All they do is criticize President Obama and ignore their own pattern of empty rhetoric and lack of alternative policies. This difficult situation requires exactly what the Obama administration is showing: real toughness instead of bluster, patience, diplomacy, sanctions, humanitarian aid to Ukraine, and international cooperation. The Republican Party has a history of showing none of those qualities during international crises.

* * *

Russia invades Ukraine, putting millions of innocent lives at risk. Naturally, good-hearted Republicans ask, "How can we twist this to make Obama look bad?" The Republican rush to somehow blame President Obama for the Russian invasion of Ukraine has been factless, clueless, and heartless. Trying to score cheap political point at the expense of reality and humanity has become a Republican reflex.

* * *

If Bush had created "Bushcare," Republicans would already have his face carved on Mount Rushmore. Obamacare even fixes the biggest problem with

Bush's major health-care reform, the "donut hole" coverage gap in Medicare Part D. But Republicans insist that Obamacare is a "train wreck." It's time to recognize that today's Republican Party is the real train wreck.

* * *

A photo proclaiming that a doctor in Texas won't "accept Obamacare" is making the rounds on right-wing Facebook pages and blogs lately. If it's real, it's pretty pathetic. Why would any patient trust a doctor who is so misinformed the he's not aware of the basic fact that Obamacare is a set of common-sense regulations, private insurance, and expanded Medicaid coverage—not some kind of separate program that he can accept or decline? Are basic reading skills not required for medical school? And all the people reposting the photo and adding supportive comments about how Obamacare will ruin the world are completely misinformed and confused.

* * *

The secret "liberal agenda" for education has finally been revealed—and it's shocking! Item #1: Help students learn to think for themselves. Item #2: Repeat Item #1.

* * *

We had a massive solar energy spill at our home today. Fortunately, we were prepared. A Republican friend tried to tell me that my newly installed solar panels took more energy to make and transport than they would ever produce. That's a favorite right-wing talking point against solar energy, and it's complete crap. PolitiFact.com rated that claim "pants on fire." Republicans probably think their flaming pants are a clean, renewable source of energy.

* * *

A Republican friend of mine said that it's wrong to call people in the Tea Party, "Teabaggers" because that's a disgusting homosexual activity. Doesn't he know that straight people can … well … you know … oh, never mind.

* * *

At age 33 in 1981, right-wing hero Ted Nugent wrote, performed, and released "Jail Bait," a song about his desire for having sex with a 13-year-old girl. Is this what Republicans mean when they talk about "family values"? It must be hard to play guitar with your knuckles dragging on the ground. Seriously, why would any Republican associate with Ted Nugent? More importantly, why would anyone associate with today's Republican Party?

* * *

Republicans are bringing back their disproven claim that the 2009 American Recovery and Reinvestment Act (the "stimulus") was a failure. But 92% of actual economists say that the stimulus worked. It created more than three million jobs and prevented another Great Depression. The only reason the stimulus didn't work even better is that Republicans fought to keep it too small, despite the fact that the nation needed extreme help after the economic collapse at the end of the Bush administration. (Let the cries of "Bush blaming" begin, but shouldn't we blame Bush for what he did? That's just basic accountability.)

* * *

Here's a simple lesson for Fox News addicted Republicans: Who's to blame for the Benghazi attack? Barack Obama? No. Hillary Clinton? No. Terrorists? Yes. Any questions?

* * *

The Republican love affair with Vladimir Putin is extremely creepy. You don't need a Ph.D. in psychology to understand what their obsession with a shirtless male authority figure says about them. Mitt Romney recently said, "Well, I think Putin has outperformed our president time and time again on the world stage." Romney and other Republicans love to praise Putin and disrespect our own President Obama every chance they get. That's quite a change from when they viewed any criticism of President George W. Bush as a form of treason.

* * *

Here's the scenario of the hit television show, *The Walking Dead:* No government. No taxes. No regulations. Lots of guns. Millions of brain-dead zombies. Well, it's a great idea for a TV show, but it shouldn't be a blueprint for Republican policy.

* * *

John Boehner and his Republican colleagues all stood to applaud President

Obama's call for equal pay for women at the 2014 State of the Union address. But several years ago, when there was an actual vote in Congress to support equal pay for women, 99% of Republicans voted against the Lily Ledbetter Fair Pay Act, while 99% of Democrats voted for it, and then President Obama signed it into law. Sure, everyone applauded the idea of equal pay, but it's clear which party actually supports equal pay for women and which party doesn't.

* * *

Republicans like to call President Obama "lawless." The president obviously hasn't broken any laws, so Republicans must be talking about the fact that they have failed to pass any laws that would help the American people for President Obama to sign.

* * *

The new report from the Congressional Budget Office contained lots of positive news about the Affordable Care Act: Millions of people are getting health insurance. Health insurance rates under Obamacare will be less expensive than originally projected. Millions of people won't have to hold onto jobs they don't want just to keep health insurance. Obamacare will significantly reduce the federal budget deficit. So what did Republicans do? Surprise! They returned to their same old lies: "job killer," "budget buster," "rate shocker." The exact opposite of the truth. How can anyone believe anything Republicans say these days? Even worse, the corporate media simply repeated the Republican lies instead of being bothered to understand the CBO report. So much for the mythical "liberal media."

* * *

Punxsutawney Phil woke up on Groundhog Day, heard about what Republicans have been doing since last February, and predicted at lest six more weeks of right-wing insanity. For Republicans, every day is like the movie *Groundhog Day*. They do nothing productive and then blame President Obama. Then the next day, they repeat the process. Unlike the Bill Murray character in the movie, however, Republicans never change.

* * *

Straight and gay couples got married at the 2014 Grammys, and some right-wingers called it "discrimination." Here's a news flash: When some people get rights that other people have always had, that's not discrimination. That's equality. That's progress. Get used to it.

* * *

Do you like the Republican position on limited regulations? If so, get used to news reports like the Gulf oil spill, the Texas fertilizer plant explosion, and the West Virginia chemical leak. Regulations can't prevent every disaster, but actively cutting regulations makes disasters far more likely.

* * *

Imagine the "Right-Wing Highway" where no one needs the horrors of government-imposed tyranny—you know, drivers' licenses, vehicle inspections, traffic laws, and lanes. Oh, yes, you'd also have to pay a toll every time you drive there. Sure, let's do that.

* * *

Apparently working hard to keep the world safe, a man recently shot himself in the butt while reaching for his wallet at Home Depot. He forgot that his gun was there, giving new meaning to the Urban Dictionary term, "Butthurt." Let's apply NRA logic to the "Butthurt Gunman": "The only thing that stops a bad butt with a gun is a good butt with a gun."

* * *

Fox News Alert: Last year, Barack Hussein Obama said it was 2014. This year, he says it's 2015. What outrageous claim will he make next year?

* * *

Remember in January 2014 when the ship carrying scientists doing Global Warming research got stuck in the Antarctic ice? A Republican friend of mine posted this on Facebook: "The EARTH MUFFINS got stuck in the ice that was TOO THICK for others to rescue them. Think they might reconsider their zealous faith in the Global Warming dogmatic religion now that they had to face some uncomfortable and inconvenient truths themselves? I kinda doubt it. Wait, was Al Gore there?" Yes, there's ice in the Antarctic, so the 97% of climate scientists who agree that evidence showing climate change is a fact must be wrong. One more time for the Fox News addicts: Cold weather in cold places does not disprove global climate change.

* * *

Ah, the joys of Facebook. Posts about important social and political issues often inspire yawning silence. But ask for the best method to keep squirrels away from bird feeders, and WWIII breaks out.

* * *

The Boy Scouts didn't actually vote to allow gay members. They just voted to stop pretending that they don't have any gay members. Sometimes progress is simply recognizing reality.

* * *

Rush Limbaugh once said, "Feminism was established so as to allow unattractive women access to the mainstream of society." Here's what Limbaugh really meant to say: "Radio was established so as to allow a man as unattractive as me access to the mainstream of society."

* * *

Republicans have sabotaged the United States Post Office. Here's why: 1) The Post Office is an example of a government agency that works more efficiently and more economically than private industry. 2) The Post Office is strongly unionized. UPS is only partially unionized, and FedEx has a long history of fighting unions. 3) The Post Office pays its rank-and-file employees more and its executives less than private delivery services. 4) The Post Office operated at a profit before Republicans passed "poison pill" laws in 2006 to destroy the agency's finances. 5) The Post Office has historically hired women and minorities since WWII when many private employers refused to do so. Nothing against the hard-working employees of UPS and FedEx, but those private companies had a hard time making deliveries every Christmas. The U.S. Post Office is a better alternative—despite the fact that Republicans have been trying to kill it. Before anyone claims that e-mail is killing the Post Office, please get the facts. The Republican Party has actively sabotaged and obstructed the Post Office, causing about 99% of its current problems. Our founders established the Post Office in Article I, Section 8, Clause 7 of the Constitution because they knew that communication between citizens enhances the public good and shouldn't be exploited for private profit. Once again, Republicans have ignored the lessons of our founders.

* * *

Why are so many Republican politicians who sit in an air-conditioned office so enthusiastic about raising the retirement age for people who do physical work for a living? Let's make every Republican who wants to raise the retirement age work construction or nursing or eldercare or shelf-stocking or fast food or farming or any other physically-taxing job until age 70.

* * *

Sarah Palin hosts a TV show called *Amazing Americans*. One of the most amazing things about America is that someone as clueless as Sarah Palin gets to host her own show.

* * *

This Christmas, I wouldn't be surprised if Republican politicians proposed a new law that outlaws giving kids presents because that just makes them dependent on handouts.

* * *

Some people have started posting memes on social media about not being ashamed to say "Merry Christmas" instead of "Happy Holidays" and not being afraid of offending all those politically correct people who want to oppress their religious freedom. Seriously? "Happy Holidays" isn't some sort of anti-Christian oppressive code word. It's an authentic wish that people experience happiness during the entire season of "holy days," whichever of the several holidays people celebrate—or none at all. Anyone offended by that is simply wishing for a way to be offended. To put it more bluntly, the opposite of "Happy Holidays" isn't "Merry Christmas." No, friends, it's "F*ck off, jerkwad. I don't give a flying sh*t." And that's why I always wish everyone, "Happy Holidays!"

* * *

Remember Festivus, the made-up holiday from the television show *Seinfeld*? This year, I'm going to combine my two favorite Festivus traditions: the airing of grievances and feats of strengths. I'm going to hoist Ted Cruz above my head and hurl him at Donald Trump.

* * *

What if God doesn't actually hate gay people? What if God actually hates bigoted people who make anti-gay social media posts with lazy thinking, poor spelling, and bad grammar?

* * *

Media pundits want us to believe that America is a center-right nation. But that doesn't explain why *It's a Wonderful Life* is America's most beloved holiday movie. Henry Potter put profits above people. George Bailey put people above profits. If Potter were a real person alive today, he'd watch Fox News, donate to right-wing organizations, and vote a straight Republican ticket. Pottersville is a right-wing paradise. America loves this movie because, at our core, we are a nation that embraces liberal values.

* * *

Remember all those upstanding conservative folks who defended the Duck Dynasty dude's anti-gay comments? The Westboro Baptist Church also defended his comments. Nice company you're keeping.

* * *

The Obama family lit the national Christmas tree in December, as presidents traditionally do. Or, as some Republicans would say, "The Obummers celebrated Benghazi with a secret Muslim ceremony from their socialist Kenyan homeland guaranteed to give American jobs to illegal immigrants just the way is says in Saul Alinsky handbook."

* * *

An optimist says the glass is half full. A pessimist says the glass is half empty. A Republican politician sees the glass and says, "How come all those lazy poor people have so much free water to drink?"

* * *

Here's what's wrong with the American economy in a nutshell: McDonald's CEO made $8.75 million last year. Average McDonald's workers would need to work one million hours to earn that much. That's nearly 500 years, 40 hours per week, 52 weeks per year, no vacation. Next time you order a Big Mac, take a look at the person serving you. Think they'll make it for 500 years?

* * *

If there really is a "War on Christmas," then crass commercialism won decades ago.

* * *

Walmart pays its workers such low wages that many of their employees have to rely on food stamps and other government benefits just to get by. Keep that in mind when you go shopping on Black Friday.

* * *

Remember the last time you worked for months to accomplish something great at your job, and within minutes, the jerks who skipped all the meetings and who don't know what they're about belittled your achievement? Yeah, that's what it's like pretty much every day for President Obama.

* * *

For years, Republicans kept asking, "If Obamacare is so great, how come Congress exempted themselves from it?" Like so many other Republican claims about the Affordable Care Act, that's an outright lie. Republican John Boehner, the Speaker of the House, who tried to repeal the law more than 40 times, signed up for it in November 2013. The sign-up process took him less than a day. Whenever Republicans talk about Obamacare, there's a very good chance they're lying.

* * *

Republicans love to say that MSNBC is left-wing and Fox News is right-wing, as if the two are equally biased. There's a technical term for that kind of comparison: bullsh*t. MSNBC is a corporate news network with left-leaning, reality-based opinion shows in the evening. Fox News is Republican propaganda. Anyone who doesn't understand the difference is accepting the big lie that allows Fox News to tell hundreds of smaller lies every day. How about a prime example when a Fox News talking head forgot that their bias is supposed to be sort of a secret? On February 12, 2012, Fox News talking head Steve Doocy read directly from a Republican Party "pundit prep" memo on the air, pretending that he was just speaking about the facts of an issue. When an MSNBC host reads a Democratic Party memo on the air, then let's talk. Until then ... bullsh*t.

* * *

A friend of mine told me that she is sick of the fighting between political parties. The political division in America these days makes me ill as well. But how did we get here? Take a look at American history. The Democratic Party

---

platform isn't much different from what it was in the 1930s. During the 1960s, southern Democrats who opposed civil rights left the party and became Republicans. Since then, the Republican Party has moved farther and farther to the right while the Democratic Party has stayed consistent. Why is there political division these days? The division might have something to do with one party promoting policies that have led to the rich getting richer and everyone else barely holding on. The division might also have something to do with one party promoting social views that demonize gay people, non-Christians, career women, immigrants, brown-skinned people, and anyone who disagrees with them. When one party considers a significant portion of our nation to be somehow less than fully human, you're bound to have some "division," to put it mildly.

* * *

The media has gone along with the Republican portrayal of Obama as a big spender, but the opposite is actually true. After an initial spending increase with the stimulus (which prevented a cataclysmic economic collapse), Obama has reduced the deficit each year and has increased spending at the lowest rate since Eisenhower. Despite the deficit hysteria in the media, we're on a path to eliminate the deficit, just as we were under Bill Clinton when Republicans ranted about spending. Clinton built a budget surplus that George W. Bush promptly destroyed. We don't have a deficit crisis—we have a jobs crisis. Obama's policies have helped with both short-term job growth and long-term deficit reduction. If Republicans in Congress would support his policies, we'd have far greater job growth and far greater deficit reduction.

* * *

Every time I read another nasty, ignorant, fact-free, confused, Fox News-inspired, profanity-laced, grammar-challenged, misspelled comment from a right-winger, I think, "Well, bless your little heart—someone taught you how to use that new-fangled computer contraption in your mother's basement."

* * *

Republicans often claim that President Obama hates our military. But in fact, the President and First Lady donated more than $100,000 of their 2012 income to the Fisher House Foundation, which supports our veterans and their families. If President Obama ever decides to hate me that much, I'll be happy with cash, a check, or a money order.

* * *

232

Stop the Republican War on Christianity! That's the kind of right-wing media headlines we would read 24 hours a day if Democrats tried to roll back Sunday early voting to keep certain Christians from voting. But that's exactly what Republicans have been doing, and no one from the right has uttered a word of protest. In several states, Republican politicians are trying to end Sunday early voting. That's when many Christian churches organize trips to the polls and vote for candidates and causes that support Christian values, such as feeding the poor, caring for each other, and creating opportunity for all people. Here's the catch: These are mostly *African-American* Christian churches whose members vote overwhelmingly for Democrats. Most Republican politicians don't really hate Christianity—they just hate the fact that African-American Christians vote their values.

* * *

In November 2013, the Senate voted on the Employment Non-Discrimination Act (ENDA). More than three-fourths of Senate Republicans voted to say that it's okay to fire someone for being gay. Let that sink in for a moment. Three out of four Senate Republicans think it's okay to fire a hard-working American human being simply for being gay in the United States of America in the year 2013. By the way, not a single Democrat made such a discriminatory and unconstitutional vote. Keep that in mind the next time you enter a voting booth.

* * *

The Republican Party has abandoned the idea of good government. Reagan told us government was the enemy, and today's reality-denying Republican Party seems intent on proving that theory true every time they hold public office.

* * *

Everyone who rants about immigrants and poor people being the source of all of our country's problems should be getting a thank-you note from the corporations, Fox News, and the Republican Party any day now.

* * *

Voting Republican is like living on a one-way dead-end street and wondering why the fire and police departments won't show up when you've set your own house on fire and you're holding a gun to your own head.

The next time a Republican complains about the cost of "welfare," remind him that the Republican-led government shutdown cost the economy $24 billion, more than the $17.7 billion yearly cost of Temporary Assistance for Needy Families (basic welfare) and only slightly less that the combined $25.5 billion yearly cost of Head Start, the Children's Health Insurance Program (CHIP), and Women, Infants, and Children (WIC).

* * *

If I had a nickel for every time I've heard a Republican rant that "Obamacare will destroy America!" I could buy comprehensive health insurance on the Obamacare exchange.

* * *

Republicans claim to be champions of "personal responsibility." But they throw a hissy-fit whenever anyone suggests that their party is responsible for the terrible Bush presidency or for the current unprecedented obstruction in Congress. Hey Republicans! Your policies are the equivalent of passing gas. Stop blaming President Obama for you own stinkers!

* * *

In 2013, for the first time in American history, Republicans shut down the federal government while our nation was a war. Remember the war? Republicans cheering the shutdown apparently don't.

* * *

Fox News recently reported that President Obama was personally paying to keep the Museum of Muslim culture open during the government shutdown. Their source for the report was a satire website. That seems appropriate: One fake news outlet quoting another.

* * *

"Republicans cut food stamps and shut down the government to stop health care? And people think I'm desperate and evil." - What Walter White of *Breaking Bad* fame might say about today's Republican Party.

* * *

Breaking Bad meets Obamacare: First episode: Walt gets diagnosed with cancer, but he has good-quality, affordable health insurance. The show focuses on his recovery and his return to an inspiring teaching career. Final episode: Twenty years later, Walt's wife, children, and in-laws throw him a great surprise retirement party catered by *Los Polos Hermanos*.

* * *

Voting for the political party that shuts down the government is like sending a thank-you note to the boss who fired you for no reason.

* * *

The folks who post the most obviously fake Facebook stories (Bill Gates wants to give you $5,000, for example) are the same ones who post ridiculous anti-Obama stories. Coincidence? No, just poor critical thinking skills.

* * *

Try to say this without laughing: "Fox News fact-checker."

* * *

If President Obama warned Americans not to eat dog poop, most Republicans would have turd breath before the end of the day.

* * *

Have you ever noticed that white supremacists are always the least "supreme" white people in America?

* * *

Why did Rush Limbaugh write a children's book? Because all con-artists need to recruit new victims.

* * *

Who would Jesus tax? Remember that Jesus loved the poor, chased the money-changers out of the temple, and said that rich people would have a very hard time getting to heaven. When Republicans claim Christian values while preaching tax cuts for the rich, they're not exactly being consistent. Just sayin' ...

*　*　*

If you think labor unions are bad for America, then you don't know American history. And you shouldn't have Labor Day off work ... or any other day ... or weekends ... or a lunch break ... or overtime pay ... or an 8-hour work day ... or a 40-hour work week ... or workplace safety ... on any of the other benefits that we take for granted today that were won by unions over the years.

*　*　*

Miley Cyrus and Donald Trump ... One of these overpaid and overrated entertainment industry celebrities does immature, tasteless, disturbing, profane, explicit, demeaning, inappropriate, performances for a national audience that no American should have to tolerate. The other's dad is the "achy-breaky-heart" guy.

*　*　*

Someday in the not-so-distant future, people enjoying the security of affordable health insurance will look back on Republican efforts to repeal Obamacare and wonder WTF was wrong with those people.

*　*　*

Homophobic right-wingers love their rhyming "Adam and Eve not Adam and Steve" anti-gay catch phrase. Bit if your role models are two people who got thrown out of the Garden of Eden for original sin, then you might want to rethink your position.

*　*　*

Fox News presents both sides of the issues: 1) The basic far-right side. 2) The factless-crazy-dishonest-angry-ignorant-regressive-corporate-far-far-far-far-right side.

*　*　*

You know who loves it when Americans blame both parties? The party that actually deserves most of the blame. Republicans blame both parties the same way Snooki blames the Kardshians.

*　*　*

"And verily I say unto thee that thou must maketh certain that the government passeth laws to control women's reproductive choices and never to alloweth those yucky gay people to marry one unto another." Thus spoke an imaginary Jesus in the Right-Wing Gospel of Misogynists and Homophobes.

* * *

Clueless Republican actor Craig T. Nelson perfectly embodied right-wing confusion about the role of government when he said this on the Glenn Beck show: "I've been on food stamps and welfare. Anybody help me out? No." Here's a news flash for Nelson and the Republican Party: Food stamps and welfare actually are help from your fellow American citizens, thanks to programs run by "we the people," our government.

* * *

Republicans keep trying to repeal Obamacare. I've lost count now, but I think there up to 50-something repeal attempts. Remember what Lloyd said in the movie *Dumb and Dumber*: "So you're telling me there's a chance."

* * *

President Obama is great with kids. He has a law degree, but maybe he should get some training in infant and toddler education to deal with the tantrums of Congressional Republicans.

* * *

If Jesus Spoke Republican: "No more loaves and fishes for you freeloaders! You'll just become dependent on handouts. And no more of this "salvation by grace" malarkey. If you can't get to heaven by your own bootstraps, then why should I help you? Who do you think I am, some kind of bleeding-heart liberal?"

* * *

To the Republicans who think that everyone on food stamps is a freeloader: Five thousand current food stamp recipients listed their occupation as "active duty military," mostly young service members with children. So be careful who you call a freeloader.

* * *

The Senate finally confirmed Richard Cordray as head of the Consumer Finance Protection Bureau after Republicans blocked his appointment for two years. Republicans didn't object to Cordray himself. They objected to the idea of a strong government agency protecting Americans from getting ripped off. Republicans are working for big banks and corporation—not for us.

* * *

The Dunning-Kruger effect is a psychological condition in which some people are so profoundly ignorant that they lack even the basic knowledge to realize how ignorant they really are. Wouldn't it be funny to see Fox News try to report on the Dunning-Kruger Effect?

* * *

I was at a wedding recently where two male guests slow-danced with each other. No one on the dance floor gave them a dirty look or asked them to stop. In fact, no one even seemed to notice except to smile at them the same way they did at every other couple. Guess what? Everyone on the dance floor was under 30. In a decade or two, gay haters are going to be very lonely.

* * *

In 2012, Ohio legislator Nina Turner introduced a bill that would require men seeking erectile dysfunction drugs to see a sex therapist, get a cardiac stress test, have a sexual partner affirm his impotency with a notarized affidavit, and receive information on the benefits of celibacy. If elected men think that they can regulate and legislate women's sex lives on the issues of birth control and abortion, then shouldn't that go both ways?

* * *

If men could get pregnant, abortions would be available in locker room vending machines.

* * *

When will Republican politicians understand the timeless economic fact that working-class American citizens who purchase a product or a service are the real job creators?

* * *

The Defense of Marriage Act never actually defended marriage. It just discriminated against gay people.

* * *

Millions of Facebook users reacted in horror at the news that Congress voted against Farmville. Later, they relaxed when they learned that it was only the "Farm Bill," not "Farmville."

* * *

Eat the rich! No, that would be morally wrong. And they're probably too touch and chewy. Let's just tax them fairly instead.

* * *

Education matters. This is not to be elitist and suggest that everyone with a formal education is automatically smarter than everyone without one. But when it comes to understanding the depth and complexity of American government, formal education can be the difference between being a real expert and being a con artist. Here are some examples to illustrate the idea: Rachel Maddow: Stanford University, B.A. in Public Policy; Oxford University, Ph.D. in Political Science. Rush Limbaugh: College Dropout. Sean Hannity: College Dropout. Glenn Beck: College Dropout. Are you getting your news from the Ph.D. or the dropouts?

* * *

I just bought a wedding gift for Robert and Michael, so now, of course, a tornado will have to strike in some southern state. Sorry folks. My bad.

* * *

The Republican-controlled House of Representatives just wasted its time passing an unconstitutional abortion ban that will never even be brought up in the Senate, let alone reach the president's desk for veto. Across the country, Republican legislatures and governors have enacted strict abortion laws, some of which have already been declared unconstitutional. When today's Republicans have control, their main focus isn't jobs, security, infrastructure, civil rights, taxes, or education. No, they seem to be fixated on the vajayjay. They claim to want small government, but they certainly love stuffing big government into women's panties every chance they get.

* * *

Here's a news flash for all the Republicans ranting about "free contraception": No employer is being forced to pay for "free contraception." Think about it: Your employer-provided health insurance is part of your compensation, just like your paycheck. No one thinks your paycheck is a gift. Why would anyone think your health insurance is a gift? It's not a gift. You work for it. It's yours. Plus you probably pay a percentage of the insurance premiums yourself, don't you? That's your money too. Your boss can't tell you how to spend your paycheck. And your boss shouldn't be allowed to tell you what health care options you can choose to buy. The Supreme Court's Hobby Lobby decision just put your boss between you and your doctor. Are you really okay with that?

* * *

It's a fact that the federal budget deficit has been more than cut in half during the Obama administration. We should have a reality-based discussion about how to achieve long-term deficit reduction without damaging the recovering economy with ineffective government austerity. But when Republicans rant about "exploding deficits" or "Obama's spending addiction," they are simply denying reality and basic math. That has to stop.

* * *

Mark Twain said, "A lie can travel halfway around the world while the truth is putting on its shoes." How did Twain know about Fox News?

* * *

In a recent survey, young Republicans were asked to name a Democratic leader. They mentioned Barack Obama, Bill and Hillary Clinton, and Nancy Pelosi—real elected leaders. When asked to name a Republican leader, they named Rush Limbaugh, Glenn Beck, and Bill O'Reilly—extremist talking heads. With actual leaders as ineffective as Mitch McConnell, John Boehner, Mitt Romney, George W. Bush, and the rest, it's no wonder know-nothing media mouthpieces rush in to fill the vacuum.

* * *

A policy passed as part of the Affordable Care Act eliminated private banks as unnecessary middlemen for federal student loans, saving taxpayers billions of dollars on wasteful kickbacks to Mitch McConnell's big bank buddies.

McConnell then claimed that Obamacare abolished the student loan program. That's a shameless lie that McConnell never corrected.

* * *

We should have a legitimate debate on government spying, But we need to remember that this specific spying publicized in 2013 was spawned by the 2001 Patriot Act, done illegally by the Bush administration in the 2000s, and supported by Congress members for more than a decade. Once again, that evil mastermind Obama has gone back in time to ruin the world before he became president. This time, he even used a George W. Bush disguise for his crime. Anyone blaming the whole thing on Obama has the shortest, most selective memory in history.

* * *

Walter Cronkite used to sign off his news broadcasts by saying, "That's the way it is." Fox News anchors should sign off with, "That's the way we pretend it is."

* * *

Fox News tried to smear the White House for its handing of the Benghazi attack by claiming that National Security Advisor Tom Donilon was missing on the day of the attack. Of course, Donilon was clearly visible in a photo dated the day of the attack right there on the Fox News screen as the talking heads lied about him. Apparently, even Fox News doesn't take Fox News seriously.

* * *

Recent natural disasters are terrible tragedies, but they could have been made much worse. Imagine these headlines: "President Romney orders FEMA to stand down and vows to veto any federal disaster aid passed by Congress." In case anyone thinks this is an exaggeration or politicizes disasters like the Oklahoma tornado or the Washington bridge collapse, please keep in mind that Romney said this about disaster relief during the presidential campaign: "We cannot afford to do those things without jeopardizing the future. It is simply immoral." Members of a political party who believe the federal government helping people in an emergency is "immoral" are already politicizing every natural disaster simply by their basic anti-government beliefs. Political positions have real-world consequences.

* * *

Republican politicians rant about how incompetent government is, and then they do their best to prove the point when they get elected.

* * *

Here's the real Benghazi scandal: Why did Congressional Republicans cut Obama's State Department requests for diplomatic security by $128 million in 2011 and $331 million in 2012, and then ignore Clinton's warnings that these cuts would be "detrimental to America's national security"? As the Republican's attempts to politicize the Benghazi attacks continue to fall apart, we should focus on the real problem: extreme budget-cutting has consequences. When Republicans cut the requested security funding, they endangered dedicated Americans doing important diplomatic work in dangerous place.

* * *

When will Republicans launch their biggest scandal attack against the president by accusing him of being a hard-working government employee?

* * *

At a recent NRA convention, a company sold ex-girlfriend and Obama-as-a-zombie shooting targets that bleed when shot. They've identified a market of cavemen morons who are willing to part with their money in exchange for demented products. This is what happens when the worst aspects of capitalism outweigh basic human decency. It's sick and inexcusable.

* * *

We need to defend the Second Amendment from the right-wing gun nuts who have no clue what it actually means.

* * *

In 2005, Sean Hannity of Fox News had this to say about Democrats who questioned President's Bush's policies: "I have had it with members of your party undermining our troops, undermining a commander in chief while we are at war." I wonder what 2005 Hannity would say to present day Hannity,, the guy who has constantly attacked President Obama since 2009—*while we are still at war.*

242

* * *

George W. Bush is actually a talented painter. Good for him. Too bad he didn't take up art around, oh, let's say, 1985. The world would be a far better place today.

* * *

Most NRA members have fairly reasonable views, such as supporting universal background checks for gun purchases. The NRA "leaders," on the other hand, are just lobbyists for the corporate gun industry who don't represent the actual members. Here's an idea: Let's all join the NRA just so we can have the pleasure of quitting to protest the organization's scumbag mouthpieces.

* * *

The stock market and corporate profits are booming again, but unemployment remains higher than it should be. Which explanation makes more sense: Millions of Americans are lazy bums, or wealth just doesn't "trickle down" like Republicans say it does?

* * *

Imagine after the Boston Marathon bombing if an organization called the National Bomb Association came forward to say that we need more bombs, that the only thing that stops a bad guy with a bomb is a good guy with a bomb. They'd be rightly laughed out of town or sent to a mental hospital.

* * *

If you actually believe that the Boston Marathon bombing or the shootings in Newtown and Aurora were "false flag" events staged by the government, then please tell us right now so that we can ignore every ignorant word you ever say. Seriously, you're just wasting everyone's time.

* * *

Killers choose their weapons. Adam Lanza, the Sandy Hook killer, left a bolt-action rifle and low-capacity magazines at home and left a shotgun in the trunk of his car. He chose a semi-automatic rifle and high capacity magazines to kill his victims. Some people think assault rifles and high-capacity magazines are no different from other weapons. Lanza knew the difference.

He chose military-style weapons that helped him kill the greatest number of people as quickly as possible. Some people claim gun-safety laws won't help prevent mass shootings. A nationwide ban on assault rifles and high-capacity magazines might have stopped Lanza. That's worth it.

* * *

The NRA has been robocalling people in Newtown, Connecticut. In other news, Hell just added a lower level.

* * *

Republicans claim that President Obama has been a terrible ally for Israel. But Israel awarded Obama its greatest honor, the Presidential Medal of Distinction, for his "tireless work to make Israel strong." Who should we believe, Republicans or Israelis? The answer is obvious.

* * *

Some Obamacare opponents are claiming that Obama will force us all to be implanted with a microchip. That's not true, but it would be great news if it were true. I'd love to replace the microchip implanted by the aliens with a new one for Obamacare. The aliens have a crappy health insurance plan.

* * *

Dear Republican Politicians: We just wanted to give you a heads-up about a fancy new invention that records sound and video. It's called a camera. Google it on the internet. They're everywhere these days. You might want to keep on the lookout for these gadgets because they can record you saying stupid stuff, and then that recording can be replayed in the future when you lie about what you said or when you say something completely contradictory. Basically, a camera is a magical machine that exposes dishonesty and hypocrisy—two words you really should also look up on the internet. You're not fooling us any longer. Sincerely, American Voters.

* * *

Can you imagine ever hiring someone who hates your company? No? They why would you ever vote for a politician who claims that government is the problem?

* * *

The U.S. Defense Department has a budget of approximately $500 billion per year, while the State Department has approximately $50 per year. We spend ten times as much on the military as we do on diplomacy, ten times as much to wage war as we spend to prevent war. What does that say about our priorities?

* * *

Worst seat for the State of the Union Address in American history: next to Ted Nugent.

* * *

Last night, President Obama advised Americans not to eat yellow snow. This morning, *Fox and Friends* unveiled the network's new official snack food: pee-flavored ice pops.

* * *

Dear Republicans: We have a challenge for you. Please find video, audio, or written evidence of all the times you claim that President Obama has directly blamed President Bush for anything. For each verified case that you present, we'll find 1,000 instances of Republicans politicians and media figures blaming Obama for things he didn't do. Your challenge begins now. We'll be waiting. Sincerely, Members of the Reality-Based Community.

* * *

Remember the good old days when Republicans cared about common-sense, long-lasting projects that helped the country? The Eisenhower Interstate Highways System is a good example. Now Republicans call building roads and improving our infrastructure wasteful spending, and they cut taxes on the wealthy to make sure we can't afford to do anything that might help working-class Americans. Republicans used to be part of the solution. Now they're just part of the problem.

* * *

Republican politicians who disapprove of Obamacare like to say that no one in America lacks "health care" because thy can go to emergency rooms. Funny how those Republicans aren't practicing what they preach by giving up their own health insurance and joining their fellow Americans in the emergency room. Emergency rooms are the last resort to keep people from dying in the street or to make sure seriously ill people don't infect al the people around then with contagious diseases. They serve an important function, but they aren't a desirable form of basic "health care." If Republican politicians had to go to the emergency room on a regular basis instead of their insurance-covered physicians, then they would embrace Obamacare in about ten seconds.

* * *

A right-wing website recently posted a photo of an attractive "woman-next-door" type person holding an assault rifle and carrying a pistol strapped to her belt. The caption read, "On his inauguration day, President Obama will be protected by the Secret Service, soldiers, and police officers. They have armor and automatic weapons. No one is assigned to protect my family." I feel so bad for this poor woman and her family who have "no one assigned to protect" them. They must live in some awful country that has no military to protect them from foreign invaders, no national intelligence to protect them from terrorists, no state or local police officers to protect them from crime, and no educational system to protect them from ignorance. I'm glad the United States is nothing like that.

* * *

"Obama-Hate-Aholic" (Noun) Someone who claims to disagree with the president's policies but who constantly misrepresents those policies and dishonestly attacks the president's character. Most often found on Fox News getting rich by lying about the president or on the internet repeating those lies for free.

* * *

On the night of President Obama's first inauguration in 2009, Republican leaders met and decided to fight everything the president proposed or endorsed, even ideas Republicans initiated in the first place, no matter how much their obstruction might hurt the country. Their purpose? To try to make the president look bad and defeat him in the 2012 election. They lost. But they're still devising desperate and destructive games well into Obama's second term. Obama's response after winning the 2012 election? "I will not play that game."

* * *

I got a robocall during the 2012 election cycle in which a voice literally shouted at me about how Obama is a socialist who is plotting to take away my guns. When I tried to call back the number to discuss the issue like adults, I got a message that the number was no longer in service. If they're so sure of their position that they would pay money to call me and shout, then why wouldn't they want to have a real discussion? Oh, wait. I know why. Because, like most right-wingers, they're a bunch of lying cowards.

* * *

If we want to be true to the Second Amendment to the Constitution, then shouldn't the first item on any background check for purchasing guns or ammunition be, "Please list your memberships in government-sponsored, well-regulated militias." How about it, strict constitutionalists?

* * *

Have you ever listened to that guy Alex Jones? Some people have guns where they should have brains.

* * *

Meanwhile, as the nation recoiled in horror at the Republican mishandling of the "fiscal cliff" in January 2013, congressional Republicans managed to block Hurricane Sandy relief and the renewal of the Violence Against Women Act. "Republican" … it's no longer the name of a political party. It's an unnatural disaster.

* * *

National Rifle Association leader Wayne LaPierre tells us that the lesson of the Newtown shooting tragedy is that we need more guns. The NRA doesn't represent its four million members, the majority of whom support common-sense gun-safety legislation. The NRA represents corporations that profit from increased fear leading to increased gun sales. Does anyone think it's a coincidence that LaPierre wants more gun sales? He's a death profiteer.

* * *

Republicans want everyone to carry a gun and shoot anyone who disagrees with them, right? No? Does that misrepresent Republicans' views on guns? Okay, then it's time for Republicans to stop falsely claiming that Democrats want to take away everyone's guns because that's not true either. Let's start the discussion with the truth instead of lies. Everyone wants to reduce gun crimes. We're all trying to find the best way to reach that goal.

* * *

I'm a teacher. I'm dedicated to educating young Americans. Anyone who says "lazy union thug" in my presence or tells me that I'm overpaid and underworked or complains that my pension is bankrupting the economy or accuses me of corrupting young minds with radical ideas had better use complete sentences and cite reliable sources of be prepared for a serious tongue-lashing from me.

* * *

I'm going to drive through South Carolina with my Massachusetts plates and my Obama and Warren bumper stickers. I've heard of "southern hospitality." What could possibly go wrong?

* * *

Question: What's the opposite of "Planned Parenthood"? Answer: Unplanned pregnancy. That's why I support Planned Parenthood and a woman's basic right to family planning.

* * *

"Wing-Nut Welfare Queens" (Noun) Ubiquitous right-wing pundits who continue to prosper in the media no matter how often they are wrong or how profoundly offensive they are.

* * *

During the 2012 election cycle, more than $200 million was secretly donated to politicians. About 80% of that secret money went to Republicans. Still think both sides are equally bad?

* * *

Tea Parties are for little children with imaginary friends. Let's leave the governing to grown-ups.

* * *

A conservative is just a liberal whose state hasn't been hit by a hurricane yet.

* * *

When the "storm of the century" hits every year, it's probably time to stop denying climate change.

* * *

America works best when both political parties agree to respect actual reality. But according to a 2010 Harris Poll, many Republicans believe that President Obama is a Socialist (67%), wants to take away Americans' right to own guns (61%), is a Muslim (57%), wants to turn the U.S. over to one-world government (51%), has done many unconstitutional actions (51%), was not born in the U.S. (45%), is a racist (42%), and is doing many things that Hitler did (38%). Is it any wonder that when I discuss issues with a Republican, I have a hard time taking the person seriously? The Republican Party is not honoring its side of the agreement to respect basic reality.

* * *

The numbers behind Mitt Romney's tax cut and spending plans add up to balance the federal budget in the same way that asking your boss for a pay cut and buying a Hummer add up to balance your family budget.

* * *

Remember when that evil dictator Obama tried to block the Violence Against Women Act, weaken the legal definition of rape, outlaw women's reproductive choices even when they were victims of rape or incest, cut contraception and family-planning access, and force women to undergo medically unnecessary transvaginal procedures against their will? No? Neither do I. That was the Republican Party.

* * *

Conservative: "I'm against welfare programs because they create dependence, just like Jesus said in that Bible verse: 'If you give a man a fish, you feed him for a day. But if you teach a man to fish, he can feed himself for a lifetime.'" Liberal: "First, that's a Chinese proverb, not a Bible verse. Second, you're also against teaching people to work for themselves when you cut funding for job training programs." Conservative: "Communist!"

* * *

A Republican friend of mine recently said to me, "You know, most people only voted for Obama because he's black, and they're afraid of being called closet racists." I replied that I voted for President Obama because I agree with him on most issues and I admire him as a person. The fact that he's black is just a bonus because it's always helpful to hear people identify themselves as closet racists by saying things like, "Most people only voted for Obama because he's black."

* * *

Pope Francis plans to issue an edict on the dangers of climate change. Republican heads will explode, which will, unfortunately, add even more carbon to the atmosphere.

* * *

Any "religion" that teaches people to hate other people isn't really a religion. It's just a hate-delivery system.

* * *

To all the nice people who believed the Republican lie about Obamacare "death panels" ... don't you feel a little silly now? Do you ever wonder what other Republican lies you believe? The same Republicans who pushed the Death Panel lie want you to believe them on everything else. Just say no.

* * *

Grown men hold hands as a sign of friendship in Zambia, but being gay is illegal there. Homophobia is a social creation, not a fact of life. Gay people are born that way. Homophobia is a lifestyle choice.

* * *

Texas and Indiana focused on "abstinence only" sex education, thanks to Republican policies. Texas got a Chlamydia outbreak, and Indiana got an HIV outbreak. Republicans want to do for America what they've done for sex education. No, thank you!

* * *

Everything's bigger in Texas—including the crazy. Dear Texans: The United States is not trying to conquer your state with the Jade Helm operation because *your state is actually already part of the United States.* You may have missed that fact in school, but it's true. Sincerely, Sane People Everywhere.

* * *

"Talk sense to a fool and he calls you foolish." Euripides (480-406 BC). Yes, Euripides was predicting right-wing internet trolls when he said this.

* * *

Right-wing "logic" says that a few isolated examples of welfare fraud prove that it's a terrible program. Here's how it works: "So-and-so saw somebody buy cigarettes and lottery tickets with food stamps, so it's all a scam!" Let's apply right-wing "logic" in reverse and see if it works: "My uncle's coworker's friend's hairdresser's cousin's neighbor says he saw somebody buy milk and break one time with food stamps, which clearly proves the program is working." Now do you see why I always put the word "logic" in quotation marks when I write about right-wing "logic"?

* * *

Republicans rely on people having very short memories ... for example, their Ebola hysterics. Remember in fall 2014 when they claimed that an Obama-caused Ebola outbreak would kill us all? Are Republicans ever right about anything?

* * *

The president said, "The freedom to worship who we want and how we want, or to not worship at all, is a core belief of our founding." Obama? No, that was George W. Bush. Look it up. Seriously, Republicans, there is no "war on religion." Please stop waging a war on common sense.

* * *

Why aren't conservatives and the corporate media blaming the mostly white biker gang violence in Texas in May 2015 on the breakdown of the white family unit or absent white fathers or white racism or whites getting welfare or white disrespect for authority or white music or white presidents or white moral decay or whatever other racial nonsense they toss out when any kind of violence happens in mostly black areas? The double standards are stunning—but completely predictable. "White-on-white violence is an epidemic in America," said no one in the corporate media ever.

* * *

The true lesson of Memorial Day is that civilized nations should wage war only as a last resort.

* * *

The real "illegals" are the corporations that hire undocumented workers to avoid hiring Americans and paying a living wage.

* * *

Some Republicans are proposing a "Religious Freedom Law" so that Christian bakers don't have to bake a cake for a gay wedding, or some such other hogwash. Actually, the United States has had a real religious freedom law for centuries. It's called the First Amendment to the Constitution, and it includes the provision that "Congress shall make no law respecting an establishment of religion, or prohibiting the free exercise thereof." It's a shame Republicans don't know this basic fact about our Constitution. Apparently, the Constitution isn't good enough for them because it doesn't hate and discriminate enough for their taste.

* * *

What's the difference between banging your head against a wall and trying to reason with a right-wing Republican? Sometimes you can make a dent in the wall.

* * *

Evangelist Franklin Graham proves that bigotry and cluelessness often overlap. Graham pulled his business from Wells Fargo Bank because the company ran an ad featuring a lesbian couple adopting a child. (It was a really lovely ad—you should look it up.) But Graham took his business to BB&T Bank without checking to see if the second bank hated gay people as much as he does. BB&T sponsors gay-pride events. How does that burn taste, Reverend Graham?

* * *

The Confederate Flag controversy points to a big difference between liberals and conservatives. Liberals are offended that the symbol of treason, slavery, and racism still flies at government buildings in southern states. Conservatives are offended when someone wishes them "Happy Holidays."

* * *

Immediately after the Charleston shooting, some disturbed people were already claiming it was a government hoax to promote gun control laws. They said the same thing about Newtown, Aurora, and the Boston Marathon bombing. Does anyone wonder where the term "gun nut" comes from?

* * *

The idea that some people are gay seemed just a little strange to me when I was ten years old. But then, you know, *I grew up.*

* * *

Right-wingers were outraged when President Obama used the "n-word" in an interview in July 2015. Funny how they don't seem nearly as outraged during the seven years and thousands of times that word has been said *about* the president leading up to that interview.

* * *

Not only was Obamacare upheld by the Supreme Court, but people who have it, love it! The approval rating among people with health insurance through Obamacare is an astonishing 86%. A similar survey one year ago showed 78% satisfaction. Yet another Republican lie bites the dust.

* * *

If you think that marriage equality will lead to people wanting to marry their dogs, then I'm scared for your dogs. Opponents of marriage equality can be some really sick puppies.

* * *

Muslim groups raised money to rebuild African-American Christian churches that were burned down not long after the Charleston shooting, proving that love, not violence or bigotry, is the best response to tragedy.

* * *

The people who hate the Iran nuclear deal loved the Iraq War. Remember how that turned out? Now we know "The Obama Doctrine": The hard work of diplomacy is better than the fake glory of dumb wars.

* * *

The "states' rights" argument might be more appealing if it wasn't used to justify terrible ideas: slavery and discrimination against people of color and gay people, for example. When states enact great ideas, such as marriage equality, better gun-safety regulations, environmental protections, marijuana decriminalization, and expanded voting access, the "states' rights" people suddenly change their tune.

* * *

"Gosh, your multiple anti-Obama conspiracy theory posts on Facebook have convinced me!" said no sane person ever.

* * *

Why do gun advocates say that you shouldn't talk about strengthening gun-safety laws after a mass shooting? Because they count on the fact that mass shootings will happen so often that no one will ever be able to talk about strengthening gun-safety laws.

* * *

Pop quiz: Most hated person in the world competition ... Lion-killing dentist or Donald Trump?

* * *

President Obama recently joked that he could win if he were allowed to run for a third term. Maybe in his third term, he could finally get around to taking everybody's guns and putting us all in FEMA camps. I heard that the tents are nice in the FEMA camps and the wifi is pretty reliable—and you get all the lobster food stamps can buy. Thanks, Obama!

* * *

Here's a suggestion: If people are going to pick and choose from their scriptures, then please follow the wonderful parts about loving one another instead of the really ugly parts about hating and killing and condemning people to hell. N'kay?

* * *

Heading into the 2016 election, the Republican anti-Clinton strategy sounds a lot like their anti-Obama strategy: make stuff up.

* * *

Expecting Republicans to provide facts is like expecting Newt Gingrich to stay faithful to any of his wives.

* * *

Denying other people their legal rights isn't "religious freedom." It's mean. It's discrimination. It's wrong. It's criminal. Kim Davis is the Kentucky clerk who refuses to issue same-sex marriage licenses because of her supposed "Christian" beliefs. Davis has been divorced three times. It must be hard to do a job where she files the paperwork to document other people's love and happiness while she seems to have little to none in her own life.

* * *

Flu season is coming. Thanks to Obamacare, flu shots are available without a copay under nearly every insurance plan. Obamacare isn't a socialist takeover. It's good public health policy that prevents illness and saves lives.

* * *

Dear Republican Politicians: You know what doesn't reduce the number of mass shooting? Doing nothing. So please do your damn job. Sincerely, Americans Who Are Fed Up With Gun Violence.

* * *

Today's lessons in Republican priorities: Obamacare saves lives by helping people get health insurance. Therefore, Republicans must repeal Obamacare immediately! Guns are killing more than 30,000 Americans each year. Therefore, there's nothing we can do about that. Stuff happens. Never mind.

* * *

When a mass murderer uses a gun to kill innocent people, Republicans send their prayers and claim that no law could have prevented the tragedy. When a woman makes the difficult, personal decision to have a legal abortion,

Republicans condemn all pro-choice people as evil "baby-killers" and demand that we outlaw abortion immediately.

* * *

When you feel bad about your life, just remember that there are people who still believe Fox News is fair and balanced.

* * *

Congratulations to our northern neighbors for their liberal election landslide in 2015! That was for sure one great Canadian election, eh? Skookum deal! Two-fours and beavertails for everyone, even Harper's keeners and hosers! Tell you what.

* * *

A Republican friend of mine recently asked me, "Ever notice that there are no liberals on Mount Rushmore? Wonder why?" Just for fun, here's a little history about the presidents on Mount Rushmore. George Washington was a liberal because he wanted independence from England. The conservatives of the day wanted to remain loyal to the crown. Thomas Jefferson was a liberal because he believed in the separation of church and state. Conservatives back then wanted a theocracy. Abe Lincoln was a liberal because he wanted to liberate the slaves. Conservatives then wanted to conserve the institution of slavery. Teddy Roosevelt was a liberal because he was an environmentalist, and he wanted to regulate corporations and the free market, as well as protect consumers from the abuses of big business. Conservatives of the time wanted the business world to control everything. So, how many conservatives on Mount Rushmore? None. Wonder why?

* * *

How do we know that Republican lies were exposed in the day-long Benghazi hearing where hapless Republicans tried to grill a resolute and presidential Hillary Clinton? Fox News cut away from the live coverage before the other news networks. What do you suppose they were scared of?

* * *

When Republicans claim that Americans don't want stricter gun laws, they're wrong. Recent Gallup polling showed that 55% of Americans want stricter gun laws, 33% want gun laws to remain the same, and only 11% want less strict gun laws. According to Republican math, 11 is bigger than 33 or 55. Maybe they should stop complaining about Common Core math.

* * *

Donald Trump whined that a three-hour debate was too long. Hillary Clinton testified before the Benghazi Committee witch-hunt for eleven hours and didn't even flinch. Our nation needs a strong leader, not a crybaby nincompoop.

* * *

Sean Hannity recently compared the Black Lives Matter movement to the KKK. Really? Hannity is too blinded by his own prejudice to notice that Black Lives Matter activists don't hide behind hoods, burn crosses, or murder innocent people because of their skin color. How can anyone take Hannity seriously? Someone should tell him that KKK members probably DVR his show and watch it at their meetings.

* * *

Every time I watch a Republican presidential debate, it looks more like a sanity hearing, and none of them could be found competent to stand trial, let along lead the country.

* * *

Hi there! I'm just checking to see if anyone has read this far in the book. If so, please go to my homepage, JohnSheirer.com, find my e-mail address there, and send me a message. I'm looking forward to hearing from you!

* * *

If people need Starbucks Christmas coffee cups to verify their religious beliefs, then their religious beliefs aren't worth the price of a cup of coffee.

* * *

Right-wingers responded to the Paris terrorist attacks by circulating a scary photo of a large group of Arab-looking men who they claimed were part of a horde of 10,000 refugees that Obama had brought into New Orleans that day. The post appeared on dozens of right-wing web sites and was shared tens of thousands of times in social media. In fact, only two refugee families had arrived in New Orleans that day, sponsored by Catholic charity groups after undergoing a long and arduous screening process. The photo of all those scary men? It was taken in Hungary nearly a year before. To sum up: lie, lie, lie, lie. We're still waiting for the retraction.

* * *

The heavily armed anti-Muslim gun advocates who march outside American mosques aren't protesting against terrorism. They are terrorists.

* * *

The domestic terrorist who shot up a Planned Parenthood clinic in Colorado has been called a "lone wolf." But that's inaccurate. He had a pretty extensive wolf pack: 1) The anti-choice zealots who made dishonest videos smearing Planned Parenthood. 2) The right-wing pundits who publicized those lies about Planned Parenthood. 3) The Republican politicians who campaigned on those lies about Planned Parenthood. 4) The NRA lobbyists who made sure he had easy access to his murder weapon. The truth is that this domestic terrorist was raised by right-wing wolves.

* * *

For all the Republicans who think that President Obama is an oppressive tyrant, maybe they should apply for refugee status and move to, oh, let's say, Syria! Good luck with that!

* * *

Have you ever heard of an agnostic committing mass murder with a rock? Of course not. Here's a simple theory: Religious extremism and easy access to guns are the real problems.

* * *

The Iowa Caucuses are so white they should be called the Iowa Caucasians.

* * *

What would you call a political party that supports guns over healthcare? Here's a hint: It starts with an "R" and ends with "epublican."

* * *

Remember when Fox was a real news channel? No one does.

* * *

Recently in India, 70,000 Muslim clerics declared a fatwa against terrorist groups. And 1.5 million Muslims signed on in support. Memo to Republicans: Muslims hate terrorists just as much as you do.

* * *

When those fake patriot militia idiots took over the federal bird sanctuary in Oregon, I had a suggestion that would have saved everybody time, money, and grief. Just cut off their internet porn access and the "standoff" would have been over in about half an hour.

* * *

Did you see the mug shots of those right-wing Bundy-led domestic terrorists once they were finally arrested? Funny how they didn't look Muslim.

* * *

LaVoy Finicum (aka, "Blue Tarp Man" from the group occupying the bird sanctuary in Oregon) tragically predicted his own "suicide by cop." As Finicum hid under his tarp, clutching his rifle in a bizarre pose, a reporter asked him, "So you're prepared to die—better dead than in a cell?" Finicum responded, "Absolutely." Unfortunately, this disturbed man got his wish. Three weeks later, he was shot as he tried to pull a gun on federal agents at the end of a high-speech chase. Finicum's death is the tragic result of the stupidity spouted by the treasonous, criminal militia movement.

* * *

President Obama said nice things at a mosque in February, so he must be the antichrist or some such nonsense. Obviously. Sheeple. Kenya. Hitler. Golf. Death Panels. Benghazi.

* * *

I didn't agree with Antonin Scalia on much (if anything), but I grieve for his family in their time of mourning. At our most basic, human level, all lives are meaningful, and all deaths are tragic. And I send out a wish to the universe that Ruth Bader Ginsberg lives forever.

If President Obama nominated Jesus Christ himself to the Supreme Court, Republicans would filibuster and demand to see his birth certificate.

* * *

No offense, but Republicans sound like a hillbilly leaning on his pickup truck chewing on a strand of alfalfa when they talk about the Supreme Court nomination. "I don't give a shit if'n Obummer went to Hafferd. I knows the Constetushun better'n him!"

* * *

Anyone who trusts Fox News is willfully ignorant. Fox News deceptively aired video of riots during a report about President Obama praising "Black Lives Matter" leaders. *Fox & Friends* anchor Heather Childers said as the clip of riots aired, "The violent riots several years ago in Ferguson and Baltimore now drawing praise from President Obama—*praise*," as if Obama were praising the riots, which he obviously wasn't. Fox News: Always unfair, always unbalanced.

* * *

Donald Trump actually said he'd like to punch a protester at one of his campaign events in the face. Now Trump knows how the rest of us feel about him. I don't actually advocate violence against Trump, of course. But no sensible person ever said, "What America needs is a president who acts like a playground bully."

* * *

There's an old saying that states, "The right-wing and the left-wing are part of the same bird." Unfortunately, the American right-wing has lost all interest in helping our nation fly.

* * *

A Republican recently accused me of poisoning my students with "progressive dribble." The word he was looking for is "drivel" not "dribble." I don't teach basketball.

* * *

Jay Fleitman, the Republican columnist for my hometown newspaper, recently wrote that, "A conservative without the drama is the prescription for our time." He's exactly right that we need a drama-free president. However, his views would be easier to take seriously if his ridiculous assessment of Hillary Clinton ("the most corrupt politician we have seen on the presidential stage in memory") wasn't based on the dramatic lies his party has been telling about her for two decades. Of course, if Fleitman really believed that we need a drama-free president, he could suggest that Barack Obama get a third term. Oh, that's right—Fleitman and his melodramatic party has been lying about Obama for years as well, leading directly to the dramatic rise of Trump. To borrow a Republican slogan and apply it to the Republican Party's current Trump crisis—"you built that." They should enjoy the fruitcakes of their labor. Sorry, but disingenuous folks like Fleitman don't get to assume the high ground when they've been wriggling in the mud with the rest of the Republican Party for so long.

* * *

Protestors are roughed up and kicked out of Trump rallies so often that they're going to start scheduling "The Two Minutes of Hate" as a regular part of the event. (If you don't know what that means, then please ask an English teacher. But ask soon before the Republican budget cuts get rid of all the English teachers.)

* * *

How do we talk to our children about the dangers of bullying and then watch the Republican presidential debates?

* * *

Marco Rubio and Ted Cruz fighting over who's more anti-anchor-baby is like Trump claiming to be the most anti-trust-fund-baby. (Note: The term "anchor-baby" is a slur frequently used by Republicans but not in any way endorsed by this author.)

* * *

Barack Obama is the most lied about president in American history, and Hillary Clinton is the most lied about presidential candidate in American history.

* * *

A March 2016 poll shows that Hillary Clinton leads Donald Trump among college graduates 52-37%, which raises the question, "What the hell kind of idiotic college did that 37% attend?"

* * *

My endorsement of Hillary Clinton was published on March 14. The next day, she swept all five Democratic primaries. Coincidence? Yeah, of course.

* * *

On March 15, the day that Hillary Clinton swept all five Democratic primaries, several corporate media commentators criticized her for using a loud voice in her victory speech, implying that she sounded harsh and shrill. When has the media ever criticized a male candidate with a loud voice for sounding harsh and shrill?

* * *

Back in 2009, Sean Hannity bragged that he would be waterboarded to prove it's not torture. Seven years later, his lying face is still dry.

* * *

While Trump and Cruz play a nasty game of family feud, the rest of America realizes how much we'll miss our current classy and dignified First Family.

* * *

Take a close look at those Donald Trump rallies. What if the Trump campaign is actually a prequel for the TV show, *The Walking Dead?*

* * *

I've seen a funny post making the rounds on Facebook lately. It shows a political yard sign that says "Everybody Sucks 2016" in huge letters, and "The U.S. is doomed." in fine print underneath. The really funny part is that I've only seen this sign being posted by Republicans. We Democrats are very happy with our great candidates.

* * *

Bernie Sanders is great, and (as I pointed out several times in this book) I'll happily vote for him if he wins the nomination. He's obviously far better than Trump, Cruz, or any Republican. But leading into the mid-April New York primary, he has exposed a major flaw in his criticism of Hillary Clinton. When a candidate bases much of his campaign on the claim that Hillary is a servant of Wall Street because she gets campaign contributions and speaking fees, then he'd better be able to offer some kind of concrete evidence that she has favored Wall Street. Through this whole, long campaign, he hasn't.

Sorry folks, but Bernie really blew this one big time at the New York debate. He was asked directly to name a case where Hillary showed favoritism to Wall Street, and he couldn't even come close. After the debate, a reporter even fed Bernie the debunked claim that Hillary changed her vote on the Bankruptcy Bill to favor big banks more than a decade ago, but he couldn't make that case either. As Hillary said in during the debate, "He cannot come up with any example because there is no example."

Here's an interesting thought experiment to illuminate the issue. According to Open Secrets, Bernie has taken significant contributions from giant tech corporations Google (through its parent company, Alphabet Inc.), Apple, Microsoft, and Amazon. Does that mean that he supports these companies' tendencies for outsourcing jobs to other countries? If we follow Bernie's theory that campaign contributions cause candidates to do the bidding of those contributors, then isn't it reasonable to assume that Bernie must be helping with corporate technology outsourcing? The logical way to test this theory would be to look for evidence that Bernie has supported outsourcing through his policy advocacy. Of course, there's no such evidence. Guess what? There's also no evidence that Hillary has advocated for policies that support Wall Street.

In contrast, we could all come up with dozens of examples of Republican showing favoritism to Wall Street, but no one has yet to come up with a single, verified, fact-based example of Hillary doing so. Democrats, unlike Republicans, base our claims on facts. Republicans reject climate change, claim that tax cuts increase government revenue and create jobs, decry the unemployed as lazy, and rant about President Obama hating America—all with no facts to support their views. That's a big reason that Democrats reject Republican positions.

Facts are important to Democrats. In the case of Hillary and Wall Street, Bernie is making a fact-free attack. An attack without a factual basis is just a smear. That's unacceptable and equally as bad in substance as Bernie supporter Paul Song calling Hillary a "corporate Democratic whore" at Bernie's big New York rally just before the primary there. Bernie condemned the nasty language but not the fact-free substance of the smear. Bernie and his supporters need to do better.

* * *

Many elected Democrats sometimes disappoint me. But the vast majority of today's elected Republicans often disgust and repulse me. I'll take occasional disappointment over frequent disgust and repulsion any day.

# # #

Acknowledgements and Notes

First and most, all possible gratitude goes to my wife Betsy Sheirer. She has more common sense than anyone I've ever met, and our discussions often help me understand current events better and lead me to my best ideas for writing. If this book meets with her approval, then I've accomplished my highest goal as a writer. Plus she always clips my columns from the newspaper and saves them in her well-organized file drawers. That's love, my friends.

Thanks to Danielle, Mike, Daryl, and Julia for ensuring that I have faith in the common sense and wisdom of the "younger generation." Every time I wonder if the world has lost its collective mind, I remind myself that you guys are out there reading books and climbing mountains and going off to work day after day and laughing and voting and making the world a better place. And I can't wait for Emily and Matthew to read this book someday when they're done with *The Very Hungry Caterpillar*.

Robin Stratton, the human tornado behind Big Table Publishing, deserves a statue in her honor for all she has done to support writers over the years. She is both an amazing editor and a wonderful writer. Please read her books and all the books published by Big Table. I'm honored to be published again by her fantastic company.

A very big thank you to Larry Parness, the editor of my hometown newspaper, the *Daily Hampshire Gazette* of Northampton, Massachusetts, for hosting my monthly column that makes up much of this book. To have 900 words each month when most national columns allow barely half that length is a bounty any writer would love to have. (Of course, I bulked many of these pieces up after they appeared in the *Gazette*.) Larry's gentle good humor and wise suggestions made the writing here better than I could have by myself.

Many thanks to the non-corporate, non-mainstream media for letting me lend my voice to discussions of our nation's common sense and confusion: Bob Flaherty, Bill Newman, and the great folks at our local radio station, WHMP; Tim Corrimal, Joe Santorsa, and the wonderful roundtable guests at the *Tim Corrimal Show* podcast; Dan Bimrose, Keith Brekhus, and Naomi Minogue of the *Liberal Fix Radio* podcast; and Scott Henderson of the *Brass Knuckle Progressives* podcast.

Just for fun, I reversed time in this book, starting with the most recent essays and moving backward. Readers can start from the beginning as the 2016 presidential primary season has gone on just long enough that we all can't wait for it to end. For the more linear among us, I recommend starting with the last sections first and moving toward the front of the book. Or, for those who enjoy random explorations, dive in at any point in the book and swim until the shore appears on the horizon.

This book presents the snapshots of my thinking about current events from 2012 and 2016. But I always strive to base these snapshots in facts, reality, and basic common sense. In my previous book on politics and current events, *Tales of a Real American Liberal,* I painstakingly provided about 800 footnotes to make sure everyone knew the fact-based sources of my views. Unfortunately, I don't think anyone bothered to read any of those footnotes. And then the book's publisher went out of business not long after that. Coincidence?

This time around, I left out the footnotes. The facts behind my views are easy to find using that terribly biased liberal invention, Google. If anyone wants to dispute any of the facts in this book, then please do your own research, get in touch with me, and let me know where I got the facts wrong. I'm happy to be guided toward better information. If anyone just wants to insult me for my views, then please form a long orderly line somewhere far away from me and have a nice day. Thanks!

About the Author

John Sheirer (pronounced Shy-er) is an award-winning teacher and author. His previous book on politics and current events, *Tales of a Real American Liberal*, gave rise to a very popular Facebook page by the same name where John posts political commentary that reaches hundreds of thousands of readers every day. At the local level, he writes a monthly column for his hometown newspaper, the Northampton, Massachusetts, *Daily Hampshire Gazette* (the 2015 New England Newspaper of the Year) and makes regular appearances on Northampton's WHMP radio station.

John is the author of many other books, including his delightful series of children's picture books coauthored with his dog Libby. His previous books also include a creative writing idea book, *What's the Story?;* a short story collection, *One Bite;* two memoirs, *Loop Year: 365 Days on the Trail* and *Growing Up Mostly Normal in the Middle of Nowhere;* and a public speaking guidebook, *Shut Up and Speak!*

Among John's multiple writing awards are three Pinnacle Book Achievement Awards; finalist medals for the Next Generation Indie Book Awards, the International Book Awards, the Sante Fe Writers Project Literary Awards, and the Eric Hoffer Book Awards; and a Pushcart Prize nomination.

John has taught English and communications at Asnuntuck Community College in Enfield, Connecticut, for more than two decades, where he has been honored several times by Who's Who Among America's Teachers and recently received the Distinguished Service and Educational Excellence Award.

John and his wonderful wife Betsy live in Northampton, Massachusetts, with Libby, their multi-talented Border Terrier. He can be found at JohnSheirer.com.

www.ingramcontent.com/pod-product-compliance
Lightning Source LLC
Chambersburg PA
CBHW060839280326
41934CB00007B/852